JEWISH SAGES OF TODAY

TOBI KAHN

Ahlom, 2001
private collection

JEWISH SAGES OF TODAY
Profiles of Extraordinary People

Edited by Aryeh Rubin

DE**V**ORA
PUBLISHING
NEW YORK◆JERUSALEM◆LONDON

A TARGUM SHLISHI PROJECT

Jewish Sages of Today: Profiles of Extraordinary People
is a project of Targum Shlishi, a Raquel and Aryeh Rubin Foundation.

TARGUM SHLISHI
www.targumshlishi.org

Also by Targum Shlishi
Toward a Meaningful Bat Mitzvah

Jewish Sages of Today Project Team

Aryeh Rubin	Editor
Andrea Gollin	Managing Editor
JoAnne Papir	Project Coordinator
Judith Dach	Editorial Consultant
Lanie Jacob	Communications
Cuqui Maya	Financial

Jewish Sages of Today Editorial Advisory Board
Judith Ginsberg
Laura Gold
Geoffrey Hartman
Karl Katz
Nathan Laufer
Deborah Lipstadt
Danny Tropper

Photography credits: Yosef Abramowitz photo courtesy Ruti Rubenstein; Mira Brichto photo courtesy Laura Griffin; Aaron Lansky photo © Patricia Williams; Jennifer Laszlo Mizrahi photo © Liz Lynch; Alice Shalvi photo © Joan Roth; Avivah Zornberg photo courtesy Debbi Cooper; Efraim Zuroff photo © Dina Mendrea.

Jewish Sages of Today: Profiles of Extraordinary People
Published by Devora Publishing Company
Copyright © 2009 by Targum Shlishi, a Raquel and Aryeh Rubin Foundation

EDITOR: Shirley Zauer
COVER IMAGES: Tobi Kahn
TYPESETTING & BOOK DESIGN: Koren Publishing Services
EDITORIAL AND PRODUCTION DIRECTOR: Daniella Barak

Soft Cover ISBN : 978-1-934440-96-4

❖

To the four women in my life:
Raquel, Felissa, Angelica, and Maya

And in honor of
the bat mitzvahs
of
Angelica and Maya

CONTENTS

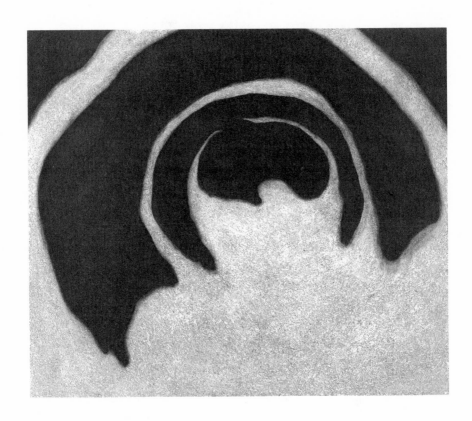

TOBI KAHN

Qinta, 1996
Ellen and Herbert Kahn

PREFACE

Our Sages: Making a Difference

A sage is more of an asset to a nation than its king.
– Maimonides, Commentary to *Mishna Horayot*

We need heroes. We need them today, more than ever. Heroes inspire us, elevate us, and motivate us to imagine and realize lives of intent and purpose. We're living in a time, in a culture, where mass opinion elevates sports stars, rock stars, actors and politicians. In this dominant celebrity culture, few seem to celebrate the real heroes – those whose lives are dedicated to making a positive difference in the world. We as Jews are no exception. Although they exist, we don't celebrate our heroes – sages who are accomplishing much that is noteworthy, living exemplary lives, espousing Jewish values, and who are willing to share their wisdom.

Many people, upon hearing of this project, have asked me to define what I mean by a contemporary sage, and have asked me how to recognize one. There is no recipe for a sage, no particular list of attributes to check off and thereby declare someone a sage. Historically, sages were people who helped guide us. In today's world, sages remain people who can help guide us, if only we would pay attention. Jewish sages are, quite simply, people who incorporate Judaism into their core, people who can serve as examples, as models, as teachers, as people for the entire community, from young children to grandparents, to look up to.

The people profiled in these pages are an eclectic group. They include: a world-renowned teacher and Jewish feminist whose doorway into Jewish knowledge has been Shakespeare; the last Nazi hunter; a rabbi whose life's work is to explain Judaism to Jews; a radio talk show host who explains Jews to the rest of the country; a scholar who explains the Holocaust to the world through museums, books and films; an internationally known, secular scientist turned

Orthodox Jew, who left the lab and now explores the nexus of science and religion; a philanthropist deeply committed to furthering Jewish knowledge, love of Israel, and to encouraging young Jews to meet, marry and procreate; a man who has spent his career rescuing and preserving Yiddish books; and a woman who left her high-powered political consulting firm to found a non-profit that advocates for Israel. These are just a few of the individuals profiled in *Jewish Sages of Today*.

Those profiled come from a wide range of professions, represent a spectrum of religious observance from Orthodox to Reform and from non-observant to secular, vary in terms of public acclaim from world famous to virtually unknown, range in age from their twenties to their eighties, and live across the U.S. and in Israel. They may appear, at first glance, to have little in common but, while the external facts of their lives differ markedly, all have motivations deeply rooted in improving the world, and all are making profound contributions to the quality of Jewish life. This book could easily have been twice, thrice, even ten times as long, and that in itself is cause for optimism in these difficult times.

．　．　．

The erosion of the hero's place in Jewish life is an offshoot of the damaging and unfortunate splintering of the Jewish world into a dogmatic, "our own particular brand of Judaism" retreat to various territorial corners. Matters have been made worse by the challenges of modern life and the subsequent emphasis by some on the letter of the law rather than a driving spiritual awe, while others have countered by drifting too far afield, espousing universalist themes while discounting Jewish values.

This deterioration of the Jewish *gestalt* was commented on by the great thinker and writer Hillel Zeitlin (1871–1942), who lived in Warsaw between the two world wars. A child prodigy who became an activist, poet, scholar and writer, Zeitlin was a major figure in the intellectual ferment of the times. His philosophical outlook incorporated a mystical and poetic faith, but was mindful of and integrated the perplexities of modernism. He rued traditional Judaism's descent into "religious behaviorism" with its lack of pathos, obsessions with minutiae, and intolerance of modernity. He believed that those who trod the path of modernity would be best served if they could nurture their inner soul to feel the majestic heritage of our people, if they could incorporate into their being the spark of Jewish heritage that would fill them with "awe and amazement."

What Zeitlin advocated almost a century ago is just as relevant today, if not more so. My aim, with *Jewish Sages of Today*, is to introduce the Jewish world and humanity at large to accomplished Jewish activists, thinkers, teachers, and the like, and to provide readers with insight as to how these individuals found "awe and amazement" in their own lives, how they accomplished their goals, how they achieved holiness. What drew these individuals to the particular work they do? What keeps them engaged, year after year? It is my hope that the examples of these remarkable people will inspire others, encourage innovative thinking, and spur the development of new ideas. I believe that we are capable of and receptive to learning from the example of others, but that in parts of the Jewish world this kind of learning has dropped out of favor.

While Zeitlin anticipated a deterioration in the Jewish gestalt, we are living that reality, a situation that has become more and more marked since the 1970s, with some responding to the upheavals of modernity by withdrawing from an interdenominational Jewish life, marking an end to even the veneer of Jewish unity. This deterioration has ushered in an era in which the letter of the law is all-important, and the long Jewish tradition of learning from others' examples has almost been obliterated. Until the early part of the twentieth century, Jewish tradition was mimetic in that it was not learned, but rather absorbed, as the brilliant scholar Rabbi Hayim Soloveitchik points out in his 1994 article in *Tradition*, "Rupture and Reconstruction: The Transformation of American Orthodoxy."

The tradition was imbibed from parents and friends and, yes, from sages. Conduct regularly observed in the home and street, synagogue and school, was absorbed. However, rigid rules of behavior were set forth in the early twentieth century with the widely accepted *Mishneh Brura* and other versions of the codes of law that formalized code and set these rules. That rigidity was partially responsible for the shift to the right and all the inherent problems that accompany it, including the elevation of leaders who are enclavist and do not pursue the interests of the wider berth of Jewry.

Other denominations contributed to the dissolution as well. Their fault lies in being too universalist, too politically correct, to the detriment of Jewish values. There cannot be an elevation of the Jewish gestalt without a focus on Jewish learning, and a stated goal of affecting one's entire being and personality Jewishly. The three times a year or one time a month religious experience, which is fleeting at best, and most often anti-climatic, will not do in keeping Jews Jewish.

. . .

I have been privileged to have lived a fully Jewish life, one that blends a mosaic of beliefs and a wide spectrum of Jewish attitudes. Hailing from a Chasidic background, my parents, both refugees from Europe, raised their children in a modern traditional household in Crown Heights, in a synagogue whose members were primarily survivors and second generation traditional American Jews. I attended a Chasidic school in Bedford Stuyvesant until the fourth grade, then a Lithuanian yeshiva in Williamsburg, then Yeshiva University, with a one-year stint at the ultra-Zionist Mercaz Harav in Jerusalem. I was exposed to right-wing Jews defending synagogues in Brooklyn with baseball bats, and was active during the days of Oslo with an organization on the left. I have learned from the haredi Rabbi Yaakov Kamenetsky and from the compassionate Rabbi Yitz Greenberg (who is included in these pages), I have studied under the intense Rabbi Moshe Tendler and the moderate Rabbi Zvi Yehuda Kook, and I have listened with admiration to the public lectures of the prescient Rabbi Mordecai Kaplan and the encompassing Lubavitcher Rebbe.

While I consider myself post-denominational, I belong to an open-minded Chabad synagogue in Miami. My wife is the child of refugees from Hitler, who was raised in Colombia in a non-observant environment. My three daughters have all attended Jewish day schools, but of different denominations – Reform, Conservative and Orthodox, depending on the school that best fit each child's style of learning. I have often described myself as having a traditional *neshama* (soul), a desire to attend an egalitarian *shtiebel* (prayer hall), and I am intrigued by sermons of relevance by the more liberal rabbis.

My own philosophy, then, espouses a Judaism that values all expressions, believes that we as a people function best when there is unity, and believes that the past fifty years have been an unproductive time of ideology gone wild, a dogmatic time when the word of the law has been elevated and the spirit of it degraded.

In many ways, *Jewish Sages of Today* is my response to the degradation of our spirit as individuals, and as a collective. I hope that this book will remind us of the value of the mimetic tradition, and that we will learn from the sages and their examples. I hope that we are all inspired to reflect on the lives of the sages portrayed here and motivated to realize a life lived according to our own values.

. . .

This book will no doubt arouse controversy as to the choice of who was included and who was excluded. I've anticipated challenges as to the choice of sages, and questions as to how these particular twenty-seven individuals were selected from among the hundreds of worthy choices. The selection of these individuals was a collaborative effort, undertaken with the help of an editorial advisory board (the names and bios of the editorial advisory board members appear in the Contributors section). Names of likely candidates were solicited from friends, colleagues and the advisory board members. Extensive research was then conducted for the hundreds of nominees, and lists of "finalists" were submitted back to the editorial advisory board. Accomplished writers in the U.S. and Israel were then selected based on a strict screening process, and assigned profiles to write.

I would be remiss if I did not mention that while all of those profiled here graciously contributed their time to the project, there were some objections to the label of "sages." More than one individual asked if the title of the book could be changed, and Avivah Zornberg, in particular, generously agreed to be included in the collection but only with the caveat that we acknowledge her strenuous objection to being labeled a "sage."

The individuals profiled were not informed of the others included in the book; thus, being profiled in these pages does not imply that those included are endorsing their fellow sages, an important point because of certain institutional/religious sanctions of affiliating with the other denominations. I hope that, in the future, we will arrive at a point where such a disclaimer will be unnecessary.

The rewards of working on this book have been many. I have had the opportunity to research and explore the work and learn about the lives of many people I have long admired. I have been challenged and inspired by their example. I have further explored the works of many of those profiled, and I hope that readers will do the same.

We, the Jewish people, have always believed that history has a purpose and that our lives have meaning. In an era in which globalization has distorted the concept of uniqueness and singularity, in which alienation and the search for meaning are the rule rather than the exception, in which the excesses of living a twenty-first century lifestyle have shifted our focus to materialism, and in which a virtual life has overshadowed the multifaceted pleasures of real human interaction, the sages profiled herein, some more than others, have experienced a redemption of their neshama, have found personal meaning through their bond with their work, their spirit, and their Judaism. Their lives have purpose and meaning; knowing their ways can only enrich us.

Aryeh Rubin
Aventura, Florida
Rosh Chodesh Adar, 5769
February 25, 2009

ACKNOWLEDGMENTS

There are many people to thank, many people who contributed to this book at every stage of the process. First and foremost, of course, are the remarkable individuals profiled in these pages. The profile subjects generously agreed to participate in the book, which involved significant time during the interviewing process and an ongoing commitment to respond to questions during editing. And while I am extremely appreciative of their time, I am even more grateful for their example, without which I never would have conceived the idea for *Jewish Sages of Today*.

The editorial advisory board members – Judith Ginsberg, Laura Gold, Geoffrey Hartman, Karl Katz, Nathan Laufer, Deborah Lipstadt and Danny Tropper (for their bios, please see the Contributors section) – were critical in helping to shape and steer the book; their guidance was invaluable during the process of researching and selecting the individuals to be profiled, and their feedback on the finished profiles proved extremely helpful during editing.

Thanks are due to the many thoughtful writers throughout the U.S. and in Israel who produced the profiles. All told, twenty talented writers wrote the twenty-five profiles for *Jewish Sages of Today* (the writers' bios appear in the Contributors section).

So many people went above and beyond in terms of contributing their expertise, their time and their help. Carolyn Starman Hessel, director of the Jewish Book Council, provided valuable advice. My friend Matthew J. Maryles, who for many years has been a sounding board and a source of guidance on matters both personal and related to the Jewish community, offered much-appreciated advice throughout this project and I owe him a special thanks. Ivan Berkowitz's friendship and his counsel on several projects over the course of our decade-and-a-half relationship has been extremely important to me, and is much appreciated.

The artwork on the cover and in the first few pages is the work of artist Tobi Kahn, who very generously allowed us to use his images. The book's elegant design owes much to the efforts of Peter Roman of Inkbyte Design for his work on initial design and Philip Brooker for his work on the photographs.

My assistants, Lanie Jacob and Cuqui Maya, have patiently lived with and provided much-needed administrative support throughout the project. Both of them have consistently responded to all requests for help with unflagging goodwill and with ongoing results – their contributions are greatly valued.

Nancy Wolfson-Moche's excellent editorial guidance in the early stages of this book helped refine the vision for the profiles. Rebecca Gollin provided much-needed research assistance throughout the project. Judy Dach's fact checking was greatly appreciated; her thoughtful and considered editorial feedback on the profiles was invaluable. I am grateful to Yaacov Peterseil and Daniella Barak of Devora Publishing who took on this book and guided me through the publication process. Thanks also to Shirley Zauer for her very thorough proofreading and Chaya Mendelson for her professional and efficient typesetting of the book.

Above all, I'd like to offer heartfelt thanks to JoAnne Papir and Andrea Gollin, who spearheaded the project. JoAnne coordinated *Jewish Sages of Today*, which was a massive undertaking; none of this would have been possible without her unflagging efforts and her ongoing championing of the project. Her work touched every stage of the process: assembling the editorial advisory board and coordinating the research of potential profile subjects, conducting the search for writers, contacting the profile subjects and securing their involvement, pairing writers with subjects, being the point person on all communications, collecting photographs, coordinating the editorial board's review process, assembling the book proposal, submitting the project to publishers, and much more.

Andrea Gollin was the book's managing editor. She, too, was involved in the initial research and selection of those profiled, reviewed the selection of writers, and oversaw the editing process as well as the design direction. The care and attention she brought to the project have been integral in shaping the book. Her editorial insight, political acumen and guidance were essential to the project. In many instances, she worked hand in hand with the writers, doing additional research, conducting follow-up interviews, fact-checking pieces, and working closely with writers on revisions; the book is stronger thanks to her hard work and dedication.

Finally, I would like to thank my family – Raquel, Felissa, Angelica and Maya Rubin – for their moral support, belief in the project and enthusiasm.

YOSEF ABRAMOWITZ

by CAROL ZALL

Yosef I. Abramowitz is only in his mid-forties but, as he's quick to point out, he has been involved in activism for decades. "I was fortunate enough to start early," he says, "and I've been doing this stuff for twenty-five years now. So it kind of adds up." One could say that Abramowitz is an overactive activist. He has a plethora of titles and is involved with a seemingly impossible number of projects. Until 2006, he was the CEO of Jewish Family & Life! (JFL), a Boston-based Jewish educational nonprofit that he cofounded in 1996 and that bills itself as the largest producer of original online Jewish content in the world. In addition to the usual CEO duties, his role at JFL included overseeing its many print and web publications – ranging from Jewish teen magazine *JVibe* and independent intellectual journal *Sh'ma*, to websites such as SocialAction.com and JBooks – as well as chairing the Koret International Book Awards.

Abramowitz – who is known as "Yossi" to his friends and colleagues – is also the president of the Union of Councils for Jews in the Former Soviet Union (UCSJ), a grassroots organization that combats anti-Semitism and xenophobia in the former Soviet states. On top of that, he's a fellow with the World Jewish Forum, has written for a large number of Jewish publications, and is the co-author of the 1997 *Jewish Family & Life* guidebook, which sold fifty thousand copies. But wait, there's more. He has been on hunger strikes for Soviet Jews, helped establish a political party in Israel (the recently formed *Atid Echad*), and received a Covenant Award for excellence in Jewish education in 2004. He has also been named by the *Forward* newspaper as one of the fifty most influential Jews in America.

Abramowitz stepped down from his CEO role at JFL in 2006 in order to spend a few years in Israel with his wife, Rabbi Susan Silverman, and their five children on a kibbutz in the Negev and to pursue new opportunities. Since moving to Israel, his activities have included advocating for Sudanese refugees in Israel and hatching plans to build a solar power plant there. Clearly, Abramowitz is a man on a mission – maybe several missions.

Abramowitz has been politically aware from an early age. Born in Brooklyn, New York, in 1964, his family moved to Israel when he was five years old. After living in Israel from kindergarten through second grade – an experience that he says left an indelible imprint of Jewish optimism on his soul – the family returned to the U.S. His parents divorced, and Abramowitz spent some of his formative childhood years living in what he describes as a "hippie commune" in Boston with his mother. He still remembers being pulled out of his Solomon Schechter school one day so he could attend "civil disobedience training" in the back room of a Communist bookstore in Cambridge, Massachusetts. The result, he says, was that by the eighth grade he not only had acquired Jewish literacy, but also "was not afraid of police dogs or water cannons or tear gas."

Abramowitz became involved with Jewish activism through the Young Judaea youth movement, which emphasizes leadership and Zionism. He attended Boston University, where he was active in student politics, created his own major in Jewish Public Policy, and helped start the campus anti-apartheid movement. He also took a course with Elie Wiesel called "Burden, Responsibility and Privilege of Rebellion: Literature of Memory" in 1986, the year Wiesel was awarded the Nobel Peace Prize. "The place was rocking," Abramowitz recalls. "I mean, it was really extraordinary – this sense that history can be changed, not just witnessed. And [the fact] that we were doing the anti-apartheid movement as he won the Nobel Peace Prize was very energizing."

Abramowitz's education as an activist took a new turn that same year when, while attending a conference of the World Union of Jewish Students (WUJS) in Jerusalem, he was unexpectedly elected to the post of chairman. (The first-ever chair of WUJS, Abramowitz is quick to point out, was Albert Einstein.) Instead of going on to law school as planned, he spent the next three and a half years chairing WUJS, "running around the world" – to Paris, Singapore, South Africa, Australia – creating campaigns with Jewish students across the globe.

According to Hillel Levine, a professor of sociology and religion at Boston University who taught Abramowitz in college and has been a mentor and close friend ever since, the WUJS experience was a crucial one for Abramowitz. Levine – who is also president of the International Institute for Mediation and Historical Conciliation – says that Abramowitz "not only developed a sense for the world Jewish polity, but also got to know all kinds of people in various strategic places in Jewish life, including various philanthropists. It was very exciting to watch and to be a part of that."

Abramowitz insists, however, that activism "has never been a vocation." Instead, he says, it's about values. "If you're going to be true to your values, you've got to do something about them, and since there aren't that many people always doing something about them, you end up somehow being a leader. I actually have a formula from my youth movement days, which is that values are what you live by, vision is what you live towards, and leadership is just simply living your values towards your vision. So anyone can do it. Anyone can be a leader."

Abramowitz next earned a master's degree in journalism from Columbia University, taking the opportunity to do coursework at the Jewish Theological Seminary and the Hebrew Union College (HUC) while he was in New York. After stints working as an investigative reporter and editor at *Moment* magazine, as well as working for the "Panim el Panim" program in Washington D.C., which runs seminars for Jewish high school students on public policy and Jewish values, Abramowitz was ready to strike out with his own publication. Searching for a topic that would "speak to a million Jews," he hit on the idea of producing a magazine about Jewish parenting and family life.

The experience of being married to a rabbi convinced Abramowitz that such a magazine would find a large and hungry audience. "One of the open secrets in Jewish life is that the spouse of the rabbi knows everything but can't say anything, and should pretend as if they don't know everything. Because the rabbi comes home and has to talk to somebody," says Abramowitz. He recounts how his wife Susan would come home each day and tell him "stories of people just wrestling with real life issues – a lot of interfaith related things – and realizing there's just a huge vacuum, a huge vacuum; that the Jewish community was completely out of touch with any of the real needs of the people. I mean, it was unbelievably crazy."

Together with Sue Laden, with whom he had worked at *Moment*, Abramowitz launched *Jewish Family and Life!* as a full color print magazine in 1996. They wanted to offer something different, accessible, life affirming – and fun. "I wasn't going to do it in a way that was going to be predictable," says Abramowitz. "So we came up with certain values that were going to really reconstitute Judaism away from the muse of Jewish institutions, and make it relevant in people's lives, in their homes."

Jewish Family and Life! had limited success as a print magazine, so Abramowitz turned instead to the Internet, transforming JFL into a multimedia company. More than a decade later, after what Abramowitz calls "an unbelievable ride," there is no question that JFL has been a great success. The organization – now headquartered in Newton, Massachusetts – has an annual budget of four million dollars and a large Web presence. JFL's Internet offerings include a dozen websites aimed at every Jew imaginable, from the blogging adolescent to the newly converted, and everyone in between. And JFL now occupies the entire floor of a building, which Abramowitz likes to refer to as "10,000 square feet of Dream Factory for the Jewish People."

Despite the successes, Abramowitz in person comes across less as a business leader who has a knack for raising large sums of money, and more like a grad student about to address a crowd at a rally. He exudes enthusiasm and energy and a certain idealistic zeal, and although he might be wearing a suit and tie, there is little doubt that he still sees himself as a rabble-rouser.

And he *is* a rabble-rouser. Referring to a series of articles first published in Boston's *Jewish Advocate* newspaper investigating fraud at the Jewish National Fund (JNF), which Abramowitz wrote in 1996, Hillel Levine calls him "the most important gadfly" of our generation. The series explored controversial allegations of questionable accounting practices at the JNF, as well as accusations that little of the money the JNF collected was actually being sent to Israel. "I mean this man single-handedly took on the JNF – *took on the JNF*. And found that it was not only using misleading rhetoric, but that it was corrupt from top to bottom. I mean, I can't tell you what a revelation that was – I mean, this was motherhood," Levine says. (The JNF was later cleared of fraudulent activity by a committee, although controversy still exists about some of its practices.)

As the investigation turned nasty, Levine says there were times when he feared for Abramowitz's safety. "I felt he was going to probably end up face down in the Charles River; I mean he was really in danger." But despite having seen "the sewers of Jewish organizational life," Levine believes that Abramowitz emerged with his ideals intact. "There's a kind of clear-eyed, optimistic, almost naïve love for the Jewish people. This is absolutely extraordinary – how this man is capable of functioning on both levels – I don't know of too many people who do it. It's part of his power, it's part of the way in which he's successful in raising money, because he really, really believes. I mean, he goes to funders with a kind of intellectual and spiritual integrity that they don't often see among the various *schnorrers* of the world."

Part of Abramowitz's success can be attributed to the fact that not only is he a man on a mission, but he's also a man with a vision. For him, his work at JFL has not been about simply building a media empire or acquiring magazine titles; instead, it has been about transforming Jewish life. As Abramowitz sees it, one of the major challenges facing world Jewry is to make Judaism relevant to people's lives. In order to do this, Judaism itself has to be shaken up, its values redefined and recalibrated in order to give it meaning and staying power in the future.

"In any kind of enterprise, organization, civilization, if you don't have a sense of purpose that's clearly defined, you start to weaken, you start to crumble," he says. "I think one can say with some degree of confidence and collective humility that the influence of the Jewish people upon civilization as a percentage of our absolute numbers is probably unparalleled. And I think we've rested a little too much on those laurels, saying, 'Oh well, look at what we have done, aren't we great?' or 'Isn't that a reason to be Jewish?' – and I don't think that translates into the future. I actually feel a special responsibility to say, 'Well, that was great, what are we going to do next? And what's the purpose of the Jewish people in the twenty-first century and moving forward?'"

Abramowitz's personal answer to the question of Jewish purpose is that the Jewish people are here to be a catalyst in the world for moral evolution. But, he asks, "If the Jewish community is meant to be a catalyst in the world, then who's going to be the catalyst for the Jewish community?" That's where Abramowitz and his various partner groups come in. Through his work with organizations such as JFL and the World Jewish Forum, he wants to reinvigorate Judaism by coming up with a core of Jewish values that have meaning for a wide variety of Jews, and then to articulate those values through various projects that will reach Jews all over the world.

One such project that has launched successfully is Jewish Social Action Month (JSAM). Abramowitz first conceived the idea for a social action month while at JFL, and then garnered support for it from the KolDor network of Jewish leaders, of which he is a member. They then gained the endorsement of the Knesset, which passed a resolution declaring Cheshvan to be global Jewish Social Action Month. (Cheshvan – which usually falls around October or November – was chosen because of the fact that no Jewish holidays occur during the month, and it is therefore considered to be *mar*, or bitter. Jewish Social Action Month aims to "take the bitterness out of Cheshvan" by transforming it into a month of positive action.) Other resolutions followed in the U.S. Congress and the British House of Commons, and the first JSAM was launched in 2005.

Abramowitz marvels at the way JSAM got off the ground. He says that two websites – www.cheshvan.org and www.socialaction.com – "were the engines that open-sourced the idea." Once the idea was out there, he said people would ask him who JSAM belonged to. "And the answer was, 'It belongs to the Jewish people' – which drives people *nuts.* But it's true, it's true, it's true. We were playing a catalytic role, with KolDor, in a new model. Not the command-control model, [but] an open-source model. Who does Shabbat belong to? Who does Pesach belong to? You know, who does Chanukah belong to? Right? So in doing this experiment, we actually came up with the next piece of the strategic plan for the Jewish people."

That next piece of "the plan" is the realization that no one institution can accomplish such goals alone. "You can't do it all yourself," says Abramowitz. "You shouldn't, you're not able to, you're not smart enough, you don't have the resources, it's just a ludicrous notion...it can't just be one institution, it has to be a global Jewish effort. And so to do that we have strategies, from the business world, of leveraging and open-sourcing."

The real value of the work he and his partners have done, he says, will be in making their ideas and strategies available for others to use. "Once we give away the key strategy pieces, someone else can come along, steal it, and do even a better job. Is that a failure or is that a success?"

Using projects like JSAM to articulate clearly defined Jewish values is also part of the big idea that Abramowitz refers to as "Peoplehood," something that is bigger – more inclusive – than nationalism, religion or culture. "Our Jewish values are the building blocks of Peoplehood, that's the DNA of it all. And imagine what would happen if you had the values run clearly through the religion, the culture, the nationalism, and that if you said, 'What do the Jewish people stand for?' you actually knew what they stood for. How about that?"

Jewish values are not just something Abramowitz wrestles with at work; he's also deeply committed to living a meaningful Jewish life at home. "This is a really extraordinary person," says Levine. "Everything is integrated: the way in which he is with his children, the way in which he is with people, his original approaches to Jewish life, his leadership, his friendships – this is a real person."

Susan Berrin, who has worked closely with Abramowitz as editor of the journal *Sh'ma* for the last eight years, agrees. "He brings his values home," she says. "To be able to synthesize your professional life and values that you're trying to put forward at work, to be able to live them at home as well, is really unusual and profoundly difficult."

One of the values Abramowitz and his wife have "brought home" has been a desire to help those less fortunate than themselves. Two of their five children, Adar and Zamir, were adopted from Ethiopia. Having worked on behalf of Ethiopian Jewry, Abramowitz felt a connection to that country, and wanted to bring something of its heritage into his family's life. And, he says, in a world in which thirty-five thousand children die of hunger each day, "the only answer is really to open your hearts and your home and your family if there's going to be a true *tikkun* (repairing [the world])."

Abramowitz is also involving his children in the kind of activism he cherishes so much. His blog (www.peoplehood.org) features a photo of his daughter, Aliza, posing with actor George Clooney at a 2006 rally for Darfur in Washington, D.C. when she was thirteen years old. And together with Aliza and his next eldest daughter, Hallel, he has cofounded WorldManna.org, which is trying to convince food manufacturers to donate one percent of their proceeds to help combat world hunger.

Following his own formula of living by his values and towards his vision, the most recent change in Abramowitz's life was his 2006 move to Israel. He and his family relocated to Kibbutz Ketura, on the Jordanian border half an hour north of Eilat, for what they expect will be a few years. The move arose out of a desire to spend quality family time together in Israel; in addition, Abramowitz and his wife were eager for their two adopted sons to have the chance to be around more Ethiopian Jews.

True to form, Abramowitz arrived in Israel in August 2006 and hit the ground running. Noticing that the sun was very intense on Kibbutz Ketura, he started asking why they weren't using more solar power on the kibbutz. He soon learned that the kibbutz's fields were located in an area that gets some of the most productive sunlight in the world, and he is now involved in plans to build a solar power plant there. If things go well, there will also be a partner plant built on the Jordanian side of the border.

Abramowitz, who likes to see the big picture, considers this latest development to be a logical continuation of his life's work. He wants to help Israel transform itself into a solar-based economy, a plan that he sees as a manifestation of Jewish values in many ways. "How can the Jewish state be a light unto the nations when seventy-five percent of its electricity is produced by coal and it is considering building a major nuclear power plant to help meet Israel's growing electricity needs?" he asks. Energy independence will, he believes, contribute to peace and stability in the region, and a by-product of the plants will be solar-powered desalination. "The more water," he says, "the more peace. For Israel to live its environmental values is a form of Zionism. We want to inspire Jewish communities worldwide to become carbon neutral by 2020."

This kind of ambitious plan, combining both Jewish values and a daring entrepreneurialism, are what led Levine to hold Abramowitz in such high regard. "If we had a hundred Yosef Abramowitzes in the Jewish community...Jewish life would be completely different," says Levine. "If we had a hundred Yosef Abramowitzes in the world, then the world would be different. One realizes just what quality people can do, people who are prepared to take risks, who are independent minded, who are honest. He's enormously powerful, enormously powerful."

In addition to working to make the solar power plants a reality, Abramowitz continues to be involved with JFL, the World Jewish Forum, and various other political and activist groups in Israel. He's working hard, he says, but his energy level is high and being in Israel has given him a great sense of replenishment. He's also hoping to write a book while he's there – its working title is *Peoplehood with Purpose* – and he'll be wrestling with the question of how the Jewish people will meet the challenges of the twenty-first century. "I don't believe that the way we're constituted now, that we can actually play our historic role in civilization," he says. "In an age of weapons of mass destruction, and in an age of real threats to the future viability of the planet, in an age in which there's six and a half billion people on the planet and a chronic scarcity of resources, if we don't step forward, then who will?"

Clearly, Yossi Abramowitz will.

RACHEL AZARIA

by SARAH BRONSON

As a child in the 1980s, Rachel Azaria was taught that the Torah is the Tree of Life, and that rabbis, especially the leaders of Israel's rabbinical establishment, epitomize goodness and exercise their authority responsibly and righteously. She still believes most of those things. In a 2006 interview in her Jerusalem office, she says Orthodox Judaism "is how I live my life and how I will raise my children. I totally believe in it."

Yet in her efforts to solve one of Israel's most embarrassing problems, Azaria is engaged in a full-time campaign to remove political power from the very rabbis she once revered. In 2004, Azaria became executive director of Mavoi Satum (Dead End), a nonprofit organization that assists Israeli women whose husbands refuse them a *get*, a Jewish divorce. Known as *mesoravot get* in Hebrew, these women are chained to bad marriages, unable to establish child custody or child support in Israeli courts, divide their assets, escape their husband's debts, or pursue a relationship with another man.

"Seeing injustice," she says, "drives me crazy." Seeing it within the rabbinical courts inspired Azaria to take the executive director position, despite the fact that at the time she was seeking a part-time job and was considering pursuing a PhD. "How often do you get an opportunity to change the world?" she says. "Anything having to do with injustice gets me going…It can't be that in Israel a woman cannot get a divorce. It cannot be in Israel that a woman must put up with an abusive relationship."

After a year and a half at Mavoi Satum, Azaria has already pushed the movement to eliminate Israel's problem of mesoravot get to new heights, achieving more media publicity and more parliamentary awareness than ever before. As board co-chairman Judith Garson Djemal says, "She has completely turned the organization around. She has put us on the map. She's a huge asset to the campaign. Things will change, and she will be one of the big movers behind it." Thanks to Azaria, she says, Mavoi Satum now has an open door to several members of the Knesset. When the state controller released a critical report about the *bet din* (Jewish Court), Azaria successfully pushed for an inquiry into the matter.

In Israel, all matters relating to marriage and divorce are subject to the regulation of the rabbinate. There is no such thing as a civil marriage or divorce. Therefore, if a husband refuses to make a divorce final, issues such as child custody and division of property are left unresolved, even in the civil courts. And, though the "recalcitrant husband," as such men are known in the world of Jewish law, can go on to have relationships with other women without penalty, a woman who finds a new partner is considered an adulteress.

The problem, Azaria says, is not that the religious court has regulatory power *per se*, but that "they exercise it unevenly, invoking Jewish law when doing so favors the husband but not when it favors the wife and children." She explains that for reasons unclear to her, most members of the Israeli religious courts opt to follow minority opinions in Jewish law that discourage forcing a husband to give his wife a get.

Of the 9,500 Israeli couples each year seeking divorce, the governmental chief rabbinate claims there are only 180 open cases of mesoravot get. But Azaria points out that the rabbinate's definition of mesoravot get is limited to women who are actively seeking a get and whose husbands refuse to grant one under any circumstances. It does not include situations in which the husband is offering to provide a get in exchange for full child custody or for huge sums of money; nor does it include women who have simply given up on the process and have resigned themselves to living in marital purgatory for the rest of their lives. When one includes such cases, Azaria said, the number of mesoravot get in Israel reaches "the thousands."

In 2006, Mavoi Satum helped twenty-five mesoravot get; this number is up from an average of just ten a year when the organization was first founded in 1995. When Azaria arrived, she says, most women who came for the first time had been without a get for years and were already so exhausted and discouraged that they had little motivation to continue fighting for their rights. As the issue of mesoravot get has garnered increasing publicity, more women are seeking help with their divorces and are approaching Mavoi Satum at earlier stages of the process. Now women come after trying to receive a get for just a few months, realizing that they have recourse other than waiting, often fruitlessly, for a resolution.

When a woman contacts Mavoi Satum asking for assistance in seeking a divorce, a social worker discusses the details of her situation and then arranges meetings with the particular staff members who may prove helpful: Mavoi Satum includes civil lawyers, lawyers for religious courts, publicity staff, and the social worker. The team works with the woman to formulate a comprehensive support plan, including anything from weekly meetings with the social worker to legal help, from therapy to private detective services to find husbands who have "disappeared."

Mavoi Satum also raises public awareness about the problem. Since Azaria's arrival, the organization has exerted pressure on the

Ministry of Justice and the Knesset to redistribute the authority of the religious courts in overseeing certain aspects of divorce proceedings. Staff members appear on morning talk shows to publicize the issue and arrange for colorful and photo-worthy street displays (such as volunteers representing "the Knesset" and "the rabbinate" playing tug-of-war with a long rope, which has a woman tied up in the middle) that glean media attention. The publicity stunts not only keep the issue at the forefront of politicians' minds, but also inspire many women to call and ask for help.

"The whole system works," Azaria says of Mavoi Satum's approach. "I believe this problem can be solved. Maybe it will take fifteen years. But it will be solved. There is momentum such as we've never had. When we approach politicians now, they know exactly what the problem is and they know that the public is angry about it. If it will be solved, it will be now."

. . .

Azaria's quiet confidence stems in part from her successful efforts lobbying to create an express train service between Jerusalem and Tel Aviv. While working toward a bachelor's degree in psychology and a master's in conflict resolution at the Hebrew University, Azaria worked for Green Course, a student environmental group with a presence on twenty Israeli college campuses. Serving first as lobbying coordinator, and later as chapter director, she coordinated dialogues with Jerusalem's municipal representatives, employees of the Israeli bus company, and members of the parliament.

The campaign for the train was long and complex, involving coordinated and strategic events and efforts to garner public support and convince the correct politicians to create a more expensive, but more environmentally sound, long-term plan for public transportation. A turning point occurred when the Minister of Transportation, trying to put the students off, agreed to support their plan if they amassed ten thousand petition signatures for it, from Jerusalem residents, within two weeks. In response, they recruited college students to stand at shopping centers and on campuses, approaching strangers to say, "Do you live in Jerusalem? Don't you want a train to get to Tel Aviv in twenty-eight minutes? So sign."

"Two weeks later we had ten thousand, and it worked," Azaria recalls, adding that they made sure to let the press know when they would approach the minister about fulfilling his promise, and that they then did so with television cameras rolling. "It was amazing. We did it. It was the most empowering thing I was ever a part of. Who were we? We were nothing. I was twenty-three, and we were a group of twenty people. I saw how you can change a law. You can campaign and change things. I was definitely empowered."

Her former supervisor, Green Course founder Eran Binyamini, says that many of the skills Azaria uses in her current leadership capacity were already evident back then, and led Green Course to hire her as a full-time fundraiser after her graduation. "She's very good at interpersonal relationships," he says. "And she's a quick learner. We trusted her that she can learn how to do it. Fundraising is different from running campaigns and being a leader who works well on the ground with people. But she did both well."

Azaria's strategies of involving the media and her unflagging efforts to effect change have worked well at Mavoi Satum. With her paid staff of seven and countless volunteers, Azaria organized an awareness rally in February 2006 that drew 1,500 participants. "We're at a peak with the press," Azaria says. "Now, when you talk about divorce, you talk about mesoravot get. It's just obvious." Before the 2006 elections, she reported, three political parties put the issue on their platforms. "That was a dream come true," Azaria says. "Okay, plenty of politicians promise things and don't come through. The fact that they think it's important enough to promise is already one step forward."

Dozens of women have finalized their divorces thanks to Mavoi Satum. In one dramatic case, the son of a religious court judge was refusing to give a get to his wife. He had moved to the United States and remarried. In March 2006, Mavoi Satum organized a demonstration in front of the religious court, setting up a marriage canopy with a happy "couple," and a bound and gagged "ex-wife" watching forlornly from the side. The woman got her get.

"Part of what we were saying is no matter how bad the divorce is, no matter what wrong the wife does, refusing a get is something you just don't do," Azaria says. "Go ahead and fight in the civil courts, but withholding a get is something you just don't do."

. . .

Born in 1977, Azaria grew up in the religious town of Bet Gamliel. She is the second of six children, four boys and two girls. She attended religious schools and chose to perform her army service as a tour guide in a special program for religious girls. She married her husband, Elyashiv, in 2001 after a whirlwind romance; their daughter Chava was born in 2003 and baby Rut was born at the start of 2007.

Azaria says her parents, both of whom are educators, instilled a sense of social awareness in their children. Her father is a native Israeli and her mother is an American who grew up Conservative and turned to Orthodoxy after moving to Israel. "My mother made *aliyah* on her own when she was eighteen. There was a sense of responsibility to the nation of Israel, the people of Israel, the land of Israel," Azaria says. "There was something in the way we were brought up – but I'm the most radical in the family." In an interesting twist, one brother has become ultra-Orthodox. Azaria says that she does not discuss her work with him.

To Azaria, the problem of mesoravot get is not only a human rights injustice, but a *chillul Hashem*, a desecration of the very religion she loves wholeheartedly. "Not all the staff members of Mavoi Satum are religious, but there is a lot of religious spirit. People are upset that religion is being abused. It touches people's deepest sense of justice. For some of us who are religious it touches the deepest sense of what religion is all about," she says.

For her, what "religion is all about" is to help the widow and the orphan as the Torah demands; to protect the weakest members of society as well as to observe Shabbat, kashrut and holidays. "I always learned that doing *mitzvot* makes us better people," she says. "Okay, a few rules are a bit complicated, but normally Judaism is supposed to be the highest level of ethics. It can't be that you are supposed to be good to the widow and the orphan, but to a divorced woman you can do whatever you want. Many women come to us and say, 'I was nervous about approaching the civil courts because who knew what they would do to me, but I felt calm before going to the religious court because my husband was having affairs and was abusive, and I was sure the rabbis – the rabbis! – would care about morals and care about the Jewish people. I didn't think there would be a problem, because it's so obvious we need a get for my husband to leave and let me raise my children in peace.' And then they are shocked at how hard it is.

"Judaism never allowed you to abuse the weak," Azaria continues. "So when did it become true that a man could withhold a get until he gets everything he wants? [The prophet] Jeremiah would certainly have something to say about it if he were living today."

Despite her convictions, her work takes a certain emotional toll, especially as she tries to reconcile her ideals with the realities of today's situation. "Sometimes I can hear her frustrations," Binyamini says, "the dichotomy between her being religious and what she sees, how the religious authorities treat women. It's not easy for her. She [and Elyashiv] are both very into Judaism. They are very connected, traditionally and intellectually. You can criticize the religious authorities but still believe in Judaism and Jewish values. They separate it in their minds. It is not easy for them."

Her disillusionment couldn't be clearer, as she discusses the judges of religious courts. "Suddenly [for me] to go against them," she says, "to see the rabbis for what they really are – all of their beauty and nice clothes and beards disappear, and the rabbis are weak people with power issues…The prophets speak of *mishpat tzedek*, judging justly. It seems to me the [judges] think they do not have to judge justly…the day the bet din takes seriously the huge job on their shoulders, you will see how all of the complaints of religious feminists will disappear, but as long as the bet din does these terrible things [allowing men to extort their wives, forcing women to try to patch up abusive marriages], their power will decrease and go to the civil courts."

Coupled with her sense of responsibility is a tenacity, a focus, that makes it difficult for Azaria to let up. The same forces that make her unable to put a book down until she has finished it, sometimes causing her to miss a night's sleep, also lead her to dwell on a social problem until she has solved it. "In a way she's too responsible," Binyamini observes. During her time at Green Course, "it got to the point that she was worrying all the time that [she was not raising] enough money, and she couldn't sleep...She cares about things deeply. She does not have a poker face. If she cares about something, you can see it. There is something very real in her, very sincere and caring."

Azaria admits to being a somewhat obsessive worrier, but says her concerns are justified. Israeli religious leaders, she believes, are violating the biblical commandment of, "Do not stand by your friend's blood," usually interpreted as prohibiting negligent behavior that may cause harm to others. "Last week a woman in Meah Shearim committed suicide after the rabbis told her to go home and make peace with her husband," Azaria says. "The rabbis do not realize they are dealing with people's lives."

She does not characterize herself as pessimistic, only fearful that her efforts will not bear fruit. She said that her work for mesoravot get has made her more nervous and overworked, less able to discuss mesoravot get calmly, and "more upset with the rabbinical authorities. I've seen things I never thought I'd see. I hear things I never thought I'd hear," she says. But Azaria also believes people can make a difference. She has seen it happen. "If you push the right buttons, you've done so much. With mesoravot get you can help so many women with one change of legislation."

.   .   .

Postscript (Spring 2008): Azaria's career recently and unexpectedly underwent a significant change. She left Mavoi Satum in spring 2007 after a disagreement with the board. She received several job offers but decided to take time to weigh her options, to determine what she was passionate about and where her efforts would be most needed. She ultimately decided to work toward a stronger Jerusalem, to address what she sees as the many challenges that detract from the experience of life in the city, a city she loves and says is deteriorating. "It is hard to see a city you love change so rapidly. If we don't fight now, it will be too late," she says.

Azaria was born in Jerusalem, lived there until the age of six, and always knew she wanted to settle there. The Hebrew University of Jerusalem is the only place she applied for college, and she and her husband live in the city.

"Jerusalem once was a very strong, pluralistic city, very cultural, very historic. Over the past ten years the city has changed dramatically. It is getting weaker and weaker," she explains. She attributes the problem to the influx of ultra-Orthodox: although the ultra-Orthodox are "very nice people," as a group she believes they are wreaking political havoc on the city. "There are many more ultra-Orthodox; the city is much poorer, less pluralistic, and although only twenty percent of the population is ultra-Orthodox, the mayor [Uri Lupolianski] is ultra-Orthodox and he basically takes care of his crowd," she says. She contends that a disproportionate amount of funding is going to ultra-Orthodox causes, that more people can't pay taxes, and that there is substantially reduced support of education and culture. Public transportation is inadequate, and traffic problems plague the city. High housing costs are driving many of the middle class out of the city, and the drain of people is weakening the city.

Azaria went to work for an organization created by the municipality to address culture, but quickly found that the organization had no true power, and she left that job after four months. After more soul searching, she decided to run for city council in November 2008. She created a political party, Hitorerut Yerushalmim (Wake up Jerusalemites), which attracted more than one hundred volunteers before she even announced it, as well as others who want to run for city council on the same platform. "We are saying that we care about the citizens of Jerusalem," she says. The central issue, as she sees it, is, "How do we turn [Jerusalem] into a pluralistic city where people enjoy their differences, instead of a place where people are fighting for their piece."

The decision to start her own party, to run for city council, is not one she made lightly. She is more comfortable behind the scenes, and she understands that politics can be ugly and take a toll on one's personal and family life. But the idea, once hatched, would not go away. "At first I kind of *whispered it to myself," she says. She thought about creating an organization to address these issues. But ultimately, she has come to believe that the way to effect change is from the inside. Her experiences at Mavoi Satum helped shape that belief. "At Mavoi Satum we really managed to change the way people in Israeli society saw the problem and the way people talked about the issue in the media, in the government, on the street. But when it came down to decision-making in the government, the decisions were always pro the ultra-Orthodox," she recalls.*

In the end, she followed her heart, going with this idea that she calls "a little crazy," and "far-fetched," but that every day is gaining momentum, becoming more tangible.

"This is what the city needs and I am going to do it," she says.

Postscript (Autumn 2008): In the municipal elections for Jerusalem held in November, Azaria's party, Hitorerut Yerushalmim, captured two seats on the thirty-one-seat Jerusalem Municipal Council.

MICHAEL BERENBAUM

by ANDREA GOLLIN

Michael Berenbaum stands at a podium at the University of Miami and he talks and talks, the words flow, his style conversational, graceful, compelling, as he relates facts and statistics he seems to know by heart. He recounts that the total staff at Treblinka was one hundred and twenty – thirty Germans and ninety Ukrainians effected the killing of between 700,000 to 870,000 Jews; there were one hundred known Jewish survivors. Chelno used mobile gas vans. Of 500,000 Jews in Belzec, two survived that we know of. Auschwitz had forty-four parallel train tracks feeding it; New York's Penn Station, by contrast, has twenty-one. Hungarian Jews – 437,402 of them – arrived primarily at Auschwitz in one hundred and forty-seven transports in the fifty-four days between May 15 and July 9, 1944, and eighty to ninety percent of them were murdered on arrival. When Auschwitz was liberated, after the Death March there were only about six thousand people left there. Also left were fourteen thousand pounds of human hair and 358,000 suits.

Before there's time to wonder what happened to the hair, he is speaking of that too, and more. He doesn't raise his voice, he is not agitated, but he is focused and urgent. "The human being was consumable raw material to be recycled. The gold went to Switzerland. The hair was used to line submarines and stuff mattresses. The human fat was used as fertilizer; there's no evidence that it was used in soap…clothing, shoes were reused. Gold and silver was melted down. It was a highly efficient, assembly line notion of killing."

This is a man who has spent the greater part of his career telling the story of the Holocaust. He has told it in many ways, to many audiences, over many years. He has told it in museums, in books, in films, in university classrooms, in lectures. He is fluent in Holocaust. He is a translator of sorts, a traveler bringing us this story, trying to teach us, hoping that something may come of the telling.

Berenbaum is a gifted speaker, verging at times on lyrical. Of the victims, he says, "When they said they were hungry, they ate in 1941 and again in 1945, and that meal often killed them. When they said they were cold, they got cold in October and warm again in May."

When he finishes speaking, there's only time for five questions, each of which he greets with interest. One man in the audience has raised his hand, not to question but to comment. "I've never heard anything discussed in such depth and in such a short amount of time – congratulations," the listener tells Berenbaum, as others nod in agreement.

"Thank you. You can collect your money outside," Berenbaum jokes.

He travels the world – he has worked on museum projects from Mexico to Japan, from Chicago to Jerusalem. He has written or edited seventeen books, not including overseeing the award-winning 2006 new edition of the twenty-two-volume *Encyclopaedia Judaica*, for which he served as executive editor. He directs a think tank in Los-Angeles, the Sigi Ziering Institute: Exploring the Ethical and Religious Implications of the Holocaust, which holds seminars and runs programs, and is part of American Jewish University, formerly the University of Judaism. He's a college professor, who taught full time at Wesleyan for seven years, as an adjunct for fifteen years at Georgetown, and for shorter stints at several other universities, including visiting professorships. More recently, he has become increasingly involved in films, sometimes as a consultant, sometimes as a narrator, sometimes as a producer.

. . .

It all began with his work for the United States Holocaust Memorial Museum, where he spent several years. He was a research fellow there in 1987–1988, became project director from 1988–1993, and was director of the research institute from 1993–1997. Of course, one does not simply become the project director of a museum being built on the Mall in Washington, D.C. It really began before that, when he was appointed to the President's Commission on the Holocaust, for which he was deputy director in 1979–1980, an opportunity that prompted him to leave his teaching job at Wesleyan.

But really, it began where things begin for most of us; it started in childhood, at a time when the Holocaust was not discussed, but was clearly in evidence. "I am not the child of survivors, but I am a product of them," he says. "I was shaped by that epoch."

Berenbaum, born in 1945, grew up in Kew Gardens, Queens, the child of parents who came to the U.S. from Europe as very young children – his mother at age one, his father at eight. American children of Yiddish-speaking immigrants, both were raised to embrace America.

Berenbaum was brought up "deeply Orthodox," as he describes it, was educated at New York *yeshivot* (he went on to receive his rabbinical ordination from the Conservative Jewish Theological Seminary in 1967), and, while growing up, attended a synagogue whose members were German and Belgian refugees desperate to make a life in America.

"It was a shattered culture," he explains. "In school we didn't study the Holocaust. I was educated by Hebrew-speaking teachers who were for the most part Holocaust survivors but didn't use the term. They were refugees. I saw things that were never explained. One teacher couldn't move his left arm and his hand had no fingers. It was a fist – he would hold chalk in it. We saw tattooed numbers on arms. We didn't know what they were. We heard words like 'children,' and 'death,' and 'murder.'"

In this world, just after the war, educated by these men, he felt that he and his classmates "were a small elite and had to make up for an entire culture that was lost."

Although the Holocaust was seldom discussed, it was a constant presence. He remembers rising at dawn as a teenager to listen to a daily 6:25 A.M. report on the Eichmann trial on his clock radio, a new invention at the time.

He attended Queens College, where he received a bachelor's degree in philosophy, then went to graduate school, first at Boston University and then at Florida State University, where he earned a PhD in religion and culture. He began graduate school with the idea of exploring the question, through the history of religion, of why some cultures are destroyed after defeat while others are not. The idea of studying the Holocaust had not occurred to him and didn't until someone else pointed out the link.

"A guy came up to me and said this was a contemporary question, and he told me to read Holocaust literature," Berenbaum recalls. He found that Holocaust literature was asking many of the same questions he was interested in, and that the literature "resonated" with him.

He had every intention of spending his career at Wesleyan when the Holocaust came calling. It was 1979, and he had just bought a house in Connecticut, which he and his family had lived in for three months, when, as he puts it, "a bizarre piece of – in retrospect – not luck but destiny" occurred. The President's Commission on the Holocaust was being formed, and Berenbaum was offered the position of deputy director. The job entailed a move to Washington, D.C. – he says he got the position because "no one else could go." Previously, he had worked at the Holocaust Resource Center in New York while he was on leave from Wesleyan.

Berenbaum began working on the conception of what ultimately became the U.S. Holocaust Memorial Museum in 1979–80,
but wound up leaving the position in 1980 after a clash with Elie
Wiesel over the issue of whether non-Jewish victims of the Holocaust
would receive attention in the museum. Berenbaum argued for their
inclusion. Wiesel "saw me as an agent of de-Judaization of the Holocaust because I told him, in the way a young man tells one's elders
[that the museum should include non-Jews]," he recalls.

Berenbaum and his family decided to stay in D.C., where he
held several jobs during the next seven years. He taught at various
universities before taking a position as the executive director of the
Jewish Community Council of Greater Washington for three years.
Then he began teaching at Georgetown as an adjunct professor of
theology, where he taught courses on modern Jewish thought and
rabbinics and offered a course on the Holocaust each year. When
he started at Georgetown, he also began working in journalism, at
the *Washington Jewish Week*, where he spent three and a half years as
editor of the Opinion Page and an overlapping year as acting editor,
a work experience he calls "a lucky break." To this day, he advises
graduate students to spend six months at a newspaper as a preemp-
tive cure for writer's block. "It helped me write quickly and well," he
says. "I suggest it to all my graduate students…because they will no
longer be afraid of the empty screen. If you don't write and you pro-
crastinate, you will get fired."

In 1987, Berenbaum once again took a position with the U.S.
Holocaust Memorial Museum, after Wiesel left as chairman. He became the project director of the museum, returning with a somewhat
different perspective gleaned during the intervening years and from
his teaching experience. "I went back to it as an agent of Judaica and
protecting Jewish memory," he says.

Berenbaum stayed at the museum for the next ten years, an
experience he calls "the opportunity of my life, which was to shape
the museum. In certain respects it was something for which my entire
life had trained me. I became the translator into America idiom and
visual idiom of what had been bequeathed to me in silence. I gave

voice to what these people [his childhood teachers] had communicated in silence but could not tell at that stage of the game."

The U.S. Memorial Holocaust Museum is a "monumental achievement of tremendous intellectual and moral magnitude that has really changed the landscape of Holocaust commemoration," says Efraim Zuroff, director of the Simon Wiesenthal Center's Israel Office. He notes that the museum has a significance and an impact that derive not only from the building's contents but from its context. "The very notion of a museum dedicated to the Holocaust, built with the assistance of the federal government on federal land, on the Mall in Washington, D.C., gave the commemoration of the Holocaust a tremendous push outside the Jewish community," Zuroff explains. "The Jewish community never had any doubts about the Holocaust's significance as a watershed event in world history, but that was not initially obvious to others." Zuroff cites the "highly effective manner in which the museum was created," and its ability to "walk a very fine line" as a government museum that "had to tell the tale in a way that was not victim-centered and not perpetrator-centered, but that had to find the right balance" as factors in both the ultimate moral resonance of the institution and its subsequent success in steadily attracting large numbers of visitors (as of 2008, nearly thirty million since the museum's dedication in 1993).

In 1997, Berenbaum left the museum, and left Washington, D.C., to take a position as the president and CEO of Spielberg's Survivors of the Shoah Visual History Foundation (now the USC Shoah Foundation Institute for Visual History and Education), created to gather video testimonies from survivors and other witnesses of the Holocaust.

The position was not ultimately a good fit for him, and he left in 1999 to work on his own, primarily as a consultant to Holocaust-themed museums, films, and other related projects. In going out on his own, his thoughts were that he "had devoted fifteen years to the creation [of institutions] but also to administration...I had done a lot of what I wanted to do. I wanted to see if I could do the creative work and not the administrative." He has since been involved in numerous projects ranging from books to films to museums and memorials, and calls this phase of his career "very productive."

. . .

Observing Berenbaum lead an afternoon planning meeting for a modest Holocaust museum in Hollywood, Florida that's in the planning stages is watching a master at work. He addresses a room full of people, explaining the museum's scope, objectives, and proposed layout, using only floor plans as visuals, yet managing to conjure a vivid, detailed image of what the institution will be. He is direct and he is honest, and he repeatedly tells his listeners that he wants to hear all of their criticism.

"A museum building is a combination of story and space. A good museum should be like a symphony with themes," he says. Yet, in the case of a Holocaust museum, certain elements function quite differently from those in typical museums. Like other museums, the idea is to "grab you, move you a continent away, a universe apart," he says. But, "museums usually show the pristine and the beautiful. With us it's the anti-pristine and the anti-beautiful. Normally you would want to see a beautiful, elegant Torah. Here, the desecrated Torah becomes more powerful."

In the case of the museum in Hollywood, the institution needs to convey not only facts and figures but also certain messages. The museum should "tell you that before they were victims, they were people. They were people like you and like me. It should create a sense of empathy." It will do this by recreating "a shadow of what the survivors experienced. [It will] shatter and shape and enlarge the human spirit and teach the fundamental values of human conscience," Berenbaum says.

On a more prosaic level, he mentions that maps are essential, because "we have kids who don't know where Europe is." Keeping the audience in mind, there is the goal that "the students should be able to answer certain·questions" after they have toured the museum. Then there's the message, the take-home lesson, and it's one that Berenbaum says must be shaped not just to its subject, the Holocaust, but to its audience, its place – to school kids in South Florida. "Kids don't need the message that the world's a lousy place and there's nothing you can do. That's nihilism, that's despair. We want to tell them – it's a little false – you can make it better. We want to teach that courage takes many forms."

And then he gets to the crux of the audience issue, which is that you simply do not know how the story you tell will affect your audience, so care must be taken. Yes, the building will be "one of the morally most important buildings in your city." Yes, it is a story that must be told. Yes, we have failed at the whole notion of "never again," but "that doesn't mean the effort is not important." Yes, we Jews "are a people who remember evil, who remember anguish, who remember suffering."

But that does not give us leave to present the story purely from the teller's point of view. It must be shaped, it must be appropriate to its context and to its audience; in this case, primarily schoolchildren. "Kids are unformed – we are formed," he says. "I, unfortunately, can no longer be a ballerina." His point? To keep in mind that the museum's objective is to impart knowledge and engender empathy, it is not to traumatize. And that children can be traumatized without much effort. Care must be taken.

. . .

Not to traumatize. How does that apply to the teller of the story? It's more than thirty-five years since Berenbaum began studying Holocaust literature as a PhD student. How does he continue to do this work, to study, to teach, to tell of the atrocities through books, movies, museums? "It's hard," he says. He mentions that he has had advantages that have helped him, primary among them being his children – he has four children, from two marriages. "When I first started I had young children, and young kids are life personified. Their life force, their zeal, is infectious," he says. Their joy helped balance the darkness of his work.

Nevertheless, he says, "You do pay a price for it. My kids did, especially my older kids." You never really know how your work, your decisions, impact your children. However, when they write their college admission essay about your work, you start to get an inkling. His oldest daughter, Ilana, who is now a rabbi, never mentioned that, growing up, she knew Berenbaum had stored a box of canisters of Zyklon-B, the poison gas pellets used at Auschwitz and other concentration camps, in the family garage, behind the ski equipment. But she wrote about it.

How the box got to the garage is a saga in itself. The canisters were the property of the Holocaust Museum, but when they arrived, staff members had a strong negative reaction. They were "a powerful symbol of evil. Some feared that their power could reach into the present," Edward Linenthal reports in his book *Preserving Memory: The Struggle to Create America's Holocaust Museum.*

One staff member claimed that proximity to the material was making him impotent and threatened to sue. Testing the pellets to see if they were toxic would cost thousands. Berenbaum took matters into his own hands – one night after work he loaded the box of pellets into his car, and drove it to his house. It was never mentioned at the museum again, he says. He hid it in his garage for years, eventually found a low-cost way to test the material, which was judged safe, and at long last brought the box to a museum storage facility, thinking that was the end of it. And it was, until he read his daughter's essay about, "what it was like to grow up where Zyklon-B was stored next to your ski boots," he says.

Humor also helps. Berenbaum laughs as he recalls the evening when his wife turned to him and said, "I don't want to see another Holocaust film. Let's go see *Hotel Rwanda*" (a film about the brutal murder of one million people in Rwanda). Irony can come in handy as well. When he drove to Dachau in 1972 there was a gasoline strike in Germany. "I couldn't get gas for my car. I said, 'Should I say that I'm the first Jew who couldn't get gas at Dachau?'" Berenbaum the scholar quickly steps in to point out that he "subsequently learned that Jews weren't gassed at Dachau."

Then, as if he's giving himself advice, he points out that balance in life is important, "so that it's not just Holocaust." For him, in his career that has become "harder and harder...I've become a victim of my own specialty. Twenty-five years ago, I got invited to speak on many more topics." That, in part, is why he recently took on the massive task of editing the *Encyclopaedia Judaica*, a three-year project to significantly rewrite the twenty-two-volume, five-million-word endeavor, first published in 1972, which had been updated a few times but never re-crafted. As he worked on it, he anticipated that it would broaden the subjects he was asked to lecture on, although that has turned out not to be the case, he says.

But there are rewards, too. "Any of us who teach the Holocaust understand that we impact in ways we cannot imagine," he tells the audience at the University of Miami. "I was in that hotel in Rwanda right after the genocide. I walked in and was greeted by a beautiful blond young woman. She had been my student in 1982, she had become a doctor, and she was volunteering for Doctors without Borders." She told Berenbaum the reason she was volunteering was because she had studied the Holocaust with him at Georgetown, and she asked him to meet with her parents and explain to them why what she was doing was important.

However, teaching is a delicate matter, one in which the lessons you impart must be carefully thought through, he says. "It is not enough to educate people," Berenbaum says, time and again, in conversation, in lectures, in presentations. "Education must be joined with values. Are we educating students to be sensitive human beings...with a respect for human rights? When I taught at Georgetown I was always afraid some student would be taking notes, thinking, 'Germany made mistakes here, made mistakes there, when I'm back in Asia, Africa, etc., I will do better.'"

That fear, the fear that in educating students about the Holocaust he is teaching aspiring perpetrators of atrocities, doesn't stop him from continuing on day after day, telling this story in every way he can think of, to as many people as he can reach, in as many different media as he can gain access to.

Why? Why keep telling the story? Why keep building museums, making films, writing books, studying the event? "People are asking that less and less," Berenbaum says. "Thirty years ago people asked why the Holocaust was relevant. The world is such that now they do understand why…It happened. It is the definitive event of twentieth-century humanity. We *have* to learn from it."

And have we?

The answer, Berenbaum says, clearly not for the first time, is, "Yes, no and maybe. We have learned, but our narrative is much more complex. Jews thought we had figured out from the history of the Holocaust that we were victims because we did not have land and did not have adequate power; we were without an army and a state. The irony of contemporary Jewish history is that Israel's weakness is its strength, and its strength is its weakness. Its greatest vulnerability is that it is perceived as being so strong that nothing it does to defend itself is regarded as just.

"But there is such a residue of victimization that the Jewish community continues to see things as having Holocaust-like peril when there is no actual relationship. This is not 1930. No one is going to ship you and me off to the gas chamber. We don't perceive ourselves the way others do. Israel is a military superpower, but it still feels victimized and vulnerable."

We have learned, too that the "political will to combat genocide is often not as strong as the political will to commit genocide," he says. "I learned this deeply in Rwanda. We could have stopped that with a very limited amount of force. The British and French left, then the Americans came in to save the Americans. The United Nations was impotent. It didn't have to happen but no one had the impetus to go against it.

"We used to think the answer was never again. But we can't say that with a straight face because we have had genocide since and indifference to genocide since. The answer is, not this time. *Not on my watch.*"

MIRA BRICHTO

by LAURA GRIFFIN

In the dank, abandoned libraries of Russia and Eastern Europe, "everything is disintegrating," says Mira "Milly" Brichto. "I saw books on the floor withering away, We're talking about hidden treasures. We sit here and these things are withering away. Libraries were victims of the war, too."

Barely five feet tall, Brichto is a tiny woman with a huge presence, a grandmother from Ohio and former literature professor who has devoted her life to humanitarian work and social activism. She is the founder of the R'fa-aye-nu Society, named for a prayer from Jeremiah 17:14: "Heal me, O Lord, and I shall be healed." She translates *R'fa-aye-nu* as simply "Heal us." Formed in 1993, R'fa-aye-nu's mission is "to help those in need of physical or spiritual healing, regardless of faith or ethnic background."

Part of that mission has been to save those hidden treasures –

Torah scrolls and Jewish texts that have undergone decades of neglect and degradation – for future generations. Brichto has been active in her work both to open archives containing Jewish texts and to encourage institutions to adopt modern techniques to preserve, catalogue and digitize these materials and to improve the conditions in libraries and archives through weatherproofing and air conditioning.

The society's mission, however, is broader than recovering, restoring and preserving the vast body of literature endangered by war and neglect. The society's work in Central and Eastern Europe endeavors to promote spiritual healing by bringing together Jews and Christians to face their complex shared history. And then there's physical healing – organizing donations from America of surplus medical supplies and equipment. Brichto has acknowledged that the dual objectives of physical and spiritual healing are confusing to some, but she feels they are integrally connected. "The medical equipment that we send is sort of like our calling card," she told the *Cincinnati Post*. "It generates goodwill."

While much of the work is comparatively quiet and behind-the-scenes, Brichto has orchestrated public celebrations, interfaith ceremonies and educational initiatives to address the history of anti-Semitic violence and the rift between Christians and Jews in that part of the world. One such celebration followed her 1996 success in restoring a century-old Torah scroll, which had been confiscated in a 1914 pogrom, to its original home in Krakow's Rema Synagogue. The celebration witnessed Jews and Catholics singing and dancing together on Krakow's ancient cobblestone streets as part of *hachnasat sefer Torah*, a welcoming of the Torah, a ritual that hadn't occurred in Krakow since the Holocaust.

"It was a very emotional, beautiful day," recalls Brichto. Of all the work she has done, bringing Jews and Christians together for a common goal is what she feels is one of her biggest accomplishments.

These days, Brichto continues her work of motivating people of different faiths to help preserve rare and disintegrating Jewish texts. A frequent traveler to Eastern Europe when she was younger –

the *New York Times* called her "a natural-born religious diplomat" – today she lives with the constant back pain characteristic of spinal stenosis, a narrowing of the spinal canal, and much of her work is done through phone calls and correspondence. A recent project, the Lviv Archives Preservation Project, a $105,000 initiative, was launched in 2005 by the U.S.-Ukraine Foundation in cooperation with the R'fa-aye-nu Society based on a proposal by Brichto.

Her one-bedroom apartment in a Cincinnati retirement home is filled with artifacts of her life: paintings by a Jewish artist from Warsaw; books of haiku and Psalms; a well-worn Bible on an end table; letters from politicians, bishops, priests, and a U.S. Army general; files of paperwork for grant applications and for reparations from the Germans for recovering books confiscated during the Holocaust. Several small, silver Kiddush cups are stacked on her dining table, a reminder of the Ukrainian bar mitzvah boys who never got to use them.

"Farmers are always finding them in barns where Jews hid during the war. They sell these in the markets – they're everywhere," says Brichto, adding that she bought as many as she could to honor those boys.

· · ·

Throughout her life, being Jewish has defined Milly Brichto. She was born in 1927, in McKeesport, Pennsylvania. Her father, Aladar Pollak, was the rabbi for a community of Orthodox Hungarian Jewish immigrants and was himself a recent immigrant. Brichto was one of eleven children and the seventh daughter in a row.

Pollak raised his children to see "everything through the eyes of being Orthodox American Jews," says Brichto. She fondly recalls him bringing the family outside during a solar eclipse. He broke a glass and put a piece over fire to darken it with smoke. Then he let the children look at the eclipse through the glass. "At that moment, he taught us a prayer," she says. "He connected everything through religion. Religious ritual was tied to the romance of our family."

Sometimes, at night, they would crawl into his bed to hear

his stories. "He wore a night cap and told us Bible stories. I can remember what he emphasized and how he told them to us," Brichto says. Those stories never left her; they even motivated her to become a storyteller herself, publishing two children's books, *The God Around Us: A Children's Garden of Prayer* (1955), and its second volume, *The God Around Us: The Valley of Blessings* (2001). "My genius, if I have any at all, is telling children Bible stories, and they're the same Bible stories he told us," she says.

Her father died of cancer when Brichto was seven. After her father died, her mother moved the family to New York, settling in the Williamsburg area of Brooklyn, with its flourishing Orthodox community. "Being Jewish wasn't skin deep, it was the opposite of that," Brichto recalls. "Even if kids were throwing stones or calling us 'dirty Jew,' we kept our pride and continued to walk. We would just remember not to walk down that street where those kids were again. We didn't see ourselves through the eyes of the kids who threw stones or through the eyes of victims.

"Everything in our whole lives was about being Jewish," she continues. "You'd get up saying morning prayers, wash your hands and say another prayer. After a while, it becomes automatic. But there is danger in that – the danger of not thinking about it."

Education was important in the Pollak family. They were part of the local Orthodox intelligentsia, and Brichto remembers philosophical discussions around the family table. "We were considered a thoughtful family. They put it this way: Even the girls were intelligent," she says, recalling that it was important to her parents that all the children, including the girls, learned. "I was the only kid I knew who was reading what her mother read. I think the fact that I was encouraged to read really explains what happened to me, how I turned out like I did."

In that atmosphere, Brichto was raised to think for herself and question everything.

And she did – eventually too much for her family. "When I reached that point where I was testing all of that, all hell broke loose," Brichto says.

She went to the first Jewish day school for girls in Brooklyn and later to a public high school, where she stood up for human and civil rights, started the first Negro History and Culture Club in 1942, and wrote editorials for the school newspaper.

"The black school was closing and some of the students were going to come to our school and there was some rumbling and unrest," she says. "I wrote an editorial saying that when they came, instead of being afraid of them degrading our school, we should welcome them. The way blacks were treated at the time was against American values."

Her younger brother, Yakov Pollak, now an Orthodox rabbi, always had a great deal of respect for his big sister. "She was an intelligent, forthright, strong-willed person. She set an example and implanted in us a great degree of liberalism," says Brichto's "kid" brother, rabbi at Brooklyn's Congregation Shomre Emunah. "Through her example, we were all for civil rights and human rights."

Nevertheless, Brichto's mother worried about her daughter's "wayward and rebellious" ways. She felt her daughter's behavior as an adolescent was not in keeping with strict Orthodoxy. "We were allowed to question and test, but only within the framework of acceptance. It wasn't *a* way of life it was *the* way," Brichto recalls. "My mother told me, 'No boy from a good family will be interested in you.'"

Then she met Herbert Chanan Brichto, who came from a well-respected Jewish family of rabbis. He liked her spunk and intelligence. "I was the girl who not only *could* think, I did," she says.

They married and Chanan went on to become a U.S. Army chaplain during the Korean Conflict, a leading Torah scholar and Reform rabbi, and a professor, biblical scholar and dean at Hebrew Union College in Cincinnati. Marrying someone who was Reform caused somewhat of a strain in Brichto's relationship with her mother and some of her siblings. Nevertheless, Brichto, who had felt constrained by the strictness of Orthodoxy, moved toward Reform Judaism, although as she has aged, she has moved back toward Orthodoxy.

Brichto began teaching Hebrew the day after her wedding and went on to teach elementary school as well, working in both Jewish and Catholic schools. However, she didn't get her college degree until after her two daughters and a son were born. Eventually, thinking it was time to do something she hadn't had the chance to do earlier in life, she also earned doctorates in literature and psychology. She created a lively home in Cincinnati, where Friday night meant a family dinner that always included a variety of friends and neighbors.

"My brother once said, 'Father had taught us to question everything and mother taught us to *experience* everything,'" says Brichto's younger daughter, Katey Brichto, a writer who lives on a farm outside of Madison, Indiana. "Our mother was always such a champion of living and doing. If we fell down or had trouble with boyfriends, or whatever, her response was, 'That's life. Experience it. Live it.' That was very wonderful in a lot of ways."

Her mother, Katey continues, "was not afraid of spontaneity, adventure, risk, or even pain that much. She is not the type of person who concedes defeat easily. I think she really is taking off at a point where people are ready to quit."

That philosophy extends to Brichto's relationship with two of her grandchildren who were born hearing-impaired. She has worked tenaciously to make sure they did not miss out on anything, helping them get into a school for the deaf in Missouri, driving them there herself when needed and helping her daughter give them the best and most fulfilling lives possible.

"My biggest challenge and my biggest accomplishment, really, were these children," Brichto says. "When I see something has to be done, I don't worry about who is going to help, I just do it. When I want something, I will it to happen, but not without a lot of work."

. . .

That philosophy, that tenacity, is in full evidence in Brichto's work through the R'fa-aye-nu Society, an outgrowth of earlier work she started at the initial request of her younger brother, Yakov. In 1979, Rabbi Pollak came to his sister with an unusual story. At the request of a dying rabbi, he had agreed to retrieve from the Soviet Union twenty volumes of work by a Talmudic scholar. Pollak had smuggled the first volume out by strapping part on his back under his coat and putting part in the lining of his wife's skirt. The other nineteen volumes remained and he needed to find a route through diplomatic channels. "I interested my sister in joining me in getting out the manuscripts," says Pollak, who is also chairman of the Jerusalem Institute of Talmudic Research. "She's a very honorable person and she had the know-how in making the right contacts with religious leaders throughout the world. The fact that she knew Cardinal Bernardin helped, too."

It helped because much of the Jewish literature she was determined to save was in the hands of Catholics and she therefore needed the cooperation of church leaders. "When villages were emptied out (under Nazi occupation), more often than not the village priest would take these materials to the monastic library," Brichto explained to the *National Catholic Reporter*. "Who else knew how to read and write?"

The cardinal had become friends with the Brichtos years earlier when he was archbishop of Cincinnati. Brichto turned to Bernardin for help, recalling, "I had to go to somebody for whom people would readily break the law. But I couldn't turn to longshoremen. Everything had to be done with an enormous amount of respect. It had to be done with clean hands and a pure heart."

Cardinal Bernardin wrote a letter on her behalf that resulted in Brichto and her brother gaining an appointment with Cardinal Franciszek Macharski of Krakow, the former see of John Paul II. Brichto recalls comparing the Jews' written legacy to paintings confiscated from the Church by the Communist government, but pointed out that as opposed to the Catholics, who had survived and could fight for the return of the artwork, all that was left of the majority of the area's former Jewish inhabitants were their documents. Little else was needed, Brichto says, to convince the cardinal that the Jewish people should have full access to documents in the Church's hands.

"You are in the right. You should have the originals. We should have copies," Macharski said, according to Brichto. "They belong to you."

When she later founded the R'fa-aye-nu Society, she made Cardinal Bernardin the honorary chairman. "Cardinal Bernardin opened a lot of doors for us. He and I made a good team – an unexpected one, so it had kind of an impact," Brichto says. Unexpected in part because of Brichto herself. "A long time ago I became aware of the stiffness with which clergy of different religions present themselves to each other…[but] I wasn't clergy and I was a woman. The rules didn't apply to me," she says. Despite the fact that she says she is "as learned as many a rabbi and certainly as committed," the clergy she worked with relaxed around her. "That woman thing works," she says. "They were sort of taken by surprise."

Once she started, Brichto wanted to continue the work of rescuing and preserving these documents. She felt that the recovery of religious texts was of paramount importance, because education and learning are so highly valued in the Jewish tradition. There were not only religious texts of course – there were documents, newspapers, letters, and other materials. "Records, correspondence, these are very important in Jewish religious life. This is our responsum, our interpretation of Jewish law…and it is scattered all over Europe," she told the *National Catholic Reporter*.

Brichto felt that to gain access to archives and libraries, she needed to give people something in return. And so the idea of sending surplus medical supplies was born. She arranged for the shipment of mammography equipment to Poland. She sent medical supplies no longer needed by the U.S. Department of Defense or American hospitals to Ukraine. In 2000, R'fa-aye-nu provided financial aid to Ukraine after a mining accident in the eastern part of the country killed eighty-one people.

"Milly always envisioned great things," says Dr. David Gilner, director of Libraries for Hebrew Union College in Cincinnati, who has known Brichto for thirty-five years and worked in an advisory role with her in her efforts to save texts. "At the same time, she was very happy to stimulate the consciousness of Eastern Europe and make them aware of what they had and the value of that."

Brichto worked with Jewish and Catholic leaders in Kiev to help restore a 102-year-old synagogue that had been a puppet theater for six decades under Soviet rule and where, during World War II, the Nazis killed many of the synagogue's members at the Babi Yar massacre. She brought that and other R'fa-aye-nu projects to the attention of legislators including U.S. senators Joe Lieberman of Connecticut and Hillary Rodham Clinton of New York, as well as Representative Marcy Kaptur of Ohio, who sent letters of support.

Kaptur worked with Brichto for years. She helped Brichto get medical equipment where it needed to go and aided in the proper disposition and replacement of Torah scrolls. "The world needs more Milly Brichtos," says Kaptur, who is Catholic. "She works in a way that builds bridges instead of walls. She's helping to piece together remnants of a glorious history. And she's unrelenting in her efforts. I never walked with her through some of the archives she discovered, but I saw the pictures and I know it was a searing experience for her," she says. "I felt when I met Milly that I had met the Old Testament in a very refined and learned way. She bridged the Old Testament to the modern era. She's a timeless individual, such a woman of history."

In part because of Brichto's work, a Ukrainian bishop sent a letter to his government, asking to restore confiscated Torah scrolls to their original synagogues. "This is probably unprecedented in that landscape, in that part of the world, that the spokesman on behalf of the religious needs of the Jewish people would be a Ukrainian Greek Catholic bishop," Brichto told the *Cincinnati Post.* "It would have been unimaginable in any other time."

"Just the idea of the thing was the exciting part – wanting to rescue all this bibliographia and wanting an exchange of ideas between Catholics and Jews," says Regine Ransohoff, Brichto's former assistant for five years. "Then giving them physical assistance in an effort to get them to help her in uncovering all this Jewish work. I'd never been involved in anything like it. Working with her was amazing. She has all these great ideas. She is one of the most brilliant women I've ever met."

Through the years, Brichto provided three million dollars worth of surplus medical supplies for the region and gained permission to access libraries. But Brichto remains frustrated that so much is still left to save and preserve.

A major obstacle is the sheer expense of preserving the works, making them accessible, and improving their storage conditions, which has kept her from achieving her goal. However, says Gilner, "She laid the foundation. Because of her, some projects are ongoing in Lviv and Poland. She was certainly very successful. She made the matter truly ecumenical – it was about saving culture, not plundering it. She had some great visions; had there been money, many great things would have been accomplished. But you do the best you can and never give up, and that's Milly."

Despite never giving up, Brichto says at times she feels like a small voice in the wind.

"I can't bring back the dead, but I can help restore their written word," she says. "The irony of this pains me: We spend so much money on Holocaust memorials, but if who died was so important to us, then their lives should be also. What did they treasure? What were their values? What was contained in their writings?"

RUTH CALDERON

by SIMONA FUMA

In Israel, there was a popular song on the radio in 2007, "Hinei Ani Ba," about a young man torn between Jerusalem and Tel Aviv. Jerusalem, the city of two thousand years of Jewish longing, is too intense for him. There is too much Israeli-Arab tension, too many ultra-Orthodox, and his secular friends are moving away. This city of stones, with its rigid conservative lifestyle, is downright boring. The young man picks up and moves to Tel Aviv, where at first he is enchanted by the openness, the liberalism, the scantily clad women. In Israel's city-that-never-sleeps, he spends his time frequenting nightclubs and befriending the in-crowd. But after two years of revelry, he begins to feel that the culture of Tel Aviv is shallow. He longs for a more substantial, authentic existence, so he returns to Jerusalem.

The immense popularity of this song is testament to the fact that in Israel these two cities are not just places, but polarities of the Israeli soul. Jerusalem is tradition, Tel Aviv modernity. Jerusalem is religion, community, learning and conservatism. Tel Aviv is secularism, dynamism, progress, creativity and change. Depending on where you fall on the religious-secular spectrum, you may love one city and find the other insufferable. For a staunchly religious Israeli, Tel Aviv evokes the image of shameless hedonists who care only about shopping and going out, who live in a "bubble" divorced from the realities of the Middle East, who lack patriotism and are ignorant of the deeper wellsprings of their past. For many secular liberals, Jerusalem is the city of the Orthodox minority, where black-hatted yeshiva boys pore over their Talmud tomes; women (both Jewish and Arab) cover themselves in modest clothing; politics are right wing; poverty is rampant, and the cafes rarely update their menus. While not all Israelis see the other in such black-and-white terms, the divide between the secular and religious is deep and, according to many, has created a serious and damaging rift in Israeli society.

And that's what makes Ruth Calderon so unusual. Based in Tel Aviv, yet immersed in the world of classical Jewish texts, the renowned Talmud scholar, who has founded two major institutions of Jewish study – Elul in 1989 and Alma, which she has directed since 1996 – has forged a career of making the classical Jewish texts accessible to the secular community.

She arrives for an interview in Tel Aviv's Ramat Aviv Gimmel neighborhood on her Vespa, clad in jeans and a black turtleneck. As she describes it, her work is to "reclaim classic Jewish texts and Jewish thought, not just the culture, but the whole legacy. I am saying to my community, the secular community, that we belong to it and it belongs to us and we can't go forward if we don't know where we came from."

Calderon, who's in her mid-forties, was raised in Tel Aviv, in "the non-affiliated community," she explains over an espresso at an outdoor cafe, and she is a huge fan of the city. "[This] is the center of Jewish and Israeli culture and creativity in music, the written word, TV, film, and the arts. I *love* it."

And yet, even as a child, she longed for something more. She felt that the ideals of Israeli secular culture were somehow lacking. "From a very early age, I felt, it is *not enough.* I felt a need for something deeper, richer," she says. "I appreciated my parents' values, I wanted to stay in my community, but I wanted to be learned in the classic texts."

Today Calderon spends the bulk of each day immersed in the world of first- through fifth-century rabbis. Dubbed the "high priestess" of secular Jewish learning by *Maariv* newspaper, she, together with Elul co-founder Moti Bar-Or, won the prestigious Avi Chai Prize in 1997, a $50,000 grant awarded to Israeli leaders who increase mutual understanding between the secular and religious. Her first book, *The Market, the Home, the Heart* (2001), quickly became a classic of the Jewish feminist bookshelf in Israel. She also hosted an innovative weekly television show in Israel, *Haheder* (The Room), in 2001 in which she brought together diverse Israelis for on-air *chavruta* (paired) study. Though not a prime-time show, it received great reviews and is currently broadcast in reruns.

One of Calderon's unique gifts is her ability to get people to fall in love with Talmud. "I see myself as a *meturgeman* (interpreter), translating complicated things into stories or things that can be understood in a popular way, without losing their heart," she explains.

Esteban Gottfried, forty-two, is a playwright and screenwriter who met Calderon several years ago when she conducted a *beit midrash* (study group) for television and film writers. "Even before I studied [with Calderon] I had a desire to connect my work with Jewish sources. It's part of our culture," he says. He found Calderon to be an excellent teacher who treats students with respect and has "a lot of passion for what she teaches. The characters in the Talmud are like her extended family. It's contagious."

While on sabbatical in the U.S. with her husband and three children from 2002 to 2005, Calderon established Alma New York, through which she initiated an annual *Tikkun Leil Shavuot* (Shavuot night learning) at New York University based on Alma Tel Aviv's Tikkun. Subsequently the venue moved to the JCC in Manhattan, and most recently drew over three thousand twenty- and thirtysomethings. The Tikkun in Tel Aviv, which takes place at the Tel Aviv Museum of Art, is Alma's flagship event. Its success has led to the development of the annual Alma *Regalim* – four mega events celebrating the Jewish calendar – Selichot, Sukkot, Tu Bishvat and Tikkun.

"Ruth has unique gifts of creativity and laser-sharp analytical skills that invite diverse people into her questions about being Jewish in the modern world," says Alisa Rubin Kurshan, vice chair of strategic planning with New York's United Jewish Appeal, who met Calderon during her sabbatical. "She makes the world of the rabbis come alive for her students and makes it real to our everyday lives. To spend an hour with Ruth is to be changed."

Despite her commitment to the texts and her goals to "make more Israelis knowledgeable about our beautiful, powerful legacy, and to make Israel an interesting, spiritual center of Judaism," you're unlikely to bump into Calderon in a traditional synagogue. "I don't pray by the book, except for very special prayers," she says.

. . .

Calderon's primary focus these days is Alma, a non-accredited institution whose goal is to create an "educated Israeli Jew knowledgeable in his culture's classics," by teaching secular Israelis Talmud and traditional Jewish texts alongside Western and Israeli classics.

Alma is located in a two-story historic building in the heart of Tel Aviv, an area recently proclaimed a World Heritage Site by UNESCO for its architecture. Multicolored flowers spill out of planters on the balconies and window ledges, and the interior is bright and airy.

Calderon seems not to dominate Alma so much as infuse it with her elegant touch. Visiting the college and meeting Calderon, you are struck by her graciousness. She is relaxed and affable as she describes the school's approach and instructs students.

The beit midrash, the epicenter of the institution's activity and the embodiment of its philosophy, seats about thirty around long wooden tables arranged in a circle. In Calderon's view, "The beit midrash as an institution relaxes the frontal style. Teachers do not stand and lecture...they are members of the study group."

The room's walls are lined with books, including the Bible, Talmud, and works of *midrash*, commentary on traditional texts through stories. But the room differs from a traditional beit midrash in that it also contains "secular" books: modern Hebrew classics by Y.H. Brenner and Ahad Ha'am as well as the works of Jean-Paul Sartre and Sigmund Freud. The aim, Calderon says, is to produce "Jewish scholars who will be well-rounded and integrated." Students at Alma spend eight to ten hours a week in the beit midrash and are also required to study philosophy, literature, history and art as part of the school's mission to study general culture along with Jewish culture. "We try to integrate, to open the curriculum so it is not only Jewish culture. Our aim is to let the books socialize with each other," Calderon says.

While the books represent a range of fields and traditions, the style of teaching is all Jewish, honed through thousands of years of yeshiva study: *chavrutot*, followed by a teacher-led group discussion, in which the text is not merely academic, but informs students' lives.

Students study in *chavruta*, groups of two to four, puzzling over a text, talking it out, and offering their interpretations before the entire class regroups. The students are not your average group of Israelis, not even for Tel Aviv. On a Wednesday morning in December, one circle consists of a young man with a rope-like goatee and hipster clothing and two middle-aged women: Kobi Oz is the lead singer of Tea Packs, one of Israel's most popular rock bands, Pazit Rosenboim is a sculptress, and Yael Mishali is a novelist and columnist for Israel's highest circulation newspaper. Many of the other students are actors, professors and people whose funky dress hints at a creative life outside the study hall. In other words, they are Israel's cultural elite.

Calderon estimates that about thirty percent of Alma's student body of about two hundred are artists, and feels that it is important to target this group as students. "Artists are agents of change in our culture. They paint and write music, poetry and television series. In teaching them, we can perhaps affect culture," she says. As for the students' motivation, Calderon says that many creative people feel a hunger for something deeper and richer from their heritage that they can own and use in their work.

At Alma, students learn *sugyot*, passages from the Talmud, which Calderon and her co-teachers organize according to themes. The theme for this year has been the idea of home – what constitutes a home in the rabbinic view? On this day, students discuss spaces that are not home, but which rabbis suggest ought to require a prayer before Jews enter and after they leave: the study hall, a foreign city, the bathhouse and a toilet. What do these four places have in common?

As the students attempt to decode the ancient text, with its puns and cross-references and subtle humor, they become increasingly engrossed. Their sense of time falls away as they experience a taste of what every yeshiva *bocher* must know – learning Talmud is absorbing and even addictive. Calderon moves from havruta to havruta, offering help with a difficult Aramaic passage or tricky logical step.

The large-group discussion that follows differs from a traditional yeshiva only in that here it's perfectly acceptable to question or criticize traditional Judaism. "The rabbis were too paranoid," says a twenty-something man. "Saying prayers before going to the bathroom is overdoing it. I'm not sure that such a paranoid religion speaks to me."

"You're wrong," counters another man. "A person can't control their anxieties. Saying the prayer is actually a tool to help relieve your fears."

The discussion next veers onto the topic of the bathhouse. Someone suggests that the danger described as "falling into the fire" in a bathhouse is actually a thinly disguised reference to homosexuality. This is the kind of risqué comment you would not make in a traditional beit midrash. But Calderon is one step ahead of her students. She mentions that the eleventh-century rabbi Rashi, biblical commentator and paragon of piety, was actually wise to this possibility. "The rabbis acknowledged homosexual attraction," Calderon explains with a smile, "It was acting on it that they considered a sin."

Calderon's approach involves reading the rabbis carefully, without the baggage of preconceptions. "An important part of my translating work involves the maxim: Don't judge [the text] from where you are, from the outside, but let's judge it from the inside, let's get inside. Once we understand it, we'll see where we can go with it," she explained in a 2001 interview.

In her book, *The Market, the Home, the Heart*, Calderon's achievement is to make Talmudic passages accessible and psychologically compelling to the contemporary reader. She takes a sparsely worded Talmudic legend, or *aggadah*, and fills in the gaps, describing the atmosphere, the motives and the inner lives of its protagonists, in a modem twist on the tradition called midrash.

Is it anachronistic to attribute such rich inner lives to those living in an age that did not emphasize the primacy of the individual? Calderon explains, "I am doing it because I need to. I want Torah to touch our lives and in order to do so I need to understand the psychological aspect of the characters."

Calderon is also adept at describing the sights and sounds and smells of everyday life in Amoraitic times. At one point in the book, Calderon even describes how a rabbi's wife removed hair from her legs with lime. "[I am interested in] how they slept, what they did, when they went to bed, what their houses looked like," she says.

. . .

Calderon was born in 1961 and grew up in the Tel Aviv neighborhood of Maoz Aviv, the youngest child of three, and the only daughter. Her secular family was nevertheless "very Jewish" and observed certain traditions like lighting candles on Friday night and reciting Kiddush. "My father was a Ladino-speaking Sephardic Jew, and my mother, Margot Kasten [an immigrant from Germany], was an elegant European lady who was always reading books in foreign languages."

Calderon's family was unusual in their Tel Aviv neighborhood where the predominant ethos was that of the Spartan, khaki-wearing "new Jew," secular soldier-pioneers, ardent Zionists who spoke only Hebrew and turned away from their Diaspora roots. The gap between the culture of her home and the ideology she observed at school and in her neighborhood, "is the gap where Elul and Alma originated," she explains. Even as a child of eleven, the early Zionist *Palmachnik* (the *Palmach* was the early Israeli military) ethos of practicality and militarism as opposed to intellectual pursuits did not sit well with her. Calderon sought out books and information on the Jewish past. In fact, she was attracted to the Talmud and other traditional Jewish texts as far back as she can remember. "We are not just heroes on the mountains," she says. "We are the People of the Book."

Calderon missed the refinement and introspection, the *luftmensch* quality or preoccupation with books and the imagination, that she identified with the world of Diaspora Jews and which the new Israeli elite was trying to root out. She set out to recapture this through the study of Talmud. After serving in the army, in 1982 she enrolled at Midreshet Oranim in the Galilee where she spent five years and received a bachelor's degree, followed by another five years at the unaccredited Shalom Hartman Institute in Jerusalem.

Despite being a trailblazer as a secular woman studying Talmud in those days, Calderon was not alone in her attraction to the past. In the period following the Six Day War, a small group of secular Israeli intellectuals decided to reclaim traditional Jewish texts for secular Jews. From this movement – dubbed the Back to the Jewish Bookshelf movement – were born both Midreshet Oranim and the Hartman Institute, new and innovative institutions that were linked to this trend in Israeli society.

In the mid-1980s, Calderon pursued a master's degree in Talmud at the Hebrew University of Jerusalem. During this time she also studied at the Hartman Institute, a modern Orthodox establishment that welcomed secular students. Calderon, while enjoying her studies, felt the need for an egalitarian institution run by both Orthodox and secular management, an institution that would promote a pluralistic approach to Jewish education that would bring together religious and secular men and women. That perceived need led her to cofound the Jerusalem-based Elul in 1989 with Orthodox rabbi, Motti Bar-Or.

Elul attracted both religious and secular young adults who engaged in dialogue over the relevance and meaning of texts. "In order to find a place where I felt at home, I needed to establish it," Calderon explains. "I was always a bit of an outsider: a city girl with the *kibbutznikim*. I was secular in the Talmud department. I was a Tel Avivi in Jerusalem."

She explains that with Elul, "It took a long time for people to understand the concept. It was like every new idea. Secular people thought we were giving ourselves over to religion, religious people questioned the validity of our approach, particularly the idea of broadening the bookshelf, to not have only the classic canon but be open to other great literature."

Calderon left Elul in 1995, in part because, as she explained to *The Jerusalem Post*, "I felt that the gap we tried to bridge at Elul was greater than me, greater than my efforts." Plus, after Yitzhak Rabin was murdered, she felt alienated in Jerusalem and longed to return to Tel Aviv, the city where she most belonged. In 1996, she founded Alma.

In addition to her current work at Alma, Calderon travels the world promoting beit midrash style Jewish text learning among the unaffiliated and spawning Alma offshoots in places such as Haifa, New York City and Warsaw. Recently, in 2007, she received her PhD in Talmud from the Hebrew University of Jerusalem.

· · ·

Calderon's major contribution is "allowing a whole segment of Israelis who were removed from their Jewish past to own it as theirs, without feeling they have to either apologize for not being religious or become Orthodox," according to Moshe Halbertal, a professor of Jewish thought and philosophy at the Hebrew University and the Hartman Institute, and one of Calderon's former professors.

Halbertal believes that this work, which today is much more accepted than when Calderon began her career, has the potential to alter both the notion of Jewish identity in Israel and the nature of Israel as a society by addressing the religious-secular ideological divide. It is "too early to see if the rifts are being healed, but it's a movement in an important direction," he says.

Calderon's work is part of a larger trend, one that she has played a pivotal role in spearheading. Today there are more than twenty egalitarian or secular batei midrash in Israel, many of which have more than one site – there are about one hundred study communities in all, Calderon says.

Clearly, there is a thirst for tradition that places like Alma have tapped into. It is, ultimately, "an identity project," Calderon says. It is this search for identity, this need for meaning, that drives many students to attend Alma. They are groping for an anchor, she says, and clearly, she teaches not only in the classroom but through her example. "Being Jewish gives meaning to my life. For me, the thought of being just another person in the world feels like a missed opportunity," she says.

DEBBIE FRIEDMAN

by DEBRA NUSSBAUM COHEN

When Debbie Friedman takes the stage, the singer-songwriter feels she is doing more than performing. For her, bringing music to people is a holy act.

"You can't imagine what it feels like to be standing up there and feel this wall of sound coming at me when everyone is singing back at me. You just know the *shechina* is there. I feel the divine presence," says the dark-haired soprano in an interview in her Upper West Side apartment. "And if people let themselves, they know it's there, too."

Friedman, born in 1952, is the first female composer to contribute significantly to popular Jewish liturgy. She began writing original music as a young woman in the early 1970s, when she first took conventional prayers and stories from the Torah and set them to completely new, folk music-inspired tunes. Her words usually blend

Hebrew and English, are based on traditional prayers and texts, and are laid out along simple, euphonious melodies.

From the start, her music has provided more than lyrics and a melody; for many listeners, her singularly accessible music is a conduit to the divine. Even people who have never opened a prayer book say they find themselves enveloped in Friedman's songs, and deeply feel their meaning. "Melody transcends intellect, transcends all the blocks that we put in our way," explains Friedman.

"People come to her services and weep, they just weep," says Angela Warnick Buchdahl, a Reform rabbi and cantor who includes Friedman's songs in every service she leads at Manhattan's Central Synagogue. "She has opened up a way of prayer-leading in which she bares her soul, in a way that invites other people to be able to do the same.

"When I was a girl I joined a Jewish choir in Tacoma, Washington. We sang Debbie Friedman songs, her early stuff like 'Sing Unto God.' For me that was a spiritual revelation, of joy of singing to God. I enjoyed singing before, but this was the way, through the music, that I connected spiritually to my Jewishness, in a way I wasn't getting when I went to services," says Warnick Buchdahl. "Debbie has this whole body of upbeat, joyous, contemporary music. She taps into this part of you that wants to leap and get up and dance. There are the two sides of Debbie – the part that can access the joy and the part of her that can access the pain."

Friedman has recorded twenty-two albums, with two more, one based on the *Shacharit* morning service and another about Chanukah, in the works. She's performed countless concerts at venues ranging from Carnegie Hall to Jewish overnight camps to intimate gatherings for healing services. Her lyrics are featured on Hallmark cards. It is perhaps because her songs are so much part of contemporary Jewish life, so ubiquitous, that people singing them sometimes don't know who authored them.

"Anywhere you go today, except in the Orthodox community, which it hasn't reached, you are sure to hear Debbie Friedman's music," says Jonathan Sarna, a scholar of American Jewish history who discusses Friedman's impact in his 2004 book *American Judaism: A History*. "She really brings a kind of soul back into Jewish music. Her music has the authenticity that comes from someone who knows Jewish music and Jewish tradition. At the same time, she offers music that resonates to contemporary ears."

. . .

As a child, Friedman was more religiously inclined than the rest of her family, which included her parents, two sisters, and a brother. Born in Utica, New York, she and her family moved to St. Paul, Minnesota when Friedman was five years old. In Utica, her father had been a kosher butcher and the family belonged to a traditional congregation, but once they moved he switched jobs and they joined a Reform synagogue. Friedman, however, insisted on going to Hebrew school at a nearby Conservative synagogue, and on Saturday mornings walked to *shul* (synagogue).

Even as a very young child she showed musical promise, singing along with symphony recordings at just eighteen months. In her teens, Friedman taught herself to play guitar one summer at Camp Herzl in Webster, Wisconsin because, "there was a person who played and I just wanted to play like she did. It looked like fun," she says. "I just picked it up and started to play." It was 1967, a time when she was listening to Peter, Paul and Mary, Judy Collins, and other popular folk musicians.

The music Friedman loved was a major influence on what was to come. "It was the message of the folk music of the time, and the music itself. It was inclusive and it had substance. [Rabbi Abraham Joshua] Heschel has this quote saying that praying is subversive to undermine all the callousness and pain and awful things there are in the world, and the music of those times did that too. Not every folksinger took that tack, but most of the people I followed did," she says.

Friedman attended a Reform movement youth group retreat the next summer, where she was asked to lead songs, and was then sent to a workshop for song leaders. That same summer she also attended an arts workshop where she was asked to cover for the song leader, who became ill. Friedman found herself in front of the youth group, explaining each song, teaching them the melody, lyrics, cadence and meaning. "I song-led, not knowing what I was doing," Friedman recalls. The next summer the camp invited her back as one of three national song leaders.

Soon afterwards, in 1970, Friedman began writing original music. The first music she wrote was "*v'Ahavta*," putting music to the second paragraph of the prayer, *Sh'ma*, which states, "And you shall love God with all your heart." She wrote it while on a bus from New Jersey to the Port Authority.

"I taught it to these kids about a month later at a regional youth convention. I was stunned when they suddenly put their arms around each other and there were tears rolling down their faces. They were reclaiming this prayer, and it was ours in a musical language they were able to understand," she says. "We were reclaiming something that we hadn't touched, that we had no access to until now."

It wasn't long after that she had a realization that set the course for her future career. She was attending a service at her family's synagogue, Mt. Zion Temple, a Reform congregation in St. Paul. "The choir sang, the rabbi spoke, and I was really passive. I realized I hadn't sung. It's like going to the gym and having someone else do the exercises for you," she says.

This insight spurred her to write music for an entire service, music that everyone could and should sing together.

At the time, Friedman, who didn't attend college, was working at Powers Associated Dry Goods, a St. Paul department store, where they put her in the Christmas Department, counting Christmas tree decorations and setting up the Nativity scene – "I had to ask people where the Wise Men went," she says, laughing. She skipped coffee and lunch breaks, instead saving up the time to leave work each afternoon and go to the high school she had attended to teach the choir the music she was writing.

When she finished enough music for an entire service, which she called *Sing Unto God*, Mt. Zion Temple let her lead it there. The tunes she wrote put new music to traditional hymns and prayers –

"*L'cha Dodi*," "*Barchu*," "*Sh'ma*," "*Aleinu*" and "*Bayom Hahu.*" She was twenty-one, and the next year, *Sing Unto God* became her first recording.

"At the time I had no idea what I was creating," she says. But others did. "People started asking me to come do services at different synagogues. From the very beginning I was traveling all over the country singing, leading services and song-leading at Conservative and Reform synagogues," she says – activities and a type of itinerary that has continued throughout her career.

"It was a whole world of text that needed to be set to music. It was wide open. Kids were singing prayers and we weren't using James Taylor tunes anymore," says Friedman of those first years. "We were using *tefilla* now, and it was really working. People were really singing and *davening* and it was exciting."

Soon after that, in 1973, Sam Karff, a Reform rabbi who had a synagogue in Chicago, commissioned her to compose a Chanukah cantata for his congregation. "He said, 'I don't want what happened to Irving Berlin to happen to you,'" she remembers. "He said, 'I want you to continue to write Jewish music and stay with us.'" His invitation spurred her to put out her second album, *Not By Might, Not By Power* (1974).

· · ·

Her creative process "varies from day to day, and minute to minute, and song to song," she says. "It's never one way. Sometimes the words come first, and sometimes the melody comes first. It's a creative process, not a fixed one."

For instance, her adaptation of "*Mi Chamocha*" ("Who is Like You, God?") came to Friedman while she was strumming the Neil Young 1970s hit "A Horse With No Name." "Playing the chords it just turned into '*Mi Chamocha*,'" she recalls.

Another early project, in 1973, was a suite based on Song of Songs – "*Kumi Lach*," ("Arise My Love") and "*Dodi Li*," ("My Beloved is Mine") among others – written to comfort her aunt and cousins after the death of her uncle.

"The thing that inspires me," she says, "is people."

When two California-based friends of hers, Savina Teubal and Marcia Cohn Spiegel, decided to mark their sixtieth birthdays in 1986 by creating a new ritual called a *simchat chochmah* (celebration of wisdom), Friedman wrote music to accompany the ceremony, songs which today are among her best-loved and most often sung.

For Teubal's ritual, believed to be the first simchat chochmah ever held, Friedman wrote *"Bruchot habaot"* ("May the Ones Who Come Forth Be Blessed"), *"L'chi Lach"* ("Go for Yourself"), and *"Kaddish derabbanan"* ("The Rabbis' Blessing"). For Spiegel's ceremony, Debbie wrote "Miriam's Song," now the classic accompaniment to women's seders, and *"Mishebeyrach"* ("He Who Has Blessed"), which has become the core of novel Jewish healing services that are springing up around the country.

Recalling the genesis of *"Mishebeyrach,"* Friedman says, "The morning of [Spiegel's] event I went to the traditional text and just translated it. We put a tallis on and I said to the congregation we were going to do it and if anyone wanted to come under the tallis they should join us. Like 150 people came up. That's the day that the Jewish healing movement began. I have goose bumps even now. It was the day people said aloud, 'I need help, I need healing.'" *"Mishebeyrach"* is arguably Friedman's most famous song, and the tune is now routinely sung in Reform and other synagogues as part of Shabbat services.

The healing movement itself has also taken off, with close to forty Jewish spiritual healing centers organized nationwide, according to the National Center for Jewish Healing, in addition to the healing services that individual synagogues may run. The services focus on prayer, singing, and group fellowship, and like Friedman's song, which is featured at almost every one of these services, they help people find a healing of their spirit as they ask God to heal their bodies.

For over a decade, Friedman and Rabbi Michael Strassfeld have run a monthly Jewish spiritual healing gathering in Manhattan, where people dealing with challenges like cancer and depression come to join her in song and meditation, and leave feeling strengthened and consoled. The gathering currently takes place at The Jewish Community Center in Manhattan.

"She really allows people to feel they can be stronger and strengthened by being able to admit and share and get support for the things that make them vulnerable. That's her great gift," says Warnick Buchdahl.

Friedman's own experience with chronic health problems has created a sensitivity to those who are ill, an ability to understand the feelings of fragility, struggle, and desperation that those with illnesses can feel. For years, she has battled a debilitating neurological condition diagnosed as paroxysmal dyskinesia, combined with ongoing adrenal and endocrine problems. In 1988, after taking an incorrectly prescribed combination of drugs, her legs suddenly went rigid. She's experienced a roller coaster of medical crises ever since, occasionally confined to a wheelchair, bed or hospital.

"My biggest challenge is this chronic battle with my body and its vulnerability," she says. "I can't do all the things I used to do. I try to keep everything in balance. My life is like a juggling act. I try to stay healthy enough to do all the things I want to do, and abide by my body's limitations."

Friedman's deeply affecting "*Mishebeyrach*," an embracing plea for healing, is sung in places large and small, in major concert halls and in cramped hospital rooms. "For people who have had illness, you look at Debbie Friedman and say wow, look what she overcame," notes Sarna. "People who have grappled with life-threatening illness but have carried on in public are tremendous role models for the community at large."

· · ·

Friedman integrates a feminist perspective in everything she writes, with mentions of the biblical matriarchs and references to God in feminized Hebrew language. Celebrating women, and filling in the white spaces in between the black letters of living Torah, where women's voices and experiences are absent from traditional texts, has spurred Friedman to write many of her best-loved songs.

In 1995, the New York Jewish organization, Ma'yan, invited her to lead their feminist Passover seders, for which she wrote "The Journey Song," "Light These Lights," the gentle "O Hear My Prayer," and her version of "*Birkat Hamazon*," the blessings traditionally sung at the end of a meal. She also integrated some of the music she had previously written, like "*L'chi Lach.*"

Once Friedman's powerful, joyous music was part of the Ma'yan seders they became enormously popular, with thousands of women attending each year. She recorded the music on *The Journey Continues* and it was published in the *Ma'yan Hagaddah*, which has sold some forty thousand copies, according to the organization.

Recently, she has written the tender new song, "Like a Rose," or "*K'Shoshana*" in Hebrew, in honor of the birth of Warnick Buchdahl's daughter, which seems sure to become the standard at Jewish baby girls' welcoming ceremonies.

Children also love her songs, especially those she has written for them, like her English and Hebrew versions of "The Aleph-Bet Song," "The Latke Song," and "The Dreidel Song." Her music has been licensed to several kid-related video projects, including *Hanukkah Tales & Tunes* and a *Barney in Concert* video, in which the ubiquitous purple dinosaur sings "The Aleph-Bet Song."

In 1996, Friedman celebrated the twenty-fifth anniversary of her singing-songwriting career by performing three consecutive sold-out shows at Carnegie Hall, where she prompted people to put their arms around one another and embrace as they swayed to her music.

"I don't think I'll ever forget what it felt like to walk out on the stage of Carnegie Hall," Friedman says. "The ambience was something to behold. The acoustics were phenomenal, the architecture elegant. All of that was seductive and impressive, but as I sang the '*Mishebeyrach*,' I was reminded in that moment that no matter where people gather for prayer it is they who create the warmth, memory and magic of any experience."

Lately, Friedman has also been taking her music and message overseas. In the summers of 2004 and 2007, she traveled with the organization Project Kesher and about 150 American Jewish women to the former Soviet Union. Among their activities were meetings with local women and an event in which Friedman sang to the assembled group of American and Soviet women on the banks of the Volga River.

She has, of course, been invited as a cantorial soloist at synagogues throughout the country; at many of them her music is now part of their regular liturgy. But her influence is not confined to the Jewish sphere – churches also use Friedman's music for teaching and worship, particularly in their music and youth groups.

In addition to performing, Friedman also teaches. She founded Hava Nashira, an annual song-leading workshop at the Olin-Sang-Ruby Union Institute, and has taught on the faculty at special programs run by a diverse set of institutions, including the Duke University Divinity School, Brandeis University, Franklin Pierce College and Hebrew Union College in Los Angeles.

She is also one of the few women appointed to the Honorary Committee for the Celebration of 350 Years of Jewish Women in North America. Among other awards, she has received the prestigious Covenant Award for outstanding contributions to Jewish education, the Jewish Cultural Achievement Award in Performing Arts from the National Foundation for Jewish Culture and the Jewish Fund for Justice's Women of Valor Award. In 2006, she was given the Burning Bush Award from the University Women of the University of Judaism in Los Angeles, which honors artists for their lifetime contributions to the community; previous recipients include author Isaac Bashevis Singer, painter David Hockney and playwright Neil Simon.

In 2007, she was invited to begin teaching at the Reform movement's cantorial school, Hebrew Union College's School of Sacred Music. Yet, despite all of these ways in which Friedman is being recognized for her contribution to American Jewish life, mainstream commercial success has eluded her.

"If it's meant to be, it's meant to be," she says. "I'm not in this work for fame. Fame is an illusion, it's meaningless. Conquering the world is not our job. Our job is to be the best that you can be. I'm never going to be more than what I'm going to be, and I'm not going to try."

As Warnick Buchdahl puts it, "She comes up with music you just can't get out of your head." But it's not just about the music. It's about how the music makes people feel.

"I love that I've been given the reward of being the *shlicha* [emissary] of this music, honest to God," Friedman says. "When I die, I want to be remembered not for all the many songs I wrote, but for helping people to feel and be empowered, to know their strengths and to know that special thing about themselves, that they are the most significant and holy being in the world, and that the person next to them is, too."

BLU GREENBERG AND IRVING (YITZ) GREENBERG

by NANCY WOLFSON-MOCHE

They are considered by many to be modern Orthodoxy's First Couple, or rabbinic royalty. Separately, each has shaped and led organizations, published books and articles, lectured widely, served as a religious and communal leader, and been recognized with numerous honorary degrees and awards from religious and lay organizations. Both endorse a more egalitarian form of Orthodoxy, encourage Jewish-Christian dialogue, and promote Jewish pluralism through intrafaith discourse. While their personal styles and approaches are different, they complement, support and respect each other wholly and deeply. Individually, Rabbi Yitz and Blu Greenberg have each influenced and given voice to a generation. Together, they have raised five children and endured the loss of one child and one child-in-law. Throughout their long and influential careers, they have been exemplars of consummate collaboration, grace and dignity.

Yitz calls the period of his adult lifetime – post-Holocaust, post-Israel – a transformative time for the Jews, "the end of Jewish exile and powerlessness and the beginning of the intent to assume power in Jewish history – a shift back to the Biblical Age..." This newfound freedom challenges Jews to make informed choices, he says. He has dedicated himself to guiding people in making these choices throughout his varied career as a university professor of history and Jewish studies; as a congregational rabbi; as founding president of CLAL (The National Jewish Center for Learning and Leadership), established to strengthen the American Jewish community through learning as well as to foster interdenominational dialogue and cooperation; as president of Jewish Life Network, an organization whose goal is to revitalize Jewish identity by creating new institutions and initiatives that will enable Jews to make "informed, balanced and inspired Jewish choices"; as the author of six books and numerous articles; and as a frequent lecturer.

Blu has been a pioneer in Orthodox feminism. Her first book, *On Women and Judaism* (1981), was the first authoritative attempt to reconcile feminism and Orthodoxy. Her second book was the widely read *How to Run a Traditional Jewish Household* (1983) in which she provided what her husband calls her "major, major unfinished contribution: Orthodoxy for the masses." Now in its thirtieth printing, it is an information-filled handbook including anecdotes, family customs and recipes – a perfectly pitched blend of objective reporting and personal storytelling. In 1997, Blu founded JOFA (the Jewish Orthodox Feminist Alliance) "to expand the spiritual, ritual, intellectual and political opportunities for women within the framework of Jewish law." She is also part of the Women, Faith and Development Alliance's *Breakthrough* Summit Leadership Council. A passionate promoter of interfaith dialogue, Blu feels that her own encounters with followers of other religions have enriched her life and deepened her Jewish identity.

Blu

A self-described "mild-mannered yeshiva girl," Blu Greenberg was "the least likely candidate to become an Orthodox feminist activist." Although it may have been improbable, Blu's evolution from yeshiva girl to feminist was a rational and progressive one. Of her path, Blu says, "I've been on an incredible spiritual and intellectual journey – without ever really leaving home."

Born in Seattle, Washington in 1936 to Rabbi Sam and Sylvia Genauer, Blu (short for *Bluma*, "flower," in Yiddish) was the middle child of three girls. She calls her father her hero, and her mother a role model. Her mother taught her to be honest, which Blu considers to be her own greatest strength in dealing with Orthodox feminist issues. Sylvia Genauer, ninety-three years old at the time Blu was interviewed for this project, was so truthful that she could not refrain from criticizing where she saw injustice or impropriety even when she knew it would not win friends or influence people. Greenberg describes her parents as opposites because, in contrast to her straight-shooting mother, her father, Sam Genauer, never said a harsh word about anyone. He was a doting father who delighted in celebrating his daughters' learning and accomplishments. Their middle-class home was nurturing and joyful, rich with the love of tradition and Jewish learning, where it was tacitly understood that being Orthodox was a privilege, never a burden. "I knew my place and liked it – the warmth, the rituals, the solid, tight parameters," she writes in *On Women and Judaism*.

Blu has no memory of becoming a bat mitzvah because it was a non-event. Bat mitzvahs simply were not a ritual practiced in American Orthodox communities in the late 1940s. They were becoming more common among Conservative and Reform Jews, but in her community having a bat mitzvah "signaled that someone had stepped over the boundaries of tradition, had violated *Halacha* (Jewish law)," she explains. Rather than envy the boys whose bar mitzvahs marked the first time they went up to the Torah, read from it and addressed the community, the girls were relieved to be excused from this "public ordeal."

In fact, the inequity built into the situation didn't really hit home until twenty-four years later, in 1972, when Blu was already a mother of five. On the last Shabbat of her husband's seven-year stint as rabbi of the Riverdale Jewish Center in Riverdale, New York, she arranged for her three sons to surprise their father by each leading some part of the synagogue service. They were rewarded with pride from their parents, praise from the community, and two dollars each from their grandparents the following morning. It was the financial reward that provoked their oldest daughter, Deborah, then eight, to complain that it wasn't fair. Her older brother, Moshe, who was ten, retorted, "Well, so what, you can't even do anything in the shul!" Recounting this exchange Blu writes, "Click, click, I thought to myself, another woman radicalized."

Blu's own "radicalization" was very gradual. Growing up in Seattle and then in Far Rockaway, New York (the family moved when Blu was ten), the only unconventional aspect about her was a tomboyish fearlessness and love of sports. Tracing the course of her radicalization, Blu cites a series of "isolated, sporadic, unconnected events" beginning in her junior year at Brooklyn College, when she spent seven months studying in Israel at a Hebrew teachers' institute. Her Bible teacher was Nechama Leibowitz, who later became something of an institution herself, famous for her *gilyonot* (Torah worksheets of guided questions) and her uniquely engaging teaching method. Leibowitz, the first woman Blu had encountered who was well-versed in rabbinic texts, was brilliant and an extraordinary role model. In fact, Blu was so motivated by her that she wanted to take a year off from college to remain in Israel to learn with Leibowitz. However, neither her parents nor friends approved, so she returned home.

Disappointed, Blu realized that had she been an Orthodox male of the same age wanting to study with a special Israeli rebbe, it surely would have been encouraged. Back in Far Rockaway, she continued to work on the gilyonot and quickly moved into the next slot on the Orthodox expectations scale. Blu cites this as an early example of her quiet discontent with the status quo, but it is also an indication of her quiet determination and her willingness to work

within the existing framework; together, these have shaped her de-
liberate – and effective – *modus operandi* as an Orthodox feminist.

Learning is an inherited passion. Ordained as a rabbi, her father did not have a pulpit but worked in the family's wholesale men's
clothing business. He was a family man; after his family, Talmud, not
tailoring, was his true passion. He spent an hour each morning studying Talmud with a rabbi friend before his commute, worked with
aspiring young rabbis, and always taught a community Talmud class.

In retrospect, Blu says, her greatest regret is not having studied Talmud with her father. It never occurred to her to ask. (She did
eventually take courses in Talmud at Yeshiva University, and, for a
period of time joined *Daf Yomi*, a daily regimen in which thousands
of Jews study a page of Talmud each day, in order to finish the whole
2,711-page work in seven and a half years.)

At that time, Talmud simply wasn't something girls generally learned. In elementary school, the girls studied Israeli folk dancing while the boys immersed themselves in Talmud. In the yeshiva
high school Blu attended, Talmud was not taught, while at the affiliated boys' branch, it was studied for three hours each day. By the
mid-1980s, many Orthodox women had become respected Talmud
scholars and teachers. To Greenberg, whose platform for Orthodox
feminism is based on the principle of "distinctive but equal," some
rituals still seem more male than female (like wearing a tallit or putting on *tefillin*, neither of which Blu does), and others more female
than male (like candle lighting), but learning, in her view, is gender
blind.

But while growing up Orthodox, Blu accepted that certain
subjects of Jewish learning were male. It was only during the time
spent in Israel in her junior year in college that she learned to question that convention. Her roommate, Barbara Edelman, took her to
a bookstore in Meah Shearim (an ultra-Orthodox Jerusalem neighborhood) where Edelman bought herself several complete sets of
"sacred texts." Greenberg followed, and felt a thrill on many levels,
which she relives each time she opens those books and sees her
name inscribed in the front flap. Ownership of the texts planted the

seeds for what would become Greenberg's controversial contention that for Orthodox women to fully own ritual and prayer, they must participate in it.

Blu Genauer, the "mild-mannered yeshiva girl," left Israel in 1955 to resume her studies at Brooklyn College, met a young rabbi named Irving Greenberg on a blind date, and two years later, at the age of twenty-one, married him. Yitz jokes that a friend gave him a list of names of four eligible girls; Blu's name was not first on the list. "But she was the most popular modern Orthodox girl in New York in the 1950s and her name sounded so exotic – I had a mental image of a bleached-blond nightclub singer – that I called her first," he says.

She turned out to be a cerebral dark-haired beauty who looked more like a concert pianist than a cabaret singer. He is three years older than she, but he claims she was emotionally more mature, more ready for marriage and a family. "Blu was certainly the teacher and the pace-setter [in our marriage]," Yitz acknowledges. "I was totally unprepared for marriage; she really trained me. And I feel, in retrospect, I didn't appreciate what I was getting into…it was just one of those gifts of life, a gift from God. Marrying Blu certainly transformed me."

Yitz

Tall and lanky with bright blue eyes, once-blonde hair, and a round face, he is quick to beam his toothy, heartfelt smile. He often dresses in preppy khakis and button-down cotton shirts, looking like the academic he was for twenty years, first at Yeshiva University (1959–1972), and then at the City University of New York (1972–1979).

Greenberg was born in Brooklyn in 1933 to Polish parents who had immigrated to the U.S. eight years earlier. "Blind luck" is how Greenberg describes his father Rabbi Eliyahu Chayim Greenberg's decision to come to America before the Holocaust that would claim one of Eliyahu's two sisters, four of his wife's six brothers and the rest of their families. Eliyahu and Sonia Greenberg arrived in New York with two daughters in their early teens; their two sons, Harold and Irving, were born in Brooklyn.

From the moment the older Greenbergs arrived in the U.S., their dream was to become all-American, although unlike many other immigrant Jews, they would not give up their religious practices. When their second son was born, they wanted to name him after his great-grandfather, Yitzhak, but they thought the name would be a stigma since it didn't sound mainstream American. At his *brit* (circumcision ceremony), they chose the name Irving, which they felt was a good white, Anglo-Saxon, Protestant name for their eleven-pound baby. "Of course, I've spent the rest of my life trying to get back to Yitzhak," Yitz says.

Eliyahu Greenberg's father had died when he was a child. His mother could not support him, so she sent him away to *yeshivot*. "My father grew up as a poor, poor orphan," Yitz says. "He lived by his wits, meaning he was brilliant; very, very sharp and talented. So, to him, learning was everything." It was his meal ticket, since the brightest students were the ones who got invited into people's homes for dinner. In exchange for the meal, they would teach at the table. Learning became his currency, taking priority over his emotional needs. Yitz's father did not openly express affection to his children and he hardly ever schmoozed or talked about daily life occurrences, but he showered them with learning.

Eliyahu's American dream was that his son become the rabbi of a large American synagogue, which Yitz realized when he became rabbi of the Riverdale Jewish Center soon after his thirty-second birthday. Ordained as a rabbi in Poland, the elder Greenberg could not get a pulpit in Brooklyn because his spoken English wasn't good enough. (The family spoke Yiddish at home.) He taught Talmud daily in an immigrant congregation "for pennies" and he became a *shochet* (ritual meat slaughterer), rising at three in the morning, coming home blood-spattered at one every afternoon. He would change into clean clothes, open the Talmud and turn to learning with his congregation and his children, including the girls. They had little money, living "spartanly," but Yitz, who keeps a picture of his parents on his desk at home, hardly noticed, since the family's values were intellectual, not financial or emotional. "My father could only translate love in terms of intellectual learning," he says. "He would love you by learning with you." His father also had a passionate love of the Jewish people and an anti-establishment streak that especially expressed itself in a fierce opposition to injustice.

As a result, "my father shaped the primordial structures of my thought at the level before ideas are grasped or put in words," Yitz says. He attributes his style of teaching to his father's model: one that integrated humor, covered a lot of ground, packing in as much material as possible, while articulating it clearly and simply so it would be accessible to everyone. Yitz's manner of speaking also may reflect his father's: he often asks a question, answering it in the same sentence; one of his most frequently used expressions is "that's the heart of it" (not surprising, since he grew up taking concepts, not feelings, to heart); his speech is peppered with "in other words" because he is adept at rephrasing and restating, just as the Talmud does; and he often prefaces statements with the words, "it's interesting," because he genuinely is interested in so many different points of view.

His father wanted to reach the group, not be a part of the group. "Hanging out" was as foreign to him, and ultimately to Yitz, as a Brooks Brothers suit. "My father couldn't understand why my brother and I would want to waste time hanging out with friends, and he influenced me," Yitz says. Birthdays were ignored and except for on Shabbat, the family hardly ate meals together because that, too, was perceived as a waste of time. His mother – "the rock of the family, a deeply religious woman with a quiet strength and selflessness, who supplied the family's stick-to-it determination" – would feed each child separately at whatever time he or she returned home after school. Yitz, a self-described "goody two-shoes and an over-achiever," would read while he ate so as not to lose any precious studying time.

Years later, as a newlywed, when Yitz brought the *New York Times* to the table, Blu did not conceal her disappointment; in her family meals were social occasions. Yitz not only conformed, but is still grateful for having learned "social skills" from Blu. Now a "pescatarian" (fish-eating vegetarian), Yitz doesn't have childhood memories around food or Shabbat or holiday meals. He remembers singing and studying on Shabbat, but not eating. "I'm not a big food maven," he says. Sitting and talking in the living room of their Riverdale home where there is always something to eat set out on the coffee table, Yitz takes two pretzels from a glass bowl and holds them for several minutes, neither tempted nor distracted enough to actually eat them. "I always joke that I don't get any credit for kashrut because I'm not really sacrificing anything," he says.

Yitz has a slight but perceptible accent traceable to the ye-shivot of Boro Park in Brooklyn where he was educated (at Yeshiva Etz Chaim and Yeshiva University High School). He went on to the secular Brooklyn College, simultaneously attending a *mussar* yeshiva (where the emphasis was on ethics and character building) called Bais Yosef. Most of the students were Holocaust survivors and Yitz considers his three years there "some of the great moments of my life." He recognizes each of the two institutions as being sound: the secular one (Brooklyn College) "much less filtered by Orthodoxy," and the religious (Bais Yosef) "much less filtered by modernity...To the strong but independent pull of both institutions, I credit my ten-dency to this day to go for dialectical approaches to religious ques-tions rather than to reach resolved positions," he told Shalom Freed-man in 1998 in a series of conversations that comprise the book *Living in the Image of God.* By the age of twenty, he had gotten *smi-cha* (rabbinical ordination) and graduated summa cum laude from Brooklyn College.

He moved on to Harvard – the only graduate program to which he applied – where he got both a master's in American his-tory in 1954 and a PhD in American intellectual history in 1960. Although he had been ordained as a rabbi seven years before, Yitz always intended to have a secular career as an academic. "There is a tradition of not making the Torah into a source of livelihood," he says. Under the influence of his mussar yeshiva, his plan was that his life would express religious values, but his career would be secular. In part, he was motivated by the American dream of economic and social mobility, after seeing his parents struggle financially.

Right out of Harvard, Yitz got a teaching post in the History Department at Yeshiva University. Although he was hired to teach secular American and general history, "YU represented the religious and secular brought together." Of this decision to alter his professional course even before setting out, Greenberg says, "the choice reflected unmet needs to work with and realize my Jewish religious urges."

The next year, Yitz was awarded a Fulbright fellowship to teach American History at Tel Aviv University. With their newborn son Moshe, he and Blu spent the academic year of 1961–1962 in Jerusalem. The teaching load was light, and Yitz immersed himself in reading about the Holocaust, which would become a lifelong passion (he served as chairman of the United States Holocaust Memorial Council from 2000–2002). When he returned to YU he began lobbying to teach a course on the Holocaust. Ironically, there was a lot of resistance to the idea – at the time, such courses were being taught in only two other American universities – and it took two years before the class was offered under the euphemistic title, "Totalitarianism and Ideology in the 20th Century."

Put off by his struggle to get the Holocaust into the curriculum at a Jewish university and by YU's general resistance to his shifting focus to Jewish studies, when the Riverdale Jewish Center pulpit was offered him in 1965, Yitz took it, retaining his position as chairman of the History Department at YU. He calls the subsequent seven years "the golden years of our lives...a time of pure happiness."

The children have since grown and left home, and Blu and Yitz have moved into a different house in Riverdale, but the newer home, now often bustling with grandchildren, still resonates with the activity and joy of the household in those early years.

In 2002, Yitz and Blu suffered a tragedy when their youngest son, Jonathan Joseph, "J.J.," died at the age of thirty-six on *Shabbat Shuva* (the Shabbat before Yom Kippur) after a bicycling accident in Israel.

J.J. was the executive director of Jewish Life Network, the organization that he helped establish in 1994 with Michael Steinhardt, its chairman and founder, and Yitz, its president. At their home after his death, Blu and Yitz spoke of J.J.'s quirky acts of kindness and integrity, like his custom of calling family and friends at 12:01 A.M. on their birthdays and anniversaries, covering his head with a towel when he couldn't find his *kippah*, and never throwing away a sheet of paper unless it was used on both sides.

At the funeral outside of Jerusalem, Yitz eulogized his son. With his characteristic ability to explain even the inexplicable, he concluded by offering the blessing of a *Kohen* (priest) to everyone present, in J.J.'s memory: "May God bless you with a child so loving, so kind, so good, so continuously supportive and protective, so wise, so Jewish, so devoted to *clal Yisrael*, so modest, so funny, so gentle, so zany, so weird, so individual, so free of spirit, so religious, so cool, so honest that even if you knew, as we now know, that at the end of thirty-six years, the life together would conclude with this unspeakable heartbreak, with this inexplicable tragedy, with this endless pain, you would still say, 'Give me this child.' Every day of our life with J.J. was a permanent blessing."

Blu

"We are all trying to hold onto J.J.'s life story," Blu says, meaning they want to remember the person (son, brother, grandson, uncle) that he was, and recognize all the work he did, large (like his work on behalf of the Birthright Israel project, conceiving Makor in Manhattan and his contribution to making Orthodoxy cool) and small (like the mitzvoth he did daily, helping whomever needed help, and donating twenty percent of his income to charity).

The family created a website dedicated to J.J.'s memory (www. jjgreenberg.org) and Blu is working on a book about her son. "I'm going to have to find a way to weave together his life and my grief," she says with typical candor. Her grief, she explains, has three pieces. First is the lack of closure. She spoke with her son nearly every day of his life, except on the last day. Second is simply that she misses him, daily. And finally, there is the sadness about the future he will not have.

When asked how he would like to be remembered, Yitz replies, "I'd like to be remembered in part as the husband of Blu and as the parent of my children. That's good enough." It was Yitz who, sometime in the late 1960s, picked up *The Feminine Mystique,* Betty Friedan's bestselling 1963 book, for Blu because he thought she ought to read it. As an associate professor of history at Yeshiva University at the time, Yitz had more than a passing interest in the sociopolitical trends emerging in America, and Friedan's book intrigued him.

Having given birth to five children in six years, Blu describes herself in the 1960s as "content and fulfilled, not in search of women's liberation." Her plate was full with childrearing, getting a degree in religious education, getting a second master's degree in Jewish history (the first had been in clinical psychology), and teaching college part-time. She says she read the book, "engaging the matter intellectually and at arm's length." She considered the issues carefully. "I did not come to feminism out of a sense of oppression or deprivation. In fact, the anger frightened me," she remembers. "Nevertheless, I understood that the underlying basis was just, and I could not easily let go of the idea."

Friedan's idea was to examine the root of the widespread malaise that was growing among American women, thus triggering change. But feminism had been brewing long before the publication of Friedan's groundbreaking book. Jewish feminists who were Orthodox and frustrated with their not being counted (literally) or being unable to participate in key rituals could walk away from Orthodoxy and become Conservative or Reconstructionist or Reform, gaining those rights in a heartbeat. Blu and many others were not willing to give up the basic tenets of Orthodoxy. Many Jewish feminists found fault with traditional rabbis and criticized the family unit. Blu, on the other hand, held rabbis as her heroes (beginning with her father and her husband) and deemed family "the defining structure and most important aspect" of her life.

The challenge for Blu became how to marry feminism and Orthodoxy without compromising or letting go of the principles of either. "I came to understand that it is far easier to destroy systems than to build them up. So when other feminists were speaking of taking down walls and doors, I was cautious about destroying what I knew had taken centuries to create," she wrote in 2005.

A team player, Blu is an enthusiastic supporter of structures and infrastructures. "An organization can change the world," she states. Since its establishment, she has helped nurture JOFA from a casual kitchen roundtable into an international alliance. Her concern for peace in Israel led her, in 1989, to help establish the Dialogue Project to promote communication between Jewish and Palestinian women. More recently, Blu also cofounded One Voice: Jewish Women for Israel and the Federation Task Force on Jewish Women. She has served and held leadership positions on boards too numerous to list in full: EDAH, Project Kesher, U.S. Israel Women to Women, *Hadassah Magazine, Lilith* magazine, the International Research Institute on Jewish Women, and the Jewish Book Council of America are among them.

Because of her respect for organizations, it is not surprising that Blu says the pivotal moment in her life was in 1973 when she was asked to be the keynote speaker at the first National Jewish Women's Conference in New York. With her characteristic humility, she describes the invitation as a "fluke" and "a call from God." In systematically researching her talk, given at the McAlpin Hotel in New York City to an audience of about five hundred women, she delved deeply into the Jewish sources on women. It confirmed her assumptions that the tradition "was filled with benevolence toward women," yet it also exposed "pockets of disadvantage, disability and discrimination."

For Blu, and for the small group of Orthodox rabbis, including Yitz, who supported her position, the key was – and still is – giving women equal status in the synagogue and the ritual within the parameters of traditional Jewish law (*Halacha*). Blu maintains this is possible if there is flexibility in interpreting the law. Blu and Yitz – and scores of other distinguished scholars and rabbis – assert that written into Jewish law is the proviso that it be contextual, reinterpreted within the context of each particular historical time; in this way the law remains relevant and vital for all generations.

"Judaism has often adapted to innovations based on the dynamic interchange between individual needs and community sensibilities, between the questions and the answers in the *halachic* literature, between new societal norms and ancient traditions," Blu says. "The full dignity of women, as images of God, is an external idea that we must integrate into our heritage." Blu's maxim became, "Where there's a rabbinic will there's a *halachic* way."

Yitz

In 2005, Yitz developed a year-long program called *Limdu Heitev* (learn goodness). The goal for Limdu Heitev, he says, is to "articulate a post-modern or pluralist vision for Orthodoxy, meaning an Orthodoxy that would not be withdrawn or triumphalist, but more embracing and affirmative of the rest of the [Jewish] community."

He continues, "That's what the Jewish people are about. There's an alternative to universalism, where we're all one great humanity, and particularism, where I'm my tribe and I kill/reject every other tribe that I don't care for. So we're trying to create a post-modern Jewry that is integrated, and it stands that it's part of humanity but it is a distinctive family and a distinctive tribe and it has its own values and its own models, but it knows its limits and it doesn't say that we are the only ones who have models or insights...or have contributions to make."

Pluralism was – and still is – the goal of CLAL, the organization Greenberg helped establish in 1974. CLAL was formed to encourage formal dialogue among rabbis of all denominations, and later became committed to promoting dialogue among the Jewish community at large. During this time, and as an outgrowth of work he did at CLAL, he wrote *The Jewish Way* (1988). His first Jewish book, it is a thorough explanation and interpretation of all the Jewish holidays. Greenberg served as president of CLAL from 1979 until 1997, although he says he only intended to work there for five years. "A lot of my life has been serendipity," he says of the opportunity he was given to establish a Jewish Studies Department at City College (which he chaired from 1972–1979), that in turn led to the opportunity to create the JJRC – National Jewish Resource Center, which later became CLAL.

CLAL was born after over a decade of active dialogue with Christian clergy. "I joined the dialogue, very frankly, not to come to love and understand Christians, but really kind of to say 'stop teaching hatred about me,'" Yitz says of his decision to get involved in Jewish-Christian exchange in 1962. He and Blu were motivated to join in this ongoing conversation as a response to the Holocaust. "How do you get Christians to reformulate their thinking about Judaism?" was the question they sought to answer. But, as he recounts in his book *For the Sake of Heaven and Earth: The New Encounter Between Judaism and Christianity* (2004), the Christians they met were so wonderful, open, sympathetic to the Jews, and ashamed of what Christianity had done in the Holocaust that as time went on the Greenbergs became more and more appreciative and respectful of Christianity in general.

Finally, Yitz concluded that, "if you can get people of such decency and quality who are willing to really criticize themselves and determined to change their own religious teaching in order to make it a vision of love...this is the key to breaking anti-Semitism." He writes of the spiritual intensity he witnessed that "lifted my Jewish religious life to a new level...Soon I felt an obligation to re-present Christianity, within the Jewish world, as a faith with independent value and dignity." Of his years of positive involvement with Jewish-Christian dialogue Yitz says, "I came to scold and I stayed to praise."

Greenberg has been criticized for this position by the Orthodox Right, but he remains grateful for the positive influence of the Christians with whom he established strong, lasting bonds. He credits them with having taught him "the techniques of dialogue," which he then brought back into the Jewish-Jewish dialogue, through CLAL. While he entered into the Jewish-Christian dialogue seeking to reformulate Christian thinking, he came out of it thinking about "how do you reformulate Jewish thinking about Christianity?"

Reformulating Jewish thinking about Judaism is part of what Yitz did as president of Jewish Life Network from 1994 until 2007. The theory behind JLN is "to create a community that has enough educational and personal, experiential Jewish experiences to choose to be Jewish in an open society. The alternatives are trying to recreate this separation [that we had in the ghettos of prewar Eastern Europe] or giving in to assimilation [as so many American Jews have done]." Whereas fundamentalism says that choice undermines commitment, JLN suggests that choice intensifies commitment. Yitz is aware of the constant conflict between the reconciliation of inherited values with new opportunities.

JLN supports Jewish day schools, camps, Israel travel and study (through Birthright Israel), youth and college (Hillel) movements, and intensive adult learning. Newer programs include extending the education push to preschoolers (through JECI – Jewish Early Childhood Initiative) and to the just-born (through participating in the "PJ Library," a Harold Grinspoon Foundation program that distributes books and educational materials to Jewish families). In the planning stages are the creation of a central Jewish Retreat Center, a follow-up program to Birthright Israel trips, and Fund for Our Jewish Future, a national fund to subsidize locally driven projects that fit into Jewish Life Network's objectives.

Unfinished Business

What are their objectives now? Both Yitz and Blu want to spend more time writing. Highly skilled masters of the craft, both note that you can reach more people through books than you can through public speaking. Blu is working on the aforementioned book about J.J.'s life, completing another that takes a new look at the ancient rite of *mikveh* (ritual bath), and beginning a book called *Kosher Friends* about how to host kosher friends if you have a non-kosher kitchen.

Of Blu's still unfinished but steadfast determination to render women distinct but equal under Orthodox Jewish law, Yitz says, "I feel that she's doing something that's very, very important, and I think historically, she will win…I don't know if [she will win] in my lifetime, but I'm highly confident that in somebody's lifetime, this will come to be."

Of Yitz, Steven T. Katz wrote in *Interpreters of Judaism in the Late Twentieth Century*, "No Jewish thinker has had a greater impact on the American Jewish community in the last two decades." As he moves to the next stage of his career and dedicates more time to writing, Yitz says he'll be addressing a tremendous backlog of unpublished ideas. "I've been so busy creating organizations that I never got my books published," he says.

Taking time off to write has been a recurring goal for Yitz. In 1974–1975, he went on sabbatical to Israel to write a theological approach to the Holocaust. His father passed away during that year and Yitz didn't write the book; that remains one of his goals. (He published several articles on the subject and co-edited *Confronting the Holocaust: The Impact of Elie Wiesel.*) Before his father's death, Yitz tape-recorded Eliyahu Greenberg's reflections and memories of his life in Poland; this is another seed of a book waiting to germinate, along with a collection of essays. Perhaps most important is a book that he has begun writing, with the working title *The Triumph of Life.* It argues that Judaism's main message is life affirming and life sustaining: Life wins.

"So what is the meaning of life?" Yitz asks rhetorically. "The Jews faced that question and they concluded that life is a partnership between God and humanity. Life is making sense of this world and improving it and doing *tikkun olam* (repairing the world) in one's own time." This seems a perfect description of his and Blu's life work, focused on developing and affirming a range of vital alternatives to encourage Jews to find their own Jewish way.

Yet, there is much to be done, and Yitz is not sanguine about the future of Judaism. "For the Jewish people it's a very scary race between disintegration and renewal…And it's not a race that I think we're winning," he says. "In fact, we're probably taking heavy losses as we talk." And with that he heads back to his desk to continue doing his best to reverse the tide.

JUDITH HAUPTMAN

by FRANCESA LUNZER KRITZ

On the wall of Rabbi Judith Hauptman's office at New York's Jewish Theological Seminary, just to the right of her desk, is a monotype that at first glance seems to be a series of brushstrokes, at once beautiful and puzzling.

Hauptman, a Talmud scholar in her sixties, recalls how the piece came to hang in her office. She was in London for a conference a few years ago, sitting and reviewing a page of Talmud in preparation to speak, when she looked up and saw the lithograph, one of several pieces of art for sale. It took her a moment to realize that it was an abstract rendering of a Talmud page.

"At first, the drawing makes no sense, but come closer and you see what it's trying to be. That's what it's like when studying or teaching Talmud. Come closer and it becomes clearer," says Hauptman. "I bought it immediately."

The Talmud has been a focus of Hauptman's life since her college days. Today Hauptman is the E. Billi Ivry Professor of Talmud and Rabbinic Culture at the Jewish Theological Seminary (JTS). The first woman to receive a PhD in Talmud, she is a prolific writer and popular lecturer on Talmud and women according to Jewish law. Although she has enjoyed a fulfilling and celebrated scholarly career, she recently broadened her focus by becoming ordained as a rabbi, while continuing to teach at JTS.

Why the Talmud? "Because I love it. It's as if I had no choice," says Hauptman. "It's as though the voices in the stories in the Talmud pulled me in. I could not have chosen any other job, because I am just addicted [to the study of Talmud]."

Hauptman began her studies at JTS as an undergraduate, in 1960, majoring in Talmud while also majoring in economics at Barnard College. She started teaching at the Conservative seminary after her college graduation in 1964, beginning as an instructor at the seminary's Prozdor High School. "I was lucky," Hauptman says. "When I graduated, the seminary offered me a part-time job teaching at the high school, which I did for six years. And then it was the feminist revolution, and they put me on the regular faculty as an instructor of Talmud in 1973."

Hauptman's commitment to teaching and enjoyment of it are strong, even after more than forty years. "Currently, I'm teaching Talmud level one and doctoral students. I love doing both but I have to say that the joy and satisfaction of taking people who can barely navigate a page is special. And leading them to where they are today, to being able to navigate a page, that's extremely satisfying," she says.

"I love being in the classroom. I can look at a page of Talmud and explain it to you, regardless of your background. People tell me I have a gift of being able to explain it in ways that you might have not understood it before."

Hauptman brings a novel style to teaching Talmud. "The traditional route of most *yeshivot* has been to study the *Halacha* (law) rather than the *aggadah* (lore). But I teach a course in which we study the aggadah because I want my students to see aggadah is a very loose term," she says. "Halacha on Shabbat tells you the principal labors you must not perform on Shabbat, but it does not tell you about Oneg Shabbat – celebrating the Sabbath. The *Mishnah* tells you how many meals to take out of your house if, for example, it's going up in flames on Shabbat and the aggadah has incredible material on meals on Shabbat, and about men and women being required to be engaged in hands-on preparation for Shabbat. And there are fifteen examples of rabbis who assisted their wives for Shabbat. I always like to point that out because we always think it's [only] a woman's responsibility. If a man wanted to take responsibility for Shabbat by taking on the candles that was permissible for him to do. It's not enough to have the halacha of Shabbat, you have to have the aggadah of Shabbat to understand it well."

Hauptman repeatedly gives credit to her early studies and her teachers in shaping the scholar and teacher she is today, adding that her college major in economics helped develop the analytical thinking style needed for Talmud study. "In theory," says Hauptman, "I could have gone into chemistry, or into mathematics. All of those would have been nice, but when it comes down to it, I can do all of those by studying the Talmud – analytic, projecting future models, and unraveling the past, with the added dimension of being Jewish."

That dimension, Hauptman says, "gives me a lens through which I look at the world, and the way I live my life. All of the aspects of my life are nice: teacher, mother, human being, but the more lenses through which you view the work, the richer your experience is."

That richness is due in large part to her immediate family, including her husband, Milton Adesnik, a professor in the Department of Cell Biology at New York University Medical School, and her three grown sons. They "continue to ask me detailed questions about my work and my writing, and, like my students in the classroom, challenge my thought process and conclusions in ways that make me think once, and then again, about my arguments," she says.

Students say Hauptman is adept at presenting complicated premises, is surefooted and receptive in class, and encourages them to question everything. "Rabbi Hauptman is able to open a class in a way few teachers do," says Rabbi Elie Kaunfer, executive director of Mechon Hedar, a New York City-based organization that provides educational and *minyan* (prayer quorum) resources for young Jews, and a former student of Hauptman's at JTS. "She doesn't shy away from presenting complex topics, and teaches to a very high level, but she [also] is incredibly open to hearing original ideas from students, even when they conflict with her own well-researched positions. On multiple occasions, I saw her change her mind as a result of what a student said in class. This takes a rare level of self-confidence to afford your students the opportunity – in the middle of class! – to cause you to reconsider long-held beliefs."

Hauptman's ultimate goal with students, Kaunfer says, is not "to teach us the strict sentences," but "to have us think with her, as though we were among the writers of the Talmud and can see their reasoning about what was included and why. That is a very powerful way to learn."

Hauptman is the author of scores of articles and the books, *Development of the Talmudic Sugya: Relationship Between Tannaitic and Amoraic Sources* (1987), *Rereading the Rabbis: A Woman's Voice* (1998) and *Rereading the Mishnah: A New Approach to Ancient Jewish Texts* (2005).

Her work over the years has explored two main subjects. As she explains, she has been most interested in "how the text of the Talmud evolved, how so many different statements, chronologically and geographically diverse, coalesced into a single, discursive text, and how the rabbis viewed women themselves, their status and their religious role."

Her work on how the Talmud evolved has been a major factor in understanding the intended meaning of many Talmudic texts. "I have demonstrated that Tannaitic texts, those from the earlier part of the Rabbinic period, lie at the base of many later units of discussion," she explains. "The Talmud was not written in a linear fashion, going from line one at the top of the page to line fifty at the bottom. Rather, a snippet embedded in the middle of the discussion may actually be the earliest element of the discussion, with later comments appended both after and even before it," a possibility that had been overlooked in the past, Hauptman says.

Her scholarship has also affected understanding of how the core document of the Talmud, the Mishnah, developed. She argues that the Tosefta, a companion volume to the Mishnah, from the same period of time and featuring roughly the same spokesmen, is not a later commentary on the Mishnah, as so many thought, but precedes the Mishnah and often serves as its basis. This theory, which is becoming widely accepted, means that many passages in the Mishnah can be understood with greater precision, she says.

In her book on women, Hauptman shows that even though Rabbinic society was configured in a patriarchal manner, men recognized that women deserved to have higher status than they had had in the past. For instance, Talmudic rabbis decided that a woman's consent be sought before she was married, that a *ketubah* (marriage contract) guarantee that upon divorce or widowhood she receive a lump payment from her husband's estate, and that her father give her a generous dowry, as she was not able to inherit from him.

· · ·

Hauptman was born in 1943 and raised in Borough Park, Brooklyn. Currently a homogeneous, right-wing Orthodox neighborhood, it has changed considerably from the diverse community Hauptman knew as she was growing up. She describes her parents as staunch Conservative Jews. Her connection to Judaism consciously began at the age of two or three when she was taken to visit an aunt who served her meat with butter, and she recoiled.

"Here I was so young and Jewish living was already so much a part of who I was," says Hauptman, who credits her parents with instilling in her the love of Jewish rituals. "As I went into the world, I was a person formed by Judaism."

Hauptman was also formed by attending Camp Ramah, a flagship enterprise of the Conservative movement, in the Poconos and in Canada, where she spent seven years as a camper, three years as a counselor, three years as a division head, and later, three years as a professor. "Ramah determined the course of my life," she says. Although her home was kosher and her parents took her to synagogue every Shabbat, the camp offered something more.

"At Camp Ramah, I discovered *Shabbos*. No lights, no talking on the telephone, no travel, and I just fell in love with the whole thing. It was a beautiful setting in the country, cold nights, sunny days. Summer camp itself was wonderful, and then superimpose on that the whole Jewish thing," she says.

When Hauptman was in graduate school at JTS, she was asked to help a newly formed group, *Ezrat Nashim* (Women's Court), go through passages of the Talmud. The group was formed in 1971 to discuss the status of women in Judaism. It was through this invitation that Hauptman's advocacy on behalf of women began, work which has ultimately helped transform women's roles in the Conservative movement by identifying Talmud sources for re-crafting women's roles and by advocating for a more egalitarian environment. "It was my job to bring to the group sections of Talmud to conduct this inquiry into how Judaism treats women," says Hauptman. "I could translate what the Talmud was saying about women; show that the seeds of change were planted in the Talmud. This was one of the most meaningful experiences of my life."

Hauptman's work with the group led her to begin speaking on these issues and championing the idea of women rabbis. "A lot of us became public speakers, and synagogues across the country were extremely open to us. Feminism in the 1960s sensitized a lot of women, so there was receptivity to accepting women by the time we came on the scene. After studying the texts, the group went to the Rabbinical Assembly of Conservative Judaism and asked for changes, and within a year, the rabbis took up our cause...Women, for example, could be counted in a minyan." Hauptman says it is one of the smartest things the Rabbinical Assembly ever did. "Without women there would often not be a morning minyan at many synagogues," she says.

Hauptman's contribution to the Conservative movement in terms of changing women's roles was transformational, according to movement leaders. The author and movement elder Francine

Klagsbrun says of Hauptman, "The fact that she taught Talmud at the seminary at a time when few women were studying texts at her level was an enormous boost. It said that a woman scholar was being taken seriously...she blazed the way for other women scholars. But she also blazed the way for all women in the movement by putting her emphasis on Talmud and texts and not on some vague 'spirituality.' Judy showed that true spirituality comes from study and a willingness to engage our texts. Judy engaged the texts in the tradition of the Conservative movement. She worked from within...Change comes about by reexamining traditional sources and showing how they can be interpreted to have meaning for our lives today."

. . .

Twenty-four years after earning her PhD, Hauptman graduated from rabbinical school. Why become a rabbi, when her career as a scholar was so full and rewarding? Actually, she wasn't entirely sure, except it was something she had thought about since JTS began ordaining women in 1983, and because in some ways she felt what she did was already quite close to being a rabbi. "In my own head, I have been a rabbi all my life. I think the way I function with students is rabbinical. I just wanted to be recognized for what I had been doing," she says. But although she had thought about it over the years, with a full teaching and research load and three young sons at home, earlier she felt she didn't have time for the coursework.

She attended the non-denominational Academy for Jewish Religion (AJR), graduating in 2003. Her studies there included pastoral counseling training and have lent another dimension to what she terms "my role in Judaism." Rabbinical school, she says, "forced me to be open to the more spiritual side of things. There was a part of me that I wasn't always in touch with that wanted to be with people, ministering to their spiritual needs and not just teaching them Talmud. I think somehow it bubbled up finally. I didn't know, when I went to AJR, that I was going to fall in love with the soft side of Judaism."

Hauptman currently serves at the volunteer Jewish chaplain for the Cabrini Home for Nursing and Rehabilitation, a Catholic nursing home in lower Manhattan. The people she works with at the nursing home would likely be shocked by Hauptman's own surprise at her affinity for this work. "Rabbi Hauptman is a people person," says Sister Doris Pagano, director of Pastoral Care at the Cabrini Home. Prior to Hauptman's arrival, the needs of the Jewish residents, from holiday services to funerals, were taken care of by rabbis of nearby synagogues when they were available. Now, Hauptman comes every other week to lead services and visit with the home's Jewish residents.

"What comes across," says Sister Pagano, "is that Rabbi Hauptman is empathetic, sympathetic, and a very caring person." Sister Pagano recalls a particular Saturday morning when she attended one of Hauptman's Shabbat services. A staff member came to tell the Sister that one of the residents had died. "Even though the person wasn't Jewish, Rabbi Hauptman insisted on coming with me to see if she could help make things easier for the family and say prayers."

Perhaps not surprisingly, Sister Pagano says some of the older men try to challenge the woman rabbi on her Talmud knowledge. "She comes right up with the answer," says Sister Pagano with a chuckle. "Rabbi Hauptman is always so well prepared, and has these wonderful stories to share from the Talmud."

Since she became a rabbi, Hauptman has become increasingly known for the free services she leads in Greenwich Village during the High Holidays as well as the low-cost Passover Seder she runs, which attract hundreds of people. This work was spurred by a chance encounter. One Yom Kippur as she was leaving the synagogue she attends regularly, the Town and Village Synagogue in downtown Manhattan, a young couple approached her and asked where they might go for services, having been turned away from the synagogue because they had no tickets. "I can do better," Hauptman thought. Since 2004 she has offered the services through a program she named Ohel Ayalah in memory of her mother. Hauptman's services are "for people in flux. Something within our attendees says they want to reconnect for the High Holidays, and what is stopping them may be the barrier of paying for the ticket. If we hold onto them now and give them these free services and try to keep them Jewish, some of them will remain within the Jewish community," she says.

.   .   .

What comes next? Hauptman's current research is about women's lives in rabbinic times, about how Jewish women lived their lives 1,800 years ago. "Having looked at laws about women, I am now trying to look at their lives. Just because men occupied the public roles in Judaism, serving as rabbis and prayer leaders and Torah readers, it is incorrect to conclude that women played no religious role at all. Rather, in the home, which was a semi-public space, women were given key religious roles to fulfill for themselves and for men," she says.

Clearly, while her responsibilities as a ministering rabbi bring Hauptman great joy, this new focus has not diminished her love for studying and teaching Talmud. The Talmud, says Hauptman, is paramount for all Jews, including those who don't realize it or are non-observant.

"The Talmud is a huge text and the text that most defines you as a Jew," she explains. "We live our lives by the Talmud. You can take a Reform Jew who says, 'I have personal autonomy, I can choose to be kosher or not kosher, but they are defining themselves against tradition, against the Talmud…If somebody came from Mars today and wanted to be Jewish, reading the Bible wouldn't make them Jewish, but living by the Talmud would."

LAWRENCE HOFFMAN

by JONATHAN VATNER

R abbi Lawrence Hoffman knows how to end Yom Kippur in style –
and with an impact. After dusk has settled, the lights in the
synagogue go out and children file in, each holding a candle that's
lit from the *havdalah* candle. The children and their parents – who
stand by to ensure that no one starts a conflagration – proceed to
the front of the synagogue, set the candles on a table, then gather
around and watch the brilliant cluster of fire.

"Remember we said that Rosh Hashanah was the birthday of
the world?" Hoffman asks.

"Yeah!" say the children.

"What do you do on birthdays?"

"We have birthday cake!"

"That's right," replies Hoffman. "We're not going to have one yet because the adults are still fasting. But what do you put on a birthday cake?"

"Candles!" they shout in unison.

"Well, we've got candles. And what do you do with the candles?"

"You make a wish and blow them out!"

So, Hoffman asks, what do you wish for in the next year?

"Peace," some kids say. "A better world," say others. "That my big sister treats me better!" someone shouts.

Then Hoffman asks the adults what they want in the coming year. Their wishes aren't so very different from those of the children.

The room is dark, except for the cluster of fire in the front, the havdalah candle towering above the others. Hoffman gives the signal and with gusts of breath all the candles flicker out except for the havdalah candle. The group makes havdalah and says the final prayers of Yom Kippur. Then the shofar is blown, and the worshippers, many of them crying, sing *shehecheyanu*.

Hoffman doesn't have a pulpit. The scene just described occurred at the *chavurah* he cofounded near Rye, New York, where he has lived since 1973. His *Ne'ilah* service, the end of Yom Kippur, is a telling example of his renowned talent at fashioning ritual. His study of and ideas about ritual have impacted a generation of Reform rabbis – and by extension, their congregations. Observe a Reform service in America and Hoffman's influence will be clearly discernable.

But Hoffman hasn't limited his focus to ritual. Through his efforts as a rabbi, a professor and a prolific author, he has played a significant role in changing the meaning of three words – liturgy, ritual and synagogue – for the Reform movement.

In speaking of Hoffman's legacy, former student Elyse Frishman, rabbi at the Barnert Temple in Franklin Lakes, New Jersey and co-editor of the newest Reform *siddur* (daily prayer book), *Mishkan T'filah*, says, "While he will certainly be known as a professor of liturgy, he's far broader than that. I think he will be seen as a pivotal thinker of our time." She continues, "He is a genius...He is a brilliant scholar and an eclectic student. He is also an extraordinarily innovative thinker."

"When they write the history on synagogues at the turn of the century, Hoffman's thinking will factor as the major influence," says Daniel Freelander, also a former student of Hoffman's and now vice president of the Union for Reform Judaism.

Many people know Hoffman as a professor who also happens to be a Reform rabbi, but he considers himself a rabbi first and foremost; his students at Hebrew Union College in New York City are his congregants. "I got my PhD but I don't have the certificate," he says. "I threw it out. I didn't care. But I have my *smicha* (rabbinic ordination) on my wall."

Before Hoffman came along, a liturgy professor was a historian, studying the way the prayer book has evolved. Hoffman's influence has played a role in expanding the study of liturgy so that it now encompasses not just the history of prayer but the study of worship. Previously, rituals – the ways in which liturgy is carried out in the synagogue – were not studied separately from liturgy. When Hoffman's teachings took hold, the field of Jewish ritual studies opened up; as a consequence, changes are occurring in the way Reform synagogues function.

In reflecting on his interests, Hoffman notes, "The history [of prayer] is an interesting thing, but it's not going to change people's lives." And changing lives is what Hoffman is after.

Much of Hoffman's focus has been to understand ritual and adapt it so that it has meaning for today's worshipers. Frishman describes him teaching "not the *what* but the *why* of liturgy."

All elements of the service, Hoffman says, should be fashioned to bring the congregants in and allow spirituality to coalesce. For example, the physical space needs to be set up to create intimacy between the rabbi and congregants. The music should fit the mood that each prayer is supposed to set. And congregants should have something concrete to focus on during rituals, such as an upraised Kiddush cup or a havdalah candle.

These concepts were practically heresy when Hoffman introduced them. At the time, the Reform service was very much standardized elaborate theater, and many old-guard rabbis, including some of Hoffman's teachers, were displeased with the liberties they felt he was taking. Today, Hoffman's approach is evident in many Reform synagogues, and students and colleagues praise his ability to create rituals that work.

Hoffman's focus extends to the very nature of the synagogue itself. Concerned that synagogues had become shops that sold religious services rather than vital spiritual centers, he cofounded Synagogue 2000 (now Synagogue 3000) in 1994, a nonprofit initiative dedicated to making synagogues vibrant centers for Jewish life. "Synagogues have to engage congregants," Hoffman explains.

The establishment has recognized the value of his ideas, and he has received multiple awards including the Berakah Award in 2004 from the North American Academy of Liturgy for lifetime achievement. The previous year, he was given the Barbara and Stephen Friedman Chair in Liturgy, Worship, and Ritual at Hebrew Union College, a position essentially created for him.

Hoffman is a fluent teacher, in his element when in front of people. He covers his topics thoroughly and with animation, introducing stories when appropriate and bantering with students as they call out questions. When he's done lecturing, he pulls a chair close to the students and sits to take questions. After his classes, most students linger for further discussion. No one seems to want to leave his presence; nor does he want to leave theirs.

"There are lots of smart people and lots of great speakers," says Ron Wolfson, a Conservative educator based in Los Angeles, who cofounded Synagogue 2000 with Hoffman. "But it's rare to find someone who combines a scintillating speaking style, superb scholarship and concern for human beings in one package. On top of that he's pretty funny."

Hoffman is also a prolific author and has written or edited over twenty-five books, with more on the way. His most known works include *Beyond the Text: A Holistic Approach to Liturgy* (1989), which looks at Jewish liturgy as a study of both text and worship; *The Art of Public Prayer: Not for Clergy Only* (1988), a textbook for directing meaningful rituals; and *Covenant of Blood: Circumcision and Gender in Rabbinic Judaism* (1995), a historical study of circumcision. He has also edited *Minhag Ami: My People's Prayer Book*, a ten-volume series that illuminates individual prayers in the daily and Shabbat services. *Israel: A Spiritual Travel Guide: A Companion for the Modern Jewish Pilgrim* (1998) explains what makes Israel's historical sites meaningful, and offers suggestions for prayer while at each one.

. . .

Hoffman was born in 1942 outside Toronto, in a town on the outskirts of a small city where cows grazed not far from his backyard and nobody bothered locking their doors. His father, a podiatrist, was deeply committed to Judaism. Beginning when Hoffman was four years old, his father taught him, along with the six other Jewish children his age in town, how to read Hebrew.

His parents created what Hoffman describes as "a warm and loving Jewish home, with candles and Kiddush every Friday night and festive dinners for Shabbat and holidays." Both his parents worked on Shabbat, but they dropped him off at the synagogue on their way to work. They instilled a love of Judaism, and Hoffman thought about becoming a rabbi from a very young age.

He attended Hebrew Union College in New York for his smicha. His father died in Hoffman's fourth year of rabbinical school, and his grief-stricken mother soon after. Years later, Hoffman learned from aunts and uncles that his father had very much wanted to be a rabbi but, like many who grew up during the Depression, never had the chance to pursue his dream. "Recognizing that he had bequeathed to me nothing less than his own calling – which by then had become my own – I became ever more committed to it," says Hoffman.

He went on to earn a PhD from Hebrew Union College in Cincinnati. For his course of study he picked liturgy, a field so new that he was one of the first ever to receive a doctorate specifically in it alone.

Armed with his degrees, Hoffman expected to become a small-town rabbi. That, however, did not happen. "I never imagined that life would've thrown me so many opportunities," he says. "I got lucky."

His first big break happened in 1973. Just as he was looking for a pulpit, HUC in New York City offered him a position as an assistant professor. He gladly accepted, eager for the chance to teach. And though he had no desire to work in a big city, he found that New York suited him, and he's been there ever since.

At HUC, he taught the history of Jewish liturgy in the traditional manner, by examining the history of prayer. Reviews were mixed. "I wasn't terribly enamored with what he had to offer us," admits Frishman. What she didn't know was that Hoffman found the purely historical approach to prayer wanting as well. The content was fascinating, but it lacked the human element. He began experimenting with a new idea: that liturgy could be best understood through the lens of ritual; that is, prayers are powerful because of how people recite them.

Part of his inspiration came from time spent studying with Christian scholars. The Second Ecumenical Council of the Vatican, or Vatican II, was in its heyday, and Catholics were examining ways to update their liturgy and rituals. Hoffman joined a new organization called the North American Academy of Liturgy. When he joined, he was the only Jew. Years later, he became its president.

Though Hoffman has always been deeply rooted in the Jewish faith, he has spent much of his life in a world of Christians. In high school, most of Hoffman's friends were Lutheran. Given the dearth of Jews his age, he gravitated to the children of teachers from the Lutheran seminary because they were serious about religion. Not long after he took the position at HUC, the University of Notre Dame invited him to lecture, and shortly thereafter to become a summer lecturer. At Notre Dame, he found that learning with Catholic scholars helped him define what he believed as a Jew.

"They'd ask you questions you had never thought of before," he says. "It sharpened my own sense of identity no end, because I had to figure out why I was different, how I was different, and how to express it."

. . .

Armed with new ideas about ritual, in 1976 Hoffman began teaching a class at HUC called Rite and Ritual. Frishman attended the class and this time, she was impressed. "In that class he revealed himself to be an anthropologist," she recalls. "He is constantly looking for something new to unveil, and he doesn't do it for the sake of novelty. He does it for the sake of figuring out why a ritual has been around for as long as it has, and why it continues to be important to us."

His students and colleagues praise him for his ability to invent rituals that work. "Larry is extraordinarily gifted at composing on-the-spot prayers. He does it with a respect for traditional forms, but he is also very creative," says Wolfson. He adds, with a note of humor, "You haven't been married until you've been married by Larry Hoffman."

A few years after that first wave of students graduated, in the summer of 1984, Rabbi Daniel G. Zemel, now the senior rabbi at Temple Micah in Washington, D.C., was back at HUC for a seminar that proved a bit dull. He and a friend of his, also a rabbi, crept out of the classroom and went to find Hoffman. They chatted, and came up with the idea of forming an alumni study group with others from those first Rite and Ritual classes. More than twenty years later, that group of sixteen students, many now leaders of the Reform movement, still meets four times a year. The group has meant a great deal both to Hoffman and his former students.

Hoffman explains that the group stretches the boundaries of Jewish knowledge by integrating areas of study into an understanding of the world. At first, the group continued its study of anthropology, beyond what they learned in Rite and Ritual. Since then, they have studied many other topics, ranging from art to quantum physics. "It's a very, very special group," says Zemel. "I cannot imagine my rabbinate without it."

. . .

Hoffman and Ron Wolfson began discussing the challenges facing synagogues the first time they spoke, in 1993. They met for coffee at a friend's urging, and spent three hours in deep conversation: Reform synagogues were losing vitality, weren't addressing the needs of contemporary Jews, were too inwardly focused and not involved in outreach, and were "pediatric," as Hoffman puts it. Families joined for the Hebrew school and the Bar or Bat Mitzvah and then stopped showing up. One of the greatest challenges, they felt, was the shift from Judaism as an ethnicity to Judaism as a chosen religion. More than ever, Jews must choose Judaism, and the synagogue must facilitate that choice. Their conversation became the seed for Synagogue 2000, a national organization dedicated to revitalizing synagogue life for all denominations. In cofounding Synagogue 2000, Hoffman also initiated a third area of career concentration, and one he feels has the potential to impact the Jewish world even more than his contributions to the study and practice of ritual.

"We have to change the nature of our conversations about Jewish community," says Hoffman. "They can't be ethnic conversations anymore. They have to be conversations about why be a Jew – honest conversations."

He elaborates, "You want synagogues to be moral and spiritual centers. We lack morality in this country, terribly, and everybody knows it. We've become a mean country. We've cut back on all the help for the poor, and we've got people living in the streets and poverty among children. Everybody knows that. And I think most Jews want to help." It's up to the synagogue, he says, to help them help the world. Hoffman also believes the synagogue must play a role in creating a welcoming spiritual atmosphere for prayer.

Synagogue 3000, as the organization is now known, in working collaboratively with synagogues to promote transformation and empower congregations, has already had a profound effect. Freelander estimates that more than half of the nine hundred Reform synagogues he works with through the Union for Reform Judaism have become more dynamic in the last decade, with a broader offering of activities, more exciting rituals and more participatory congregations.

Both Hoffman and Wolfson have extended their impact by writing on the topic. Each published books about Synagogue 3000 in 2006 – Hoffman wrote *Rethinking Synagogues* and Wolfson contributed *The Spirituality of Welcoming.* "The single greatest success is that we've changed the nature of the conversation," Hoffman says. "When we started, almost nobody was doing this work. People are now talking about the sacred. People are now saying services don't have to be boring; they can be compelling."

And yet, despite his accomplishments, despite having changed the Jewish world in many ways, Hoffman underplays his impact.

"Traditional Jewish life would say that our transcendent purpose as Jews is to bring about *tikkun olam*, to bring about the messianic age," he says. "I've reached the conclusion that the amount of good that I can do in terms of bringing about the Messiah is so tiny that it seems to me if it's going to happen, we may work for a million years, but God's going to have to do something someday or other. The most important thing that we as Jews can do is to use the gifts that God has given us to help the people around us. So I've influenced, I think, the people who are around me."

The people around him have influenced him as well, including his three adult children, Joel, Rob and Shira – especially Shira, who suffers from severe epilepsy. The fact that God did nothing to prevent this illness has caused Hoffman to struggle with his conception of God.

"There's plenty of evidence in the Talmud that we see God suffering with us rather than entering to heal all of us. The rabbis are perfectly aware of this. They were the ones who put Job in the Bible, after all. The question of Job is: Why do the good people suffer? And God doesn't answer him. God avoids it. But one of Job's friends comes to visit him and says, 'You must have sinned. Obviously God wouldn't let bad things happen to good people, so what did you do wrong?' And the only thing God says at the end of this story, He says to Job, 'By the way,' He says, 'Your friend who said you must've sinned? He's wrong. I don't work that way.'"

Hoffman explains, "I believe with Maimonides that we can't ever do justice in describing God...I don't like even saying, 'I believe in God' or 'I don't believe in God'; I think that's not a Jewish question. A Jewish question is, is there such a thing as the 'God-ly' – a reality of God in the world – and how can I act God-ly? When I say 'God heals,' what I mean is, I should try to be a healer, and therefore to concentrate on the God-ly...

"So my concern is not drawing a detailed picture of God. My concern is not expecting too much of God, because you'll be disappointed. The way I have come to imagine it is, there are three key aspects of God in traditional theology. One is that God is omniscient, God knows everything. Two, God is omnipotent, God can do everything. Three, God is beneficent, God is all good. Now, I don't think you get to keep all three. I think you have to give up on one.

"I give up on God's all-power," he says. "I think God created the universe, and in doing so had to create a natural world, and in creating a natural world, God had to create the laws of nature and set us free now to learn them. God doesn't change the laws of nature. That's the way it is, folks."

.   .   .

Clearly, Hoffman isn't content to sit back and accept the accolades that come his way. At a point in his career when many people slow down, he's looking forward to starting an institute for synagogue studies, to elucidate what makes synagogues unique and to serve as an incubator for ideas that will change them for the better. "Imagine if we had a hundred people studying this, instead of one or two!" he says.

And then there's the world at large, a source of constant concern. When questioned as to what he worries about, Hoffman, after denying he's much of a worrier, begins to list concern after concern, a litany of them. He fears that there aren't enough good people in the world, that some of his students graduate without being qualified, that Israel's wars will never end, that people don't think deeply enough. Then there's the frustration that so many people want to limit freedom and turn the clock back to the "good old days," which Hoffman calls "old but not necessarily good."

And there's more. "I worry when I hear the news," he says. "Almost always, I worry when I hear the news about what the world's coming to. But I try my best to work on a one-to-one basis. That's the only thing in my power to do."

AARON LANSKY

by NANCY WOLFSON-MOCHE

Talk about a blizzard. Fat flecks of snow swirled outside the small plane, affording pilot and passengers little visibility. It was mid-January, 1991 and Aaron Lansky, his wife Gail, the architect Allen Moore, and Myra Fein, the president of the Board of Directors of the National Yiddish Book Center (NYBC), Lansky's then-eleven-year-old nonprofit organization, were aboard a private plane destined for Martha's Vineyard. When the plane finally landed, the first thing Lansky spotted was a flashing yellow light next to the words: "DAN-GER. When light is flashing it is unsafe to take off or land."

   Frazzled, they climbed out of the plane and into a car. They drove past one palatial home after another, pointing to each one and repeating, "Is that it?" Finally they reached a small salt marsh and overlooking the marsh they saw what appeared to be a small, unremarkable house. As the car came to a stop Lansky thought, "For this tiny house I just risked my life?" They went inside. The whole space was oriented toward the marsh and a pond, and beyond the pond you could see the ocean. It was one of those houses that you want to move into on the spot. In that moment, Lansky knew it was *bashert* (meant to be): the non-Jewish architect who had designed this non-ostentatious, magical house was the perfect pick to design the permanent home of the National Yiddish Book Center.

Lansky, who relishes a good story, and who has gathered plenty of them in the course of his unexpected and surprisingly adventurous career as the man behind the rescue of 1.5 million Yiddish books, explains that they made the trip in order to check out a summer house designed by Moore, a Newburyport, Massachusetts–based architect.

Moore was in the running for the commission to design the NYBC's headquarters in Amherst, Massachusetts, on the campus of Hampshire College. It would be a Yiddish cultural and educational hub, housing a small portion of the then-million Yiddish *bicher* (books) that Lansky and his crew of *zamlers* (volunteer book collectors) had been gathering since 1980. And it would be a permanent home for the NYBC, which had been housed in seven different borrowed or rented buildings since its inception (including a former elementary school, a former roller skating rink, and a defunct shopping mall), before buying the land from Hampshire College.

Moore worked on the NYBC project "for four and a half years, six days a week, for almost no money whatsoever. It was a labor of love for him," Lansky says. The cluster of unpretentious, low-lying linked wings of the NYBC building designed by Moore has an unmistakable *shtetl* style yet blends organically into the rolling New England landscape. Like the Martha's Vineyard house on the salt marsh, the exterior does not reflect the interior. While small-scale and dark, with disconnected Old World references on the outside, the inside of the thirty-seven-thousand-square-foot, climate-controlled, fire-protected center, completed in 1997, is light, almost loft-like, and modern. And yet the building seems perfectly balanced and whole.

The architecture makes reference to the Diaspora: Jews may

have dispersed in small groups yet still remain connected and strong as a people. Lansky sees the building's architecture as a metaphor for his organization, which has managed to revive a deep-rooted yet widely scattered bygone culture by taking a forward-looking, modern approach. Book by book, small teams of volunteers rescued tens of thousands of Yiddish volumes that would otherwise have landed in the trash.

Actually, many of the books *had* already landed in the trash, and retrieving them was no easy feat. In *Outwitting History* (2004), Lansky's absorbing memoir of his often outlandish book-collecting adventures, he compares his perseverance to the United States Postal Service, as stipulated in their maxim, "Neither snow, nor rain, nor heat, nor gloom of night stays these couriers from the swift completion of their appointed rounds."

He took note of that inscription on Manhattan's General Post Office early one sleety morning in 1980. He had been awakened at midnight the night before by an emergency phone call from his former Yiddish teacher, who had spotted thousands of Yiddish books in a dumpster on Sixteenth Street in New York City. Within hours the dumpster company was scheduled to pick up the overflowing container and render its contents landfill. To make matters worse, rain was forecast.

Lansky took an overnight train from Northampton, Massachusetts, where he was living, and made it to the dumpster seven hours later. The rain had beat him to it, and the books on top were already wet. With sixty dollars in his pocket and no credit card, he needed to rent a U-Haul A.S.A.P. Only one local U-haul dealer was willing to rent to him – contingent on a $350 cash deposit. His Yiddish teacher came up with the deposit. After rallying six friends to help load, they began packing the books into the rented twenty-four-foot truck. Their clothes turned red, yellow, blue and green, splotched by the book covers' running dyes. By nightfall they had saved about five thousand books, and sacrificed another three thousand that were thoroughly waterlogged. Lansky landed in bed for the next three days with a fever, his body depleted but spirit reinforced.

· · ·

Twenty-five years later on an early September afternoon Lansky sits in his large, light-filled corner office at the NYBC and reflects on a career spent rescuing endangered books written in a vanishing language, creating a home for them, preserving them, and promoting Yiddish culture – the center's work has gone far beyond simply collecting and storing books.

Yiddish may be a lost language, yet the NYBC claims to be the "largest and fastest-growing Jewish cultural organization in America." At last count, the NYBC had collected 1.5 million books, boasts thirty-five thousand members, attracts ten thousand visitors a year, and operates on a four-million-dollar annual budget. The Center publishes *Pakn Treger* (The Book Peddler), a thrice-annual magazine exploring Yiddish culture, history, art and life; offers internship programs; and is a pioneer in the innovative application of technology – thanks to an initial grant from his Righteous Persons Foundation, the Steven Spielberg Digital Yiddish Library scans every page of every Yiddish book in the Center's collection.

It took two and a half years to digitize the fourteen thousand individual titles that are currently available. This amounts to something like 3.5 million pages, all of which are preserved in digital files and, within the next few years, will be accessible online through a searchable database that Lansky believes will revolutionize Jewish scholarship. Printouts of all digitized books are available – it takes a few minutes to print out an on-demand reprint. In addition, surplus copies of the rescued books are made accessible by distributing them to libraries and educational institutions – the NYBC has provided Yiddish volumes to six hundred major university and research libraries. Recently, the process of translating selected volumes has begun and a Yiddish dictionary is in the works.

When Lansky established the NYBC in 1980, he was told a lot of things – he was told that there were only seventy thousand Yiddish books existing in the U.S., a number he collected in the first year alone. He was told that Yiddish was dead. "I must have gone to every major Jewish organization in America looking for help. And I sat in front of these expansive desks, and people would look at me in a rather condescending way and say, 'Don't you know that Yiddish is dead? Forget it.' Well, I didn't believe them, and I appealed directly to everyday Jews, and the response has been sort of astonishing," he says.

He wasn't told that one day he would have 222 zamlers stationed throughout the U.S. and Canada collecting books. He wasn't told that the NYBC's internship program would routinely receive hundreds of applicants, or that approximately half of the center's interns would go on to further study or professional work related to Yiddish. He wasn't told that one day the NYBC would have a full-time staff of twenty, or that in 1989 he would be awarded a MacArthur Fellowship, or that Yiddish would be the first literature to be digitized, becoming, as the *New York Times* reported, "the most in-print literature in the world."

The driving impetus behind the entire endeavor was that it was great literature that was being lost. "The literature had enough intrinsic worth that no matter what anybody told me about how Yiddish was dead, and how no one cared about Yiddish anymore, what I knew was it's just an extraordinary world literature that needed to be saved, no matter what," Lansky says. "All the other virtues, the fact that it's a critical part of defining contemporary Jewish identity, that's sort of secondary...great books need to be saved."

When Lansky began, he thought it would take three years to collect all of the books. Almost thirty years into the adventure, he's still at it. "Jews are just far more avid readers than I think anybody understood or anybody imagined," he says. "Books have a lot of meaning for Jews, unlike anything else. They allow for reflection, they allow for deliberative thinking, and so I think books have a real role to play. We are a People of the Book...because books are big enough and powerful enough to define and contain identity. Dispersed and landless throughout most of our history, Jews venerated books as a 'portable homeland,' the repository of our collective memory and identity."

Physically, the man who has been called the "Indiana Jones of Yiddish" does bear a slight resemblance to Harrison Ford. Lansky is 5'6", slim, bright blue-eyed and bespectacled with a lightness of being that defies his purposeful strength. With curly light brown hair that is graying at the temples, he appears much younger than his early fifties (he was born in 1955). He speaks with a Massachusetts accent, slower than you would expect, and his sentences are peppered with Yiddish words, inflections and humor. The Yiddishisms have a way of softening his sharp intellect and wit, bringing out his *haymish* (likeable, friendly) qualities. He is quick to quote Lenny Bruce, Bob Dylan, Abbie Hoffman, Mordechai Kaplan and Isaac Bashevis Singer.

The blonde wood furniture in Lansky's vaulted-ceilinged office is white oak (hand-built by Suzi Moore, Allen Moore's wife), and light pours through the floor-to-ceiling windows that face the "Yiddish Writer's Garden," commemorating 120 of the greatest Yiddish writers. The clean, sparely appointed office contrasts with the spaces described in *Outwitting History*, in which he depicts every place he inhabited, including his car and his parents' home, as being in a constant state of *hefkeyres* (chaos), crammed beyond capacity with his treasured Yiddish books.

Because the book collection has grown so large, Lansky explains, almost ninety percent of it is stored in a warehouse in Holyoke, a neighboring town. "Sometimes I walk into that warehouse and just get this sense of the weight of it all," Lansky says. "I don't mean because we crack beams – which we do – but just a sense of the weight of history and what an incredibly vibrant and intellectually engaged culture all of this was."

He is referring to the fact that until 1939, Yiddish was the first language of seventy-five percent of the world's Jews. Between 1864 and 1939 (the heyday of this thousand-year-old culture, when there were eleven million Yiddish speakers) thirty thousand Yiddish titles were published. "It was effectively sort of just ripped out of the fabric of Jewish life and nobody even knows that it exists anymore," he says.

Well, now they do, thanks to Lansky's drive to revive it. Recently, some college students have even deemed Yiddish "hip." Lansky calls it "the 'in' language of a people on the outs." *Yiddish*, which means

"Jewish," emerged in the tenth or eleventh century among Jews on the Rhine River. It is an East European vernacular that is a *mishmash* (hodge-podge) consisting of twenty percent Hebrew and Aramaic mixed with German, Latin, French, Italian, Polish, Ukrainian, White Russian and Slovak.

It is written in the Hebrew alphabet, but until the second half of the nineteenth century, Yiddish existed mostly as a spoken language. By the early twentieth century, there were Yiddish newspapers and magazines, films and plays, politics, art, music, and what Lansky calls "a free-wheeling literature that marked one of the most concentrated outpourings of literary creativity in all of Jewish history."

Among the best-known authors were Sholem Aleichem (who wrote *Tevye the Dairyman*, which later gained fame as the musical *Fiddler on the Roof*), Isaac L. Peretz (author of *The Golem*), Mendele Mocher Seforim (a pseudonym for Solomon Abramowitsch, meaning "Mendele the Bookseller"), and Isaac Bashevis Singer, the Nobel Prize–winning, Polish-born author of thirty-six books, including *Yentl the Yeshiva Boy*. They chronicled the average *Yankl* (Jack) and his outer and inner life, with angst-centered recurring themes like unrealized dreams, unarticulated worries and wants, and universal hopes and frustrations.

.   .   .

Lansky was drawn to Yiddish as a child in New Bedford, Massachusetts, where his grandparents spoke Yiddish to each other, and to Lansky's parents (it was his mother's sole language until she was six) when they wanted to keep something from the children. He became intrigued with this secret language of the past. His mother's parents, both from a shtetl in what is now Poland, were educated Jews who spoke five or six languages.

"They weren't great intellectuals or great scholars, but they were intellectuals in the way many Jews were intellectuals: they valued learning, there were books and a piano in the house. Even though my grandfather worked as a junkman all his life, he had a tremendous depth of education, both Jewish and non-Jewish," explains Lansky, who also collected junk for a few months after high school. His grandfather came out of retirement to accompany him on his junk hunt, and as they talked, Lansky discovered his grandfather's "inherent radicalism, inherent sense of justice and inherent sense of humor."

His grandmother had arrived in America at sixteen, alone, carrying one cardboard valise containing her most valued possessions, including books, Shabbos candlesticks, and photographs of her parents, whom she would never see again. After her brother picked her up at Ellis Island, they boarded the ferry to Manhattan and he flung her suitcase overboard, explaining that embarking on a new life meant "leaving the Old Country behind." Although he hasn't scoured the harbor bottom for his grandmother's baggage, Lansky satisfied his curiosity about his roots by collecting a significant portion of the Yiddish books that did survive the crossing.

His father's father peddled fruit and vegetables and chickens on Cape Cod and owned a local baseball team. Lansky's own father became a lawyer. His mother's family was "more active, more socially conscious and funnier," than his father's, and a large part of why he so values Yiddish culture. "My mother used to say to me, 'You have to marry a Jewish girl, so that when you tell a joke she'll get it,'" Lansky laughs. He did. He met Gail Sharpe at the end of 1989 and although on the surface they seemed worlds apart – she was well-dressed with polished nails, and not academic; he was perpetually scruffy, jeans-clad, and book-obsessed – they shared a sense of humor and common spirit. They were married a few months later, in 1990, and had two daughters, Sasha and Chava, born in 1991 and 1993, respectively.

Growing up in New Bedford, Lansky perceived the difference between what he terms "the front and the back of the shul." At the front of the shul were the mink-stole-clad, designer-conscious, well-assimilated congregants, while at the back were the old guys who used to *fabrengen* (eat, drink and argue). They would sit and drink *schnapps* out of paper water cups, eat raw onions and herring, and talk constantly, always in Yiddish. Lansky preferred the "out" crowd at the back. "If you can understand the tension between the front of the shul and the back of the shul then you begin to understand what Jewishness is all about," he claims.

If Lansky has an intellectual fixation other than Yiddish books, it is this notion of duality and dialectical relationships. He sees "Jewishness" as a "religion of incongruities. It's high culture brought down to earth, and it's the tension between the two that gives Jewishness its oomph, that makes it funny when some people perceive it, but also makes it profound," Lansky says.

Duality was the theme of the "very small book" that Lansky credits with having determined his destiny, *The Schlemiel as Modern Hero*, by Ruth R. Wisse. Lansky's synopsis of the book's thesis: "The *schlemiel*, the familiar protagonist of much of Yiddish and, later, American-Jewish fiction, appears foolish only insofar as he is out of place – a Jew who ventures into the mainstream world and asks 'the wholly spontaneous questions of a different culture.'"

Lansky read the book after his junior year of college, and immediately resolved to study with Wisse – now at Harvard – who was just starting a graduate program in East European Jewish Studies at McGill University in Montreal.

In 1973, in his first semester as a freshman at Hampshire College (where the NYBC is now headquartered), Lansky had taken the course, "Thinking About the Unthinkable: An Encounter with the Holocaust." At the time, it was uncommon for such a course to be offered in the U.S. – the Holocaust was not a topic of academic inquiry. By the end of that semester Lansky had become fascinated not so much with the Holocaust *per se* as with the Jewish people and culture as targets of German destruction. "What was there about Jewish culture that was so antithetical to fascist ideology that the Germans literally lost the war to pursue the death of the Jews? Who were these Jews? What was it about them, anyway?" he asks. He constructed his own undergraduate curriculum and in so doing taught himself Yiddish in order to read the primary sources. He "became enamored of it," he says, and perceived the language as a "key to a civilization," the mid and late nineteenth- and early twentieth-century Jewish culture.

Casually, Lansky and assorted friends and girlfriends began a search for Yiddish books. They struck gold for the first time in the late spring of 1975 on their first pilgrimage to New York's lower East Side when, after much finagling, the bookseller J. Levine on Eldridge Street led them to a basement where he had stored his father's library of one hundred Yiddish books. The highlight of that initial group of books was a fourteen-volume "deluxe" edition of the complete works of Sholem Aleichem. And so the *schlepping* unofficially began.

When Lansky got to McGill in the fall of 1977, the biggest challenge was not *reading* the assigned Yiddish books in the original, but *finding* them. All were out of print, and libraries had few. (This was, of course, long before the existence of Internet search engines and online book emporiums.) Once the Montreal Public Library's single copy of a work had been claimed, the other students often had to Xerox the whole book in order to take it home. David Roskies, a professor at the Jewish Theological Seminary in New York and also Ruth Wisse's brother, joked that Jews were no longer the *Am hasefer* (the People of the Book) but were now the *Am ha-kseroks* (the People of the Xerox).

If there was an "Aha!" moment for Lansky, it happened on a bleak, snowy winter day at McGill while he was sitting in a classroom. The assignment – *Fligelman*, a novel by Hirsh Dovid Nomberg – was announced and suddenly it occurred to him that while he was scrounging for the assigned books, at the same time, in other places, those very titles were being destroyed at an alarming rate. "If we don't save them soon, what in the world is the next generation going to do?" Lansky wondered.

"I knew how to drive a truck and I knew how to organize and make things happen, and I figured I could probably do this," he says of his decision to leave school and look for books. He never expected the process to be so enlightening, demanding – or enduring. What began as a short-term book-gathering leave of absence from graduate school has occupied three decades of Lansky's adult life. His book-collecting odyssey (for which he could not solicit a penny in 1980 but was able to raise $8 million in 2004 alone) is itself a *bobbe mayse* (improbable tale).

Within a short time, the only thing he learned to expect was the unexpected. With zamlers stationed all over the New York area on the lookout for Yiddish libraries large or small, these treasured collections were often discovered just hours before the demolition crew was to come, spurring late-night calls and last-minute rushes to their rescue. Books were rescued from places like the Newark Public Library, where unsupervised workers were indiscriminately throwing away about two thousand books a day, including many of the library's three thousand Yiddish books. By the time Lansky and his crew arrived to spirit off the library's collection, about one-third of the Yiddish books had already been discarded. There were books to be rescued from small, informal libraries set up in apartment buildings, and of course, there were many, many books owned by individuals.

With a core crew of about three friends, he initially solicited books by hanging posters in laundromats, synagogues and senior centers. Lansky went from stores to homes to institutions, scouring attics, basements, dumpsters and demolition sites for Yiddish books. The individuals who called him to come and pick up their books were old at the time and are now mostly deceased. They fed him, serenaded him, told him stories, *kvetsched* (complained), *kibbitzed* (chatted), cried and laughed with him, and then thanked him, kissed him, and reluctantly, let him leave. "They sat me down at their kitchen tables and poured a *glezele tey*, a glass of hot tea, which they served with homemade cookies, *lokshen kuglech* (noodle puddings), or Entenmann's cakes," Lansky writes at the beginning of *Outwitting History*. As you read on, you accompany him as he *noshes* (nibbles) on gefilte fish, pickles, sauerkraut, bagels, bialys, lox and more, developing warm, deep friendships with many of the donors.

Throughout his active book collecting years, Lansky took notes and often tape-recorded the people he met – he wanted not just to preserve their books but to preserve their stories. "I understood that this was a moment in history, it really was the passing of one epoch to the next," he says. "These people were pouring out their hearts and telling me their stories. I bought a little tape recorder, which I'd put on the kitchen table between the horseradish and the gefilte fish."

The time was right for the endeavor, Lansky says. "I think things happen at the right moment in history. It was just my good fortune that I entered graduate school when this was finally possible. If I had started ten years earlier, I don't think anybody would have cared – there were Yiddish books everywhere. Yiddish was still too present for people to take it seriously. I don't think anybody had a sense yet that we had lost a culture, because we hadn't lost it yet, it was still 'Big deal, all old people speak Yiddish, what's the problem here?' and if I started twenty years later, of course, the books would have been lost, it would have been too late. I consider it the great blessing of my life that the work was there waiting for me."

. . .

Twenty-eight years into the adventure, Lansky is raising funds to expand the NYBC by almost doubling the size of the Amherst building. Allen Moore designed the addition, scheduled to open in spring 2009, which will include a climate-controlled library to house half a million volumes, a two-story "Yiddish academy" with classrooms, a performance hall that can seat 275, a student commons, a distance learning studies area, galleries and exhibition space, a kosher kitchen, office space and an outdoor "big top" tent for large summer audiences.

If there was anybody who imagined all of this, it might have been Max Weinreich, a founder of YIVO (Yiddish Scientific Institute), considered by many to be the greatest Yiddish scholar of his generation. Weinreich came to New York in 1939 at the age of forty-five, narrowly escaping the Holocaust. He then taught Yiddish to American students, though he had almost no takers. When a student asked him why he persevered, Weinreich responded, "Because Yiddish has magic, it will outwit history."

As you enter the vestibule of the National Yiddish Book Center the Weinreich quote is printed in English on the left wall, and in Yiddish on the right. These words could be Lansky's motto (they inspired his book's title), for he is fascinated with the magic of the unexpected. "I've seen [Yiddish] work its magic already, and I have great hopes for the future. This was a thousand years of Jewish experience," Lansky says. "The wonder is that it took so long for us to come to terms with what was lost."

DANIEL LIBESKIND

by DENISE COUTURE

When Daniel Libeskind won an international competition in 1989 for the design of a Jewish museum in Berlin, he was largely unknown outside architectural circles. It was the first commission for the Polish-born professor who had been more interested in exploring architecture theoretically than in practice. When completed a decade later, the museum – a haunting, zigzagging structure that evokes a broken Star of David – was hailed by many as a masterpiece, a work of genius. Libeskind, at fifty-three years of age, suddenly found himself thrust onto the world stage.

The spotlight has shone on Libeskind ever since. In 2003, his design for a master plan to rebuild Ground Zero – the gaping pit where the Twin Towers of the World Trade Center once stood – was selected from a crowded group of renowned contenders. In the fall of 2006, the Libeskind-designed Denver Art Museum in Colorado opened to fanfare and acclaim. His much-anticipated addition to the Royal Ontario Museum in Toronto opened in the summer of 2007. A fairground redevelopment in Milan and residential skyscrapers in Singapore are among myriad high-profile projects in the works.

Libeskind has come a long way from Lodz, where he entered the world in 1946, the son of Polish Jews who lost most of their extended families in the Holocaust. Today, his architecture firm, Studio Daniel Libeskind, occupies the nineteenth floor of an elegant lower Manhattan office building overlooking Ground Zero. There are satellite offices in Zurich, Bern, San Francisco, Denver, Toronto, Hong Kong and Tel Aviv, employing 150 people.

Now in his early sixties, Libeskind is frequently described as boyish and ebullient. When he talks, his hands often fly up toward his ears as he exuberantly voices his thoughts. He smiles often, a wide toothy grin, and his bright blue eyes are intelligent and friendly. He exudes an infectious, youthful optimism and love for life, qualities he says he owes almost entirely to Judaism and especially to his beloved parents, the late Dora Blaustein and Nachman Libeskind. Even after the horrors they experienced during the war, part of which they spent in Soviet prison camps, "they truly believed the world was worth fighting for," he says.

Libeskind took their life lessons to heart. Generous helpings of optimism and a fighting spirit were required in order to see the Jewish Museum Berlin through to completion. The obstacles were immense – hostile city officials and an undercurrent of anti-Semitism. "At one point in 1990, the city government voted unanimously to scrap the entire project," says Libeskind.

In 1999, when Libeskind accepted the German Architecture Prize for the museum, he told the audience: "The cultivation of naiveté, the feeling that one should remain a beginner worthy of entering the 'cloud of the unknown,' is what motivated me to continue this work across the vicissitudes of the past ten years: six governments, five name changes, four museum directors, three window companies, two sides of a wall, one unification, and zero regret."

From the beginning, Libeskind was determined to design a

structure that would serve as a memorial to victims of the Holocaust. The East German Senate's invitation to enter the competition called for an extension of the Berlin Museum to house a Jewish Department, a *Jüdische Abteilung*. Those two words horrified Libeskind, who recognized them as the very words used by the ss officer Adolf Eichmann, mastermind of the policy of transporting Jews to ghettos and death camps.

"Something rebelled in me against that idea that you could compartmentalize Jewish culture in Berlin rather than see it as part of the everyday life, both its successes prewar and the tragedy of the complete extermination of Jews from Berlin, throughout Europe," says Libeskind, whose slightly accented English retains traces of Polish and Yiddish syntax.

Libeskind felt a sense of darkness, "because I understood who I was dealing with. I was dealing with a generation that was also a perpetrator of those crimes." Sustaining him was "a kind of desperate faith that silence around me would be given a voice and there would be something positive, something that could educate someone about what Berlin was, what Germany was, what the Holocaust was, and what the future was for a democratic new kind of city. But there were bleak days."

What Libeskind designed – and what the Berlin city government finally approved – is virtually a separate museum that incorporates symbolism of both the connection between Jews and Gentiles, as well as the fragmentation of their tortuous history. One axis, a path of continuity, connects the old baroque museum to Libeskind's new building. A second axis leads to the Garden of Exile and Emigration. A third axis dead-ends at the Holocaust Tower, a bare concrete structure, dark, damp and empty to recall the experience of Nazi Germany's Jewish victims. A series of empty rooms, the Voids, run throughout Libeskind's museum, evoking the emptiness in Europe following the mass genocide of World War II.

Among the survivors of that genocide were Libeskind's parents. Not sure what to do after the war, they returned to their Polish homeland. While many members of Poland's small community of postwar Jews hid their Jewishness and assimilated, Dora and Nachman did not. They were "indefatigably and proudly Jewish," says Libeskind. "They continued to speak Yiddish. They continued to be Jewish in their outward identities, not only inwardly. I always admired them for that. I admired their stance in life." Libeskind considers himself and his older sister, Ania, to be lucky that their parents transmitted to them Jewish values of life and tradition, even though they were not observant, nor is Libeskind himself.

"Our Judaism was an everyday thing," he explains. "It was in the way that you saw the world, and the way you talked about it; it was the way you reacted to other people and the way you embraced realities that are often rejected by others." Of himself, Libeskind says, "I would say what I *do* is Jewish…it's a Jewish approach to reality."

In 1957, the family left Poland for Israel. Libeskind was eleven. Two years later they moved again, this time to the Bronx in New York City. Libeskind often speaks of the visceral feelings he had upon entering New York harbor aboard the S.S. *Constitution* and setting eyes on the Statue of Liberty for the first time. "As we saw it coming out of that mist on that late August day, we stood there with our… jaws dropped, just like all the other immigrants," he recalls. "You could see the beauty and optimism and the power of thought in America in this city."

Nachman Libeskind found work as a printer not far from where the World Trade Center eventually was constructed. Libeskind's mother, Dora, who had run a corset shop in Poland, became a sweatshop seamstress. The family lived in a one-bedroom apartment in garment workers' union housing where nearly everyone spoke Yiddish. Yet in spite of meager circumstances, their daily life was rich with art, culture and learning. "They were very intellectual and scholarly people," says Libeskind of his parents. "They read books. They saved their money to go to the theater. They represented really what Jews in their makeup are."

The arts, especially music, have always been a large part of Libeskind's world. He listens to classical music every morning over coffee and counts the complete works of Bach among his prized possessions. As a boy in Poland he was a serious accordion player. Not long after moving to Israel, he won an America-Israel Cultural Foundation scholarship, also awarded the same year to Itzhak Perlman. The two pudgy prodigies played alongside each other at a recital in Tel Aviv. But as a young teen in New York, where Libeskind attended the acclaimed Bronx High School of Science, he began to turn to drawing, something he had always loved.

It was his practical mother who first suggested that he try architecture. Worried by her son's obsessive drawing, she urged him to give up any notion of becoming an artist, as Libeskind recounts in his delightful 2004 book, *Breaking Ground: An Immigrant's Journey from Poland to Ground Zero.* When young Libeskind offered up the name Andy Warhol as an example of a successful artist, his mother responded: "Varhole? For every Varhole there's a thousand penniless waiters. Be an architect. Architecture is a trade, and an art form."

The idea stuck. For Libeskind, it was a way to combine all of his passions and interests – the arts, philosophy, mathematics, science.

After high school, Libeskind enrolled in the architecture program at New York's Cooper Union, graduating in 1970. Two years later, he earned a master's degree in the history and theory of architecture from Essex University in England. A short-lived entry-level position at a New York architecture firm left him with a distaste for the actual practice of his chosen profession.

So for the next couple of decades, Libeskind spent his time as a theoretical architect, moving frequently to take various teaching positions, accompanied by his Canadian wife, Nina, whom he had married in 1969. When he was thirty-two, Libeskind accepted an offer to become head of the highly respected architecture department at the Cranbrook Academy of Art in Bloomfield Hills, Michigan. The couple settled into academic life and started a family.

For a time they were pleased to be there. Gradually, they weren't. Each of them wrongly assumed the other was happy with their Michigan life. Finally, in 1985, Libeskind came clean: He wanted to leave Bloomfield Hills; he was restless and eager for new adventures.

Nina responded by opening a bottle of cognac to celebrate. ("I can still, to this day, remember the taste. I was so happy," says Nina.) The next year they found themselves in Milan, Italy, where Libeskind started Architecture Intermundium, a kind of alternative school that attempted to bring together his disparate ideas about architecture and life. Libeskind, working from his home, was the sole teacher.

When Libeskind learned he had won the competition for the Jewish museum, he, Nina and their children were preparing to leave Italy for a stint in sunny California, where Libeskind had been awarded a prestigious resident scholar position at the Getty Center in Los Angeles. First, however, they made a detour to Berlin to pick up Libeskind's award. Shortly after their arrival, Nina, the worldly daughter of a Canadian politician, told her husband that if he ever wanted to see a Jewish museum actually built in Berlin, they would have to stay. He knew she was right.

Of the many crossroads in Libeskind's life, none would have as dramatic an impact on his career as the path he took toward Berlin.

Recalling that fateful first day in the city, Libeskind says, "We checked into a hotel. Rachel was just an infant and Noam and Lev were six and eight or something. And to this day, I remember the hotel. I remember the man at the desk said, 'How long are going to stay in Berlin?' I said, 'Until the Jewish Museum is built.' And he burst out laughing. He had never heard something so funny in his life. He thought it was kind of a joke.'" For the Libeskinds, of course, it was anything but funny.

Nor did Libeskind's extended family find it humorous. They were horrified to learn he was living in Berlin and swore they would never set foot in the city where the Holocaust had been conceived. Libeskind's father was the exception – he visited, eager to see everything. In one of the most moving passages in *Breaking Ground*, Libeskind writes of his father stopping suddenly on a Berlin street and proclaiming, "'Look at me. Here I am. Hitler is nothing but ashes. But I am here, and I am living, eating, sleeping in this city, and below, Hitler's bones are rotting!' His eyes glistened with tears, but he sounded victorious."

Other family and friends eventually visited as well, in 2001, when Rachel Libeskind had her bat mitzvah, the first such ceremony at Berlin's Oranienburger Strasse Synagogue since 1933.

Berlin was where Nina Libeskind became a full partner in her husband's career, something her husband made a condition if he were to see the Jewish Museum project through. Certainly, she was more than capable. As a girl she worked on the political campaigns of her father, David Lewis, who grew up in a Russian shtetl and went on to become a Rhodes Scholar and the founder of Canada's New Democratic Party. Every ounce of Nina's considerable political savvy would be called upon not only in Berlin but also in the couple's next stop, New York City.

Though construction on the Jewish Museum was completed in 1999, the official opening of the fully installed exhibition space came two years later – on September 11, 2001. When Libeskind heard that the World Trade Center had been struck by terrorists, "I instantly at that point said, 'I'm going to lower Manhattan. I want to be there.'"

The timing was right. His work in Berlin was done. And America, his adopted homeland, beckoned. Almost the first thing he did upon arriving in Manhattan was to visit the slurry wall – the World Trade Center's foundation, which held fast during the inferno. Before leaving Berlin, Libeskind had roughed out a plan for Ground Zero. After visiting the wall, he immediately called his team in Germany and said, "Change everything."

To Libeskind the slurry wall was symbolic of the strength of America's democracy and the value of people as individuals. He wanted to acknowledge the tragedy that had occurred, but he was equally determined to imbue the site with hope. To those ends, he incorporated the exposed slurry wall into his design of two large public spaces: the Park of Heroes to commemorate the fallen and the Wedge of Light to mark the time that each of the Twin Towers was hit by terrorist-flown airplanes. A third major element, dubbed the Freedom Tower, is a skyscraper that soars a symbolic 1,776 feet in the sky.

While the opening of the Jewish Museum in Berlin "instantly made [Libeskind] one of the most sought-after architects in the world," as *Time* magazine critic Richard Lacayo wrote, winning the master plan competition for developing Ground Zero propelled him to near-Hollywood-star status.

Like most celebrity, however, it has come with a price. Libeskind soon found himself embroiled with other architects on the project – and nearly anyone else who had a strong opinion about it – in a battle to retain the integrity of his master plan. As with the Jewish Museum, with its many references to the Holocaust, Libeskind's architecture tends to be deeply, sometimes overtly, symbolic. His harshest critics have called aspects of the Ground Zero master plan corny, kitschy, even ghoulish and ghastly.

"Libeskind's main contribution has always been to integrate history and meaning into design, which was more or less a revolution from modernism, which was much more straightforward," Arjen Oosterman, an editor for the Netherlands architectural magazine *Volume*, recently told the *International Herald Tribune*. "That produces strange, weird and sometimes uncomfortable buildings."

But for Libeskind, true symbols, such as the Jewish flame or the American flag, hold great meaning. "Very often symbols become hollow when they are not really lived, and people take them for granted as if they were just objects," says Libeskind. "Certainly, as an immigrant, one would feel it more profoundly because you would never take for granted what you can find in America," especially, he says, "when you grow up under Communist dictatorship, when you grow up under hardships where you don't have those opportunities."

Libeskind says he was open to making changes on other aspects of the master plan, but he would not compromise on the 1,776-foot height of the Freedom Tower, derided by his harshest critics as empty symbolism. "Definitely not. I fought for it! I had to fight very hard. What's more important than that date?"

In *Breaking Ground*, readers are given a fascinating play-by-play of the World Trade Center battle, complete with insider details (from Libeskind's position, of course), such as the bullying behavior of the lead architect hired to execute the master plan and ego-driven bickering more befitting little boys on a playground than grown men.

The Ground Zero architectural controversy continues, even as rebuilding has begun. Notes one architect who is acquainted with and likes Libeskind, "There's usually a fair amount of turmoil around him." For many people, Libeskind's appearance on the international stage has been cause for welcome, even celebration. Certainly he has contributed to enlivening the sometimes overly staid architectural scene.

Despite – or perhaps partly because of – the controversy, Studio Daniel Libeskind is flourishing. "We just keep getting project after project in the office," says Nina, who runs the firm's business operations. "The challenge is to remain small."

The eternal optimist isn't complaining. "It's my passion," says Libeskind. "It's not something that you can do between nine and five. It's not something that's even work in any secular sense of the word."

Libeskind, whose grandfather was an itinerant storyteller in Poland, believes memory is the force that drives Jewish life forward and gives it a future. He also believes that every building has a story to tell. "A great building – like great literature or poetry or music – can tell the story of the human soul."

SHOLOM LIPSKAR

by OREN BARUCH STIER

"We're all *shluchim* (emissaries) of the *Aibishter* – we are all emissaries of God," says Rabbi Sholom Lipskar, the dynamic founder and spiritual leader of Miami's Shul of Bal Harbour. "Each one of us is an emissary of God [created] to fulfill a unique purpose of creation. We each have a fundamental, monumental mission that is incredible and that touches on the core of our being, and that gives us the single most important reason for existence, and which gives us passion for existence."

One of the rabbi's many missions is to "touch every single Jew" in his Bal Harbour congregation's zip code "in a way that is not aggressive and is neighbor-to-neighbor" and thereby make the shul the center for the entire community. His ongoing Project 33154 designates "block shluchim," a representative on each block. Six times a year, each *shliach* goes to all his Jewish neighbors and makes sure they know about the coming Jewish holiday. There are about forty block shluchim, and the shul has identified close to a thousand Jews in the area who have "never participated in Jewishness," says Lipskar, who launched the program in 1998.

It's necessary to understand the context in order to grasp the magnitude of the goal. Lipskar founded the Shul of Bal Harbour in 1981. In its early years, the shul met in the card room of a hotel, and later moved into a storefront. The Bal Harbour community was less than welcoming – the local Homeowner's Association did not allow owners to sell their property to people of "Jewish and Syrian descent." Today the Chabad synagogue is housed in a nine-million-dollar structure, offers a myriad of programs and educational opportunities for all ages, and is known for its pluralistic, welcoming nature.

How did this change occur? How did Lipskar move from a storefront to a multi-million dollar building that can accommodate the thousand people who attend weekly classes in multiple languages in any given week?

Lipskar is always counseling, reaching out, bringing in. He "works harder and longer than anyone I've ever met," says Mitch Feldman, a congregant and member of the shul's executive committee. "And it isn't for business – his whole purpose is to bring Jews back to Judaism."

Lipskar pays particular attention to three areas of outreach. There's the Shul of Bal Harbour itself, home to a congregation of five hundred families. The shul hosts a dazzling array of Jewish activities – daily minyanim (including a Sephardic minyan), a community *kollel* (study group), men's and women's mikvehs, the Chaim Yakov Shlomo College of Jewish Studies, a Montessori-style preschool, singles' activities, and over fifty weekly adult education classes taught by Lipskar and others, including Spanish language classes for the shul's Latin contingent, which comprises a third of the congregation.

Then there's his outreach among South Florida's elderly and underserved. Lipskar's program for the elderly, essentially a yeshiva for the elderly, meets twice weekly for learning and lunch. Finally, there's the focus he puts on reaching out to Jews who are in prison and in the military through the Aleph Institute.

Despite the broad scope of his outreach, Lipskar is intensely focused on people as individuals. "He has a certain penetrating look, almost into your soul," Feldman says. "He'll even ask, 'How's your soul?' And it stops you for a moment – How *is* my soul?"

"Lipskar knows what's going on with every person he relates to, and he keeps track of every single event in a person's life – rich or poor, it doesn't matter," says Arturo Colodner, another congregant.

Mitch Feldman shares a story that underscores this point: "Whenever Lipskar visits the Rebbe's *ohel* (the Lubavitcher Rebbe's gravesite), he brings the entire shul membership list along and reads through it, picturing every single person and family member as he does so."

That passionate involvement characterizes Lipskar's role as a shliach. In addition to being a *chasid* (follower) of the Lubavitcher Rebbe, the late Menachem Schneerson, as a shliach Lipskar is one of the Rebbe's personal emissaries to the Jewish world, and, in many respects, the non-Jewish world as well. Being a shliach means caring for every individual Jew, and not letting anyone fall "through the cracks," Lipskar explains. "Being a shliach of the Rebbe is almost a professional sounding term, because you have a job to do, to wake up all the other shluchim of *Hashem* (the Name, a respectful title for God) to make sure that they get it done. Being a shliach is like being in the army."

He continues, "*Shlichus* is dealing with an extended family." Lipskar gets calls from all sorts of people in all sorts of situations at all sorts of times. Sometimes it's a person who just needs to hear a friendly voice; sometimes it's someone calling from jail, or someone who's gravely ill. Friends have told him to get an unlisted number. Lipskar replies, "So who should I give it to? My family? My closest friends? Who do you think calls me in the middle of the night? I get a call from a brother or sister who's lost."

. . .

Perhaps Lipskar's drive arises from his family's suffering and sense of purpose during and after World War II's nine-hundred-day siege of Leningrad. His father's father was killed, and his grandfather and father arrested for *Yiddishkeit*, for practicing Judaism. His family realized they had to flee their home to sustain their Jewishness.

Lipskar was born in the Uzbekistan capital of Tashkent, in 1946. When he was only weeks old, his grandfather smuggled him across the border into Czechoslovakia in a suitcase to avoid the per-person charge for crossing the border.

Until he was four years old, he lived with his family in three separate displaced persons camps in Germany, where he started *cheder*, traditional Jewish religious school. Early memories of people "really damaged" from the events of the Holocaust are mixed with fond reminiscences of accompanying his grandmother to a nearby farm to milk cows so they could have *Cholov Yisrael*, milk supervised by observant Jews, and of course Shabbos, which always felt like a feast even if they didn't have much to eat.

The family moved to Canada in 1951 and settled in Toronto. Lipskar continued learning, tagging along with his older brother to his advanced *Gemara* (Talmud) class in the evenings. One of his teachers, upon finding out that Lipskar intended to be a rabbi or a teacher, advised his parents that Lipskar shouldn't waste his life studying to become a rabbi but should instead become an accountant, since he was so good at math. Lipskar didn't heed that advice. "The selflessness of numerous family members on behalf of Yiddishkeit, along with a long rabbinic lineage, implanted a desire to be effective in the public domain," he says.

In 1961, after he turned fifteen, he left home to attend the Lubavitch yeshiva in Crown Heights, where he stayed until his marriage in 1968. A year later, he moved to Miami as a shliach.

The rabbi took what he describes as a "running start" when he went on shlichus, going into it "full time" as a twenty-two year-old. At twenty-three he was already the principal of a Jewish school. He says he quickly mastered the "technical questions" of his job, such as "where was God in the Holocaust," replicating the classic rabbinical responses, describing God as responsible for everything in the universe. Although we are allowed free choice, we see only a small piece of the picture, and the issue of the Holocaust is an unanswerable question, beyond our intellectual capacity.

Lipskar developed successful relationships with donors: one gave the "single largest gift Chabad had ever received" in 1974. However, after eleven years in Miami, a number of issues were troubling him, particularly those related to the theological perspective on the Holocaust. He felt challenged in his ability to internalize these religious responses and thereby represent them authentically. Other areas of concern were Jewish attrition, inertia and attraction to cults. His search for answers initiated a period of radical change.

With the help of a philanthropist and the support of the Rebbe, Lipskar took a year's sabbatical. During his 1980 sabbatical, he had no obligations. He kept notes and traveled widely. When the year ended, he requested and received another six months. Throughout that year and a half, every Friday, wherever he was, he would fly back to New York to spend Shabbos in Crown Heights with the Rebbe. Each week he also would question the Rebbe on various issues, and the Rebbe would respond, speaking about it then or the following week, often in his public *fabrengen* (bringing people together). During that time, the Rebbe was no longer meeting with people privately as a rule, but in 1981, after *Pesach*, the Rebbe's secretary called to schedule a meeting with Lipskar.

The custom for *yechidus* (private meeting) with the Rebbe was to write one's questions on a piece of paper and submit them. Lipskar explains that at that point he had seen the Rebbe more than forty times and would usually submit long reports in his position as shliach. But this time was different. He wanted the Rebbe to see him in a different way. He thought, "What am I going to ask the Rebbe? Where is God? Whatever I ask him, five years later I'm going to have another question, so I said to myself, 'This is the Rebbe, his soul knows my soul, so I'm not going to ask him anything.' The only thing I put on that note was my name."

The Rebbe looked at the piece of paper for a long time, and then he spoke to Lipskar for an unheard-of forty-six minutes (someone outside timed it). The Rebbe emphasized the significance of every single positive act done with sincerity, and reminded Lipskar that one's expectation of oneself should not exceed what God expects.

"That meeting changed my life, changed my perspective, changed my thinking," says Lipskar, using his hands for emphasis. "There was nobody in the room, just he and I, and just to be in the presence of that extraordinary energy, my whole experience of Jewishness took a dimensional leap. It was much more internalized, every aspect of my prayers, my outreach. It was not any longer an intellectual commitment that I understood and I had to convey; it was something that came from my inner being that used my intellect in order to express it."

Lipskar says this experience was not so different from that of a *ba'al teshuvah*, one who "returns" to Judaism, rediscovering his connection to God. He thinks of this meeting as a "great gift from the Rebbe. It felt transformational – a dimensional change, not a linear change – it was a different perspective."

Lipskar then asked the Rebbe what he should do, and the Rebbe said, "Hashem will give you a good thought." That Shabbos in his public talk, the Rebbe said, "There are thousands of Jews who are waiting for someone to come and to teach them Torah, to change their lives, and to elevate them...and nobody is paying attention...I'm addressing Jews in jail and their families, and nobody cares about them."

. . .

Here was the "good thought" Lipskar had been waiting for. He launched three programs in 1981 for Jews in three overlooked areas – those in prison, the elderly and in the assimilated community of Bal Harbour. He thought of it as an experiment, to see if the "language of Jewishness" with an updated communication system would be effective. This focus helped resolve his internal struggle and repair the "disconnect between the intellect and the emotion" that he had experienced. He returned to work more effective, more driven towards outreach than ever before.

A donor helped start the prison program, now known as the Aleph Institute. It operates in five hundred prisons and military facilities and has served ten thousand Jews, plus their families, according to Rabbi Menachem Katz, director of Prison and Military Programs. The organization runs a host of programs designed to provide moral and ethical education, rehabilitate inmates, and give those in isolated environments the opportunity to learn and to pray.

"It's wild, because we're sitting here in Miami and serving the needs of people who, without us, really can't get it done. I'm putting two guys on a base in Iraq together right now, neither of whom knows the other, and hooking them up with a Friday night minyan, all via e-mail," says Katz. "The main idea of Aleph is serving Jews separated from their communities – we become their resource, their base."

"I will never forget that the Aleph Institute helped me during the only time in my adult life when I felt helpless," a former inmate wrote. "You helped me to find my real self – reassess my values, what is really important."

Lipskar's education program for the elderly program currently exists as the Senior Torah Academy. In addition to its concentration on education, the program focuses on combating serious illnesses through Torah and studying the results through research projects Lipskar has initiated.

When Lipskar started the Shul of Bal Harbour, he would often have to "schlep people in from the street" to make a minyan, according to Sami Rohr, one of the shul's original members and a key benefactor instrumental in establishing the shul's permanent home.

While those early years were challenging, ultimately the shul exceeded even Lipskar's expectations. "The thirst for spirituality and Jewishness was so enormous, so palpable, and people were so eager to absorb anything that you would give them that had authentic Jewish content, that was not dressed in pageantry and formality," he recalls. Lipskar strives to have the shul embody what Chabad-Lubavitch stands for. "Non-compromising, yet non-judgmental, inclusive, Torah-based, filled with Jewish love," says Lipskar, whose sense of inclusiveness extends to the women of the congregation. Women actively participate on the board and in the shul itself. They participate in special women's services, and during regular services they benefit from better sight lines in the second-story gallery than the men have below.

The congregation is eclectic and well-rounded, ranging from black-hatted scholars to assimilated Jews with little background in Halacha and observance. "We don't perceive any Jew as marginalized," says the rabbi. Indeed, Lipskar has served as a tireless spiritual guide for many of the community's ba'alei teshuvah.

More recent endeavors include the ongoing Project 33154 to reach out to Jews in the Bal Harbour community and the geographically more far-flung Million Mitzvah Campaign launched in 2004, "to get people to do acts of goodness and kindness in order to make the world a better place."

Rabbi Mendy Levy, the shul's outreach director and campaign coordinator for the Million Mitzvah Campaign, explains the project involves almost thirty institutions, not all of them Chabad-affiliated, in twenty-five states and ten countries. With over eight hundred thousand mitzvahs to date, it's well on its way to meeting Lipskar's goal. Another, unrelated initiative is Lipskar's personal goal for the Bal Harbour community to raise over a million dollars so that every Jewish child can get a Jewish education, free if necessary. Once happy to support ten scholarships a year, now Lipskar aims for a hundred.

"From my perspective, as much as I've done, there's much more that I haven't – much, much more," says Lipskar.

"I sometimes feel that Hashem has really given me a gift, because the fact of the matter is that each of us can have some improvement. I watch some of these people make radical changes in their lives and I think to myself, look, they...change their lives," Lipskar says. "Watching intelligent people make changes in their Jewishness validates it for me. It works. Jewishness works. We're so lucky to be Jewish, can you imagine? It's better than winning the lottery."

The goal for Jews today, he believes, is to keep focused. "Living outside of history, in history, influencing it, but not being influenced by it. When we get influenced by it, it's our downfall. When we influence it, the world moves tremendous strides."

JENNIFER LASZLO MIZRAHI

by DENISE COUTURE

The résumé of Jennifer Laszlo Mizrahi is so dense with experience and accomplishments, it seems surprising that it belongs to someone in her early forties. A media and political consultant, Laszlo Mizrahi has advised presidents, prime ministers and political candidates; managed the winning campaign of a U.S. congressman; made a gutsy, though unsuccessful, bid for Congress herself; published hundreds of articles as a weekly newspaper columnist; and held leadership posts in a variety of Jewish and civic organizations.

And that was all *before* 2002, when she cofounded The Israel Project (TIP), a Washington, D.C.-based nonprofit organization whose mission is nothing short of making the world a safer place for Jews.

Drawing on the expertise of a five-star board of directors and a six-million-dollar budget, TIP uses the weapons of strategic communications – polls, focus groups, targeted advertising – to educate the press and public about Israel, fight anti-Semitism, and promote peace and security in the Jewish state. A large part of TIP's focus is on educating journalists. The organization has found that most people today form opinions about Israel – and therefore Jews – based on what they read in the newspaper and see on television, according to Laszlo Mizrahi.

It was television that compelled Laszlo Mizrahi to take action.

"I started the Israel Project when I was watching a lot of CNN after the birth of our first child, Max [in 2001]," recalls Laszlo Mizrahi, who lives in Annapolis, Maryland, with her second husband, Victor Mizrahi, a scientist-businessman, and their two children. "I would see Israel in the news and I was disgusted, frankly, with the horrible image that they were portraying. And having been to Israel many times, I knew that what I was seeing on television was dramatically different from the real Israel." This was all the more troubling to Laszlo Mizrahi because she had come to believe that if Israel was at risk, so too were Jews throughout the world.

She and her husband decided they would donate money to an organization that was doing smart, proactive, strategic work to strengthen Israel's image. But after conducting a diligent search, she came up empty.

"There was nobody who was bringing cutting-edge communications skills [to the task]. There was no polling or focus groups being done. There was nothing modern or strategic about how the research was being done," she says. During her search, many people suggested she take on the challenge herself. "Since I worked in communications, everyone I talked to saying, 'I want to donate money,' would turn around and say, 'Well, what we need is your time and your brain power and not your money. Somebody needs to do this.'"

So, at a conference of the Jewish Funders Network in Houston, like-minded philanthropists informally pledged financial support if Laszlo Mizrahi could get such an organization off the ground. She put her strategic communications and public policy firm, Laszlo

& Associates Inc., on hold, contributed fifty thousand dollars of family money, and donated her time.

"I recruited my friend Margo Volftsun, who's a terrific philanthropist and leader. And she recruited Sheryl Schwartz, who's a young attorney and a friend of hers. And the three of us founded The Israel Project together in March of 2002," Laszlo Mizrahi says.

With Laszlo Mizrahi as president, Volftsun as secretary and Schwartz as the group's treasurer, TIP was launched.

Since then, TIP has run major media campaigns to influence attitudes on thorny topics such as Israel's security fence, gathered reams of opinion research data through polling and focus groups, informed thousands of Jewish professionals on how to better advocate for Israel, and worked with hundreds of journalists to educate them about Israel in general and about important policy issues in particular.

Today TIP has fifty thousand journalists worldwide on its e-mail list, from those at major U.S. news organizations to reporters in India and Scotland. Laszlo Mizrahi estimates that two thousand journalists a week use TIP's services. "Sometimes that just means opening an e-mail from us, sometimes coming to a briefing with an Israeli official, sometimes they come to us for research," she explains.

Another goal of the organization is to put a human face on Israel, giving the world images of the nation that are more multidimensional than the aggressor it is often portrayed as in the news. One campaign orchestrated by TIP brought a delegation of bereaved Israeli Jewish families to the International Court in The Hague in 2004 to share stories of suffering and loss caused by suicide bombings and other attacks. The campaign was part of an effort by various pro-Israel groups to support the building of a security fence. Ron Kehrmann was one of the bereaved. His seventeen-year-old daughter, Tal, was among the seventeen people killed in a bus bombing in Haifa in 2003.

"The Israel Project does a lot to make our voices heard," Kehrmann writes in an e-mail. "TIP shows the other side of Israel. It enables people not familiar with all the small details of the Middle

East conflict to learn and understand our side of the story. TIP teaches people that the Israelis would like to live an ordinary life, without killing and being killed."

Sheryl Schwartz, TIP cofounder and now its vice president, says the campaign has had a lasting impact. "Pictures of the terror victims and their stories went around the world," she says. "It was very exciting to see that the world was listening. Before that, it wasn't." Since then, the media has given more attention to the plight of Israelis, says Schwartz, so that now at least "you hear there *are* terror victims in Israel."

Or, as Laszlo Mizrahi puts it, "tens of millions of Americans changed their mind on Israel's security fence." According to TIP polls, prior to the campaign, only forty-three percent of Americans thought Israel had a right to erect the fence. Afterward, the figure jumped to sixty percent.

In interviews at TIP's offices on K Street – the hub of Washington lobbyists – Laszlo Mizrahi exudes supreme confidence and a kind of suffer-no-fools competence. She favors classic jacket-and-skirt suits, wears little make-up and keeps her dark blond hair in a low-maintenance shoulder-length cut sometimes pulled back in a no-nonsense ponytail. She's tall and slim. Her look is professional but not Wall Street, feminine but not frou-frou (this is not a woman with time to accessorize).

Numbers, percentages and poll results roll off Laszlo Mizrahi's tongue as easily as if she were reciting what she had for breakfast that morning. She is *uber* media-savvy, speaks in complete sentences and seems always at the ready with a well-formulated, lengthy argument or a succinct sound bite – all in support of Israel.

When asked what she believes are TIP's greatest accomplishments thus far, she mentions several successful media campaigns, such as the one waged at the time of Israel's decision to withdraw from Gaza. "We saw that there was going to be an immense amount of goodwill given to Israel because of this policy, and we worked very, very hard to make sure that reporters covered this," she says. Among other things, TIP set up a media center in Gaza to work with reporters. "We were very proud of our [Gaza withdrawal] campaign. There were thirty thousand press mentions, 760 page-one stories in the United States. By a ten-to-one margin, Americans feel better about Israel as a result of that."

Just how much of that media coverage and goodwill was the direct result of efforts by TIP is, of course, difficult to measure. But Laszlo Mizrahi – with her staff of about twenty, not including the scores of interns and others who come on board to help out in a crisis – knows how to mobilize quickly and take action when the need arises.

. . .

Reared in Durham, North Carolina, by a cancer specialist father and community activist mother, Laszlo Mizrahi displayed an early affinity for challenging work. When just thirteen and continuing through college, she began spending occasional summers in France, working at her great aunt's skin care products company, Ella Bache Inc. Unlike many teens who put in time at the family business, Laszlo Mizrahi skipped stocking shelves and other menial tasks and went right to marketing and communications, something she immediately liked.

Bache was an important role model for Laszlo Mizrahi, who named her second child, a daughter, Ella. Her great aunt represented what a woman with intelligence, determination and courage could achieve despite enormous odds, such as those faced by Jews in pre- and post-World War II Europe.

Laszlo Mizrahi made her first trip to Israel around the age of ten, then spent her junior year of college at the Hebrew University. After college, she found herself in Israel again, contemplating becoming a rabbi or Middle East expert. But her interests in communications and politics won out and she returned home to work as a legislative assistant for the U.S. Congress. She spent two years in a leadership role at the District of Columbia Jewish Community Center and then landed a job as a political trainer for *Campaigns & Elections* magazine. All the while, she kept her hand in volunteer work for Jewish and non-Jewish community groups, earning recognition as one of President George H.W. Bush's "1,000 Points of Light."

Soon, Laszlo Mizrahi was leading campaign training seminars around the world, working with Vaclav Havel in Prague, Boris Yeltsin in Moscow, and other emerging heads of state. She struck out on her own in 1993 and founded Laszlo & Associates, building an impressive client roster that included the White House, sixty U.S. senators, more than one hundred U.S. representatives and various Fortune 500 companies and notable nonprofits.

She also decided to practice what she preached, so to speak, and made a bid, at age twenty-nine, for U.S. Congress when the seat became vacant in her home state, North Carolina, where, she says, a Jew had never run for federal office before. When asked what compelled her to make the bid at such a young age, Laszlo Mizrahi says, "I had been working at my [great aunt's] business in a role where there were a lot of high expectations. I had had my own company and I had worked for Congress, so I didn't think of myself as being particularly young when I was twenty-nine. I had a lot of experience."

Nevertheless, she lost in the 1994 Democratic primary – and admits to no regrets. "I saw a chance to try and make a difference and so I made an attempt. And I got shellacked. But I will never be an old person sitting in a rocking chair, looking back on my life and saying I didn't try." For the next six years, as a "hobby," she wrote a weekly column for the *Daily Record*, a small newspaper in Dunn, North Carolina. "It was an outlet for creativity and for a lot of opinions that I had," she says. "I published literally hundreds of columns, mostly on foreign policy or on American politics or issues of need."

Laszlo Mizrahi's critics have at times construed her doggedness in getting the message out and willingness to put herself in the public eye as arrogant and self-aggrandizing. When questioned about this, she sighs as if she has heard it before but knows she has to address it. "Look, I'm just trying to do something positive to make a difference," she says. "If somebody wants to spend their time criticizing or if they want to spend their time differently, they can certainly do that. That is not going to get me down or upset me. I mean, we're doing things that are dramatically different here, and change is not always easy for people."

She truly enjoys working collaboratively with various groups, Jewish and non-Jewish, that share her dreams for Israel, that are willing to exchange good ideas, "so that everybody can do a better job. And for me that's what it's all about."

Moreover, Laszlo Mizrahi says she is deeply grateful to many people who have guided or mentored her throughout her life. She ticks off a list of rabbis, former professors at Emory University, where she earned degrees in international relations and Judaic studies, and people she works with at TIP, among others. "I have been really blessed with really good, intellectually outstanding Jewish role models," she says.

High on the list is her mother, Nancy Laszlo. Originally Baptist, she converted to Judaism before marrying Laszlo Mizrahi's father. "She embraced Judaism fully and is a very terrific Jewish leader in her own right, and that's very important," says Laszlo Mizrahi. "She frequently, in my community in Durham, North Carolina, represented the Jewish community on interfaith church councils and interfaith organizations, where she really helped bridge the gap between northern Jews, who had moved to Durham to be doctors at Duke, and southern Christians, who had a very big culture gap with the Jews."

Her mother was also active in local nonprofits. She started and ran a hospice for the terminally ill, as well as a center to house out-of-town cancer patients at Duke University and a community Meals on Wheels program. As a child, Laszlo Mizrahi and her two siblings, a brother and a sister, sometimes helped their mother make sandwiches and deliver meals to homebound seniors. "She would see a need in the community and she couldn't stand idly by and watch the need not be filled," says Laszlo Mizrahi.

Although her parents divorced when Laszlo Mizrahi was in college, she remains "incredibly close" to each of them, she says. Her father, John Laszlo, who had a prominent career at Duke University's medical school, was indirectly a factor in Laszlo Mizrahi's fascination with communications and her founding of TIP.

As a new mother, she found herself thinking, "I don't want my son to have happen to him what happened to my father," she recalls. "My father, who lived in Vienna, had two very successful parents who came from very successful families and they went from having everything to having most of their family murdered. My father was there during the Anschluss, and when he was five, which is the age that my son is now, he literally wanted to join the Brown Shirts, which is the Nazi youth. They had made it so socially acceptable and so cool and so hip that a five-year-old Jewish kid in Vienna, Austria, wanted to be a Brown Shirt, and these were the people who pushed him out of Europe and ultimately murdered most of his family.

"And it didn't happen overnight. It came through sophisticated, strategic communications. They had messaging, they had delivery systems, they had Nazi radio. They had rallies, they had uniforms, they had posters, they had banners, they had newspapers. They sold their message to the public. And what most people don't realize is that in Austria where my father lived, Hitler was democratically elected. People say it couldn't happen again, well those people don't see the handwriting on the walls. What we see today in terms of propaganda in the Arab world about Jews is worse in many cases than what the Nazis had. And if you don't stop it before it's deadly, then it's too late."

Laszlo Mizrahi is adamantly opposed to any suggestion that American Jews should stay behind the scenes to avoid fueling negative stereotypes about Jewish influence over the media and policymakers. She says she rejects the informal consensus reached some years ago among many Jewish leaders to keep quiet on sensitive issues affecting Israel. "It was the wrong strategy!" she exclaims. "Americans have the right to speak freely, and Americans who are not Jewish feel that people who are Jewish or who just know a lot about Israel have as much right to educate reporters about Israel as they have to educate reporters about the Boy Scouts or their opinions about abortion or taxes or guns or whatever."

TIP accepts neither funding nor direction from the Israeli government (or that of any other country), says Laszlo Mizrahi. "We are a completely independent, nonprofit organization, completely controlled by our board of directors, who are all American citizens." But it does work closely with Israel's political elite. "We visit very regularly with Ehud Olmert, with Shimon Peres, with [then] Ambassador [Daniel] Ayalon, with [then] Ambassador [Dan] Gillerman," says Laszlo Mizrahi. "We work very closely with Silvan Shalom and Bibi Netanyahu. So, across the political spectrum, we're sharing data and sharing ideas. Just like in the United States we work with a whole host of pro-Israel groups and the same in Europe."

. . .

Although as a youth she was very active in the Reform synagogue her parents founded in North Carolina, where Eric Yoffie was her rabbi, these days Laszlo Mizrahi finds there is little time in her schedule for religious observance. "I don't go to synagogue very often anymore. I used to go a lot," she says. "For me, Shabbat is about just being with my kids and my husband."

Even so, juggling her family's needs with those of Israel is a constant balancing act. She's frequently at her home computer into the wee hours responding to TIP e-mails or quietly text messaging on her Treo while sailing with her family. "Israel, a democracy defending itself from terror while working for peace, is so important to me. But both our children need special attention and love, and being a good parent is the hardest and most important thing I do," she writes in an e-mail.

And despite her commitment to Israel, she misses the work she did while running Laszlo & Associates – the variety of political campaigns and projects – and dreams of one day re-opening the firm. When asked when she envisions that day will come, she pauses for a moment. "You know, when there's world peace and Israel is secure," she says. "But right now is a time of crisis for Israel so I can't make any changes now, because the threat of Iran is so severe and the other threats that Israel faces are so significant."

And off she goes, delineating the various threats – with focus group and poll results flowing from mind to tongue with matter-of-factness and ease.

HANKUS NETSKY

by KEN GORDON

Hankus Netsky is a piano player. A saxophonist. He squeezes the accordion and blows the clarinet with equal parts soul and *chutzpah*, and can if necessary modulate into the key of oboe and English horn. He's a composer and an arranger and, when he jumps onstage, a purple-suited emcee. Netsky's day job is instructor of Improvisation and Jewish Music at Boston's venerable New England Conservatory, where he has mentored musicians such as clarinetist Don Byron – *Downbeat Magazine*'s 1992 Jazz Artist of the Year – and trumpeter Frank London, whose band, the Klezmatics, won a 2007 Grammy award. Since 1980, Netsky has led the Klezmer Conservatory Band (KCB), which has toured the world, recorded ten albums, and even provided music for movies, including the 1991 children's film, *The Fool and the Flying Ship*, narrated by Robin Williams, and the 1989 Oscar-winning *Enemies, a Love Story*.

From 1987 until 1999, Netsky was the unofficial (read: unpaid) producer of Ben Gailing's Boston-based *Yiddish Radio Show.* "I recorded the show, made half the announcements – anything in English that had to be read – mailed the bills, and paid the radio stations," says Netsky. He regularly appears at KlezKamp and Klez-Kanada, two major gatherings of players and listeners, adult and children, who have an interest in *klezmer* music. He plays improvisational and world music with flautist Linda Chase, does the odd gospel gig, and recently helped out with his twelve-year-old daughter's middle-school musical.

It took a while for people to appreciate the diversity of Netsky's work. Growing up in the Mount Airy section of Philadelphia in the 1960s (he was born in 1955), he led marching and jazz bands and arranged and wrote music, which prompted a reporter at his high-school newspaper to ask when he was going to make a choice between, say, classical and jazz. Decades later, he recalls saying that he was a little confused but thought he wanted to do "something with Jewish music." Netsky says the paper ran a photo with a caption saying, "Confused."

Today, the only people who are perplexed about the multi-faceted musician are those twentieth-century souls who can't listen to music unless it is carefully labeled and filed in some record-store bin. If you really want to know Netsky, consider the derivation of the word he is almost synonymous with: *klezmer.* The term comes from the Hebrew phrase *k'li zemer,* which means "instrument of song," and this nugget of etymological poetry suggests that Netsky is a conduit between the musical past, present and future. It doesn't matter if he's performing or teaching or writing or arranging – all the activities are of one piece: Netsky's mission to rescue the lost tunes of Jewish history and to drag them into the twenty-first century.

He realized his calling early. In 1972, at the age of 17, he attended The Lighthouse, a summer arts camp in Philadelphia. His counselors put on a play culled from the work of Bertolt Brecht, which contained the line, "I feel like a man who carries a brick around to show the world what his house was like."

On hearing these words, Netsky "just totally lost it" and cried the whole night. "I felt like I had the brick and I needed more. I needed to – you just can't carry a brick around to show the world what your house is like. You have to rebuild the house."

Why such emotion? For Netsky, the survival of Eastern European Jewish music is a highly personal matter. A family affair. His grandfather, a drummer, ran a Jewish wedding band called the Kol Katz Orchestra, and his Uncle Marvin played with a number of klezmer outfits. The young Netsky wanted to learn more. His Uncle Marvin suggested he call his cornet-playing Uncle Sam. To which Netsky's grandmother said, "Don't call your Uncle Sam!" His mother added, "You're not allowed to call your Uncle Sam!"

"So I called my Uncle Sam," says Netsky, "and he invited me over."

Netsky's maternal Uncle Sam regaled his nephew with the true family musical history and played him scores of old records. "The first time we met, he was born in Philadelphia," says Netsky. "The second time we met, he was born in Kishinev." But these sessions weren't simply about kibbitzing and knocking the cobwebs off old Naftule Brandwein '78s. His elders didn't understand Netsky's enthusiasm for their music. "They just were bitter about it," says Netsky. They told him, "That market is gone. This stuff is gone. And you don't want to learn that. There's no reason."

Netsky is, in some ways, avenging himself on a world that tried to bury Ashkenazi culture as quickly as it could after World War II. There were some good reasons Jews wanted to forget the culture of the Old World. The tragedy of the Holocaust was fresh and endlessly disturbing. Many people wanted to sing non-European songs, ones that focused on, say, Israeli strength and independence. Netsky, ever the pedagogue, explains this last desire has its foundations in Abraham Z. Idelsohn's 1927 book, *Jewish Music*. "He basically proclaimed that the only Jewish music that has any value is Jewish music that can be linked to Palestine."

Netsky responds to that kind of musical revisionism by offering an impression of Idelsohn's blank-slate approach to musical history. "So it was like, 'Yiddish theater, nothing; Yiddish folk song, nothing. This is nothing. This is all nothing. This is meaningless.'"

But Netsky, and the music he plays, is hardly bitter. Or if there's bitterness, it's a joyful bitterness, a comical bitterness, a mish-mash of emotions you can hear in the music itself. Just consider the lyrics of "*Di Mechutonim Geyen/Tants a Freylechs*" ("The In-Laws Are Coming/Dance a Freylechs"), from the KCB's album *Dance Me to the End of Love* (2000):

> *Ot geyt der feter Mindik,*
> *Vos hobn mir gezindikt – shat nor, shat!*
> *Er blozt zich vi an indik,*
> *Shpilt a lidele dem chosen's tsad.*
> There goes Uncle Mindik,
> What did we do to offend him? – hush now,
>   hush!
> He's strutting like a turkey,
> Play a song for the groom's family!

The word *klezmer*, Netsky explains, "is a pretty new term. Traditionally, you just call something Jewish music, or you just call it 'music' – if you're Jewish you don't have to say 'Jewish.'" The traditional wedding stuff, songs like "*Chasene Tanz*" ("Wedding Dance"), are a major part of his repertoire, but it "goes alongside the music that you would play in the synagogue or that you would sing in the synagogue. And it goes alongside the music that you would sing around the house: the folksongs and the theater songs and all that."

If you were to meet with Netsky in, say, a conference room at the Newton Centre Library in Massachusetts or at his modest teaching space at the New England Conservatory, he'll talk about canto-rial chanting, Chasidic *niggunim* (tunes), the relationship between Yiddish and jazz, the "Yiddish Cab Calloway"; in fact, he recently put on a show featuring the vocal talents of Calloway's grandson, C.B. Calloway Brooks – and even people like John Zorn and the folks he has signed to his Tzadik record label.

Netsky has the soul of both a jazzman and a professor. And maybe a little rabbi, too. He's the kind of guy who wears a leather jacket *and* glasses. When he sits down at the piano, he makes a major jazz face, bobs his head of wavy hair as the music dictates. Doesn't matter if he's doing a concert for a jammed house or playing a few illustrative riffs for a journalist, it's obvious, from a mile away, that jazzy Jewish music courses through Netsky.

Says Theodore Bikel, who worked with the KCB on the 1998 CD, *A Taste of Passover*: "While Hankus is one of the finest all-round musicians, at home in many styles, he is arguably one of the finest klezmer musicians on the American scene. In this type of music he not only excels, he is a fountain of knowledge, a veritable encyclopedia of Jewish repertoire and styles."

Netsky's wide-ranging approach to music applies to his Judaism as well. He says that while many American Jews like things organized – "You belong to synagogue and you belong to the Rotary Club" – he tries not to be rigid in his religious practice. "If I want to go to the Hasidic Center next week, am I suddenly Chasidic? I mean, I do that sometimes. I live two blocks from The Adams Street Shul." Then he ends his riff with a few pungent phrases: "The last thing I would want to do is define myself by a denomination. No, denominations have really killed Judaism."

He sends his kids to a Reconstructionist synagogue, for the education. He attends a Jewish Renewal synagogue called B'nai Or, "for the purpose of having a spiritual, exciting, Carlebach-like experience." He's also drawn to Temple Beth Israel in Waltham, Massachusetts, because he loves the work done by their *ba'al tefillah* (prayer reader). Netsky says that the chanting he hears at Temple Beth Israel "moves me so much that it's like the deepest thing in the world."

When asked about his most meaningful gig, does Netsky dust off a memory of working with legendary violinist Itzhak Perlman (the KCB played in Perlman's 1994 PBS documentary, *In the Fiddler's House*, recorded live albums with him, toured, the whole *shmear*)? Does he reminisce about being the musical director and arranger for Tony- and Oscar-winning actor Joel Grey's *Borscht Capades '94*? Not at all. Netsky doesn't dismiss the experiences – "they're good projects," he says, "high-profile projects" – but he describes them as "footnotes" in the careers of Grey and Perlman. He says that collaborations "with people who really were from the tradition" are "much more exciting for me."

Theodore Bikel, for instance. "If I had to pick a concert that was the most exciting, it would probably be playing with Theo at the Berkeley Jewish Music Festival in 2005."

Netsky also mentions German Goldenshteyn, a now-deceased klezmer clarinetist from Moldova. Goldenshteyn stayed at Netsky's house for a week in the summer of 2001 and did some workshops with Netsky and his students at the New England Conservatory. Goldenshteyn told a lot of stories, which put some oral history to the music. "I really felt like I was doing something then," Netsky says.

But he's just as jazzed about imparting musical traditions to his students. Ask about his students and he's like a proud papa passing out photos of the kids. Here's fiddler Lily Hinley; there's trombonist Daniel Backsbrug; and just look at clarinetist Michael Winograd.

"It is Hankus's innate, informed and passionate ability to understand what someone needs to hear and to provide them with this that makes his teaching skills legendary," says Klezmatics trumpeter Frank London. "It doesn't feel like hyperbole to say that Hankus's influence was one of the major causes of the renaissance of new Jewish music in the last twenty-five years."

The renaissance, of course, had to do with Jews getting in touch with their roots. In the same way Irish-Americans turned to Celtic folk music, Jews rediscovered the musical world of their grandparents.

Netsky's own role was sort of accidental. He formed the KCB while teaching at the New England Conservatory. In 1980, he put together a band comprised mostly of NEC students for what was to be a single concert. The crowd went absolutely *meshugge*, wild.

Ingrid Monson, a former student of Netsky's and a founding member of the Klezmer Conservatory Band – she's now the Quincy

Jones professor of African-American Music at Harvard – says that being in the original KCB involved quite a bit of back and forth between the band and its founder and musical director. In the course of listening to the scratchy old recordings, Netsky and the other band members would sometimes disagree about "what was *really* on the '78s," she says, and then reconstructs the scene: "Hear that! Hear that!"

And of course, new students come into his class each September – ready to learn, ready to argue, ready to play. Just like their teacher.

Which is to say that Netsky is profoundly driven. "I don't give up, at all," he says. "That's the main thing. My wife would say, 'Ridiculously stubborn.'" And ridiculously hardworking. He talks about his course load at the New England Conservatory, which involves teaching five days a week, as a "twenty-four hour workday," which, when you add in all the performing and recording, probably isn't too far off the mark.

He's also working on a digital Jewish music archive project with Florida Atlantic University and the Dartmouth Sound Archive. "Recordings are a major way that the Jews have documented their cultural history in the twentieth century. Some kinds of Jewish recordings – cantorials, especially – have been fairly well-preserved, but others have been sorely neglected and there's a very limited time window for doing something about it."

When asked about his goals, he says that the archive – not performance or composition or even teaching – is extremely important. "I really want to help to build a Jewish musical, a Yiddish – especially a Yiddish music archive, an Eastern European Jewish musical archive." He doesn't know how long the project will take; he only knows he's totally committed to it.

Also important is his recently assumed role as the vice president of Education at the National Yiddish Book Center, which he began in fall 2007. As part of his work there, he has been forging collaborations with other organizations involved in the rescue of Yiddish culture and he initiated the Discover Project, a cultural rescue project whose aim is not only to preserve, but to "bring alive again, get into circulation again" the works that are rescued, such as music that's been lost or neglected. He notes that time is of the essence in this work. "There's a huge Yiddish revival now. People are starting to notice that it's gone, and we have to be really busy to get after it while it's still there to collect," he says.

Exhausting. And yet, all this work seems to invigorate him. At his first interview for this profile, Netsky said he was on "half-sabbatical," which he explained was "the only reason I'm here." Later, he managed to pencil in interviews at his school and at Peet's Coffee House in Newton Center. Between doing his various jobs and obligations, carpooling his two daughters, and grocery shopping, he's a busy guy.

Netsky says he feels most fulfilled when he can make music and preserve the Jewish tradition at the very same time, as when he works with his Uncle Marvin at the big yearly KlezKanada festival.

"We're teaching my grandfather's tradition," he says. "We're really teaching the stuff that I grew up not hearing. And my uncle remembers it all and he can still play it. And he plays it the same way. And getting that down is very important."

ROBERT POLLACK

by HARVEY SIMON

Robert Pollack's parents were adamant. They were Communists, proud atheists, and no son of theirs was going to have a bar mitzvah. The boy's grandparents – observant, Orthodox Jews – demanded that the tradition go on. The result was the uniquely American compromise known as the "quickie bar mitzvah." In place of years of Hebrew School, young Robert took a crash course in reading the Torah phonetically.

"I didn't know what the hell I was doing," says Pollack, recounting his coming of age in the early 1950s amid an intergenerational tug-of-war. Pulled one way by parents and another by grandparents, it would be many years before he fully chose his own path.

From this crucible, Pollack, now in his late fifties, emerged as a renowned molecular biologist who, in recent years, has become a deeply religious man. His embrace of Orthodox Judaism has led to a new career path in which he's stepped out of the science lab to explore the connections between religion and science.

And he's helping others do the same. In addition to his many articles and award-winning books that investigate the nexus of religion and science, including *The Faith of Biology and the Biology of Faith* (2000), he is founder and director of Columbia University's Center for the Study of Science and Religion (CSSR). The CSSR is an interdisciplinary initiative dedicated to examining the juxtaposition of scientific and religious beliefs. Pollack describes the CSSR as "an experiment in being religious and dealing with nature."

Not quite what you would expect from your typical biology professor – and Pollack's scientific credentials are impeccable. Born in 1940, he has spent thirty years as a biology professor at Columbia and was the dean of Columbia College from 1982–1989. He's the author of more than one hundred research papers on the oncogenic phenotype of mammalian cells in culture. He's also held a Guggenheim Fellowship and put in time as a research scientist at the Weizmann Institute and at Cold Spring Harbor Laboratory, as an assistant professor of pathology at NYU Medical Center, and as an associate professor of microbiology at the State University of New York at Stonybrook.

But Pollack isn't typical. He is also a lecturer at the Center for Psychoanalytic Training and Research, an adjunct professor for science and religion at Union Theological Seminary, and an adjunct professor of religion. And then there's the CSSR, which he founded in 1999, five years after he decided to step out of the lab and concentrate on inquiries at the junction of science and religion, and after he and his wife, Amy, decided in the early 1990s to become observant Jews.

. . .

Columbia University has been Pollack's home, literally, intellectually and professionally, almost since the day in 1957 when he traveled across town, from Coney Island in lower Brooklyn to the Upper West Side, for his first classes as a freshman. At Columbia, Pollack became an accidental scientist. The Soviet Union had won the opening round of the space race with the launch of Sputnik and the U.S. began training a new generation of scientists. If Pollack, who had perfect college-board test scores, would study physics, New York State would pay his way with a Regents Scholarship.

Columbia's physics instructors trained Pollack to ask probing questions – something his devoutly Communist parents didn't welcome. Asking questions was "intrinsically subversive" in his household because it challenged the fundamental assumption that Communism was the one true path. "I grew up in a household whose religion was Marxism, not Judaism," says Pollack.

It was a household absent of doubt, a household of great certainty. That certainty gradually, perhaps subconsciously, steered him toward Judaism. Questions of certainty and choice would become a theme Pollack would later explore more deeply, after becoming Orthodox. No Jew, Pollack believes, can be content only with what he knows for certain. Running through Jewish texts, he says, is a "rich vein" that concedes the difficulty of obtaining certainty "and the obligation to live properly despite uncertainty."

Pollack's path toward Orthodox Judaism is not a linear narrative. "I don't think there's a straight line of greater observance, but there is episodic going from rock to rock in the river, where each rock in the river represents a different way to be Jewish and more engaged," he says.

The next rock was marriage. He met Amy during his senior year at Columbia. She, too, came from a non-observant Jewish family. Her parents were "afraid of being too Jewish and afraid of being noticed – the usual burden of living in a large Christian world if you're not really tough," he says.

Together these two offspring of Jews without religion decided to have an Orthodox wedding ceremony. They insisted that the rabbi from his grandfather's shul perform the ceremony – despite his parents' objections. "We both had the sense, if we were going to do this we were going to do it right," he explains, which for them meant in accordance with the traditions of Jewish law.

Their choice might seem surprising, but Pollack saw himself and his wife re-enacting the choices Jews through the ages had to make between continuing to practice their religion and blending into Christian society. By choosing an Orthodox wedding, they were "doing a reconstruction in our lives of the continuity that was broken by our parents." The ceremony also expressed an inner religious feeling that had found no outlet. "I don't think we were ever non-observant Jews, I think we were deeply religious people who were not given any context for it until we made [that context] ourselves," he says.

After receiving his PhD in biology from Brandeis University, Pollack returned to Columbia to teach and to do research. He began writing extensively about molecular biology, including the findings of the research lab he headed at the school for many years, where his work examined the genetic development of cancer cells. Soon, he was receiving commendations and awards for his work.

At the same time, Pollack was becoming something of an anomaly to his fellow biologists. He believed that science should be part of the core curriculum for the school's undergraduates, along with courses in the humanities. His colleagues, by contrast, thought they would be wasting their time teaching science to students destined to become art historians or lawyers. "I was known in the university as a bit of a 'nutter' for that reason," he says.

But those outlying beliefs about education gave him just the right qualifications, as the university president saw it, to lead Columbia College. And so it was that in 1982 Pollack became the first Jewish dean of an Ivy League school. "When I was given the chance to become dean, I grabbed it," he says. It gave him the opportunity "to serve kids, not my own career."

His major accomplishments from those years are two campus buildings that now face one another across 115th Street. One is a four hundred-bed undergraduate residence hall; the other is the six-story Hillel Center. The dormitory was part of Pollack's decision to make Columbia College co-ed, which increased the size of the school. The university leadership was content to accept the extra tuition and have New York City students live at home. But Pollack fought hard for the principle that all students should be allowed to live on campus.

The Hillel Center also faced strong resistance, in this case from those who believed that "Jews have enough stuff here already," as one university official insisted, although just a generation before, a quota limited the number of Jews who could attend. "Columbia, like most Ivy League schools, was a place in which the Jewish chaplain kept you functional in Jewish ritual but you understood you were at a place, but not of a place, if you were Jewish," says Pollack, who had virtually no Jewish life as an undergraduate.

Today Columbia is considered one of the best Ivy League schools for Orthodox Jewish students, according to Simon Klarfeld, who directs the Robert K. Kraft Family Center for Jewish Student Life, as the Hillel Center is known. Klarfeld was hired in 2004, when Pollack was president of Hillel's board of directors, where he still serves as a member.

"Anything that is Jewish on campus, Hillel is responsible for. So we are 'the synagogue,' we are the community center, we are the cultural center, we are the advocacy organization, we are the welfare, we offer counseling services to students," Klarfeld says.

Working at the heart of Jewish life on the Columbia campus, Klarfeld is in a unique position to understand Pollack's influence at the school: "He's an incredibly magnetic, charismatic lover of people and lover of engaging people in intellectual and social ideas – an extrovert in the best and truest sense of the word. He gives a huge amount of energy to people and I think he gets an enormous amount of energy and excitement from sharing ideas with others."

Much of that sharing of ideas is facilitated through the CSSR. With offices in Columbia's Department of Biological Sciences and the nearby Union Theological Seminary, the CSSR is an institutional home for people of all faiths who are navigating the crosscurrents that some believe make it impossible to reconcile the scientific method with God. The CSSR sponsors seminars such as: "Blame it on the

Genes? The Challenge of Behavioral Genetics and Free Will," "Evolution, DNA and the Soul: A Week-Long Seminar for Religious Leaders," and joint seminars with Hillel including "Dignity of Life at the End of Life; Jewish Medical, Religious, Legal and Personal Perspectives," in which the speakers included seven rabbis (one with a law degree and a doctorate) and four medical doctors.

"Bob integrates these issues constantly," says Klarfeld, adding that combining matters of "the head and the heart" in this way "can be incredibly rich for the participants," though it is rarely seen in university settings.

Another rarity is Pollack's decision to teach at the Union Theological Seminary, which is unaffiliated with the university – he is the only scientist teaching at a seminary, he says. At the seminary, he serves as adjunct professor of science and religion and teaches the course "DNA, Evolution and the Soul." "My contribution is the contribution of nature to the Christian study of Christian ethics," he explains.

Students in his seminary class describe Pollack as "magnanimous" and "wildly lucid." One student says, "Sitting next to him I feel I'm in the presence of greatness." There is no disagreement around the seminar table when, in their professor's absence, a student states, "It's a truly remarkable class."

During one class session, Pollack speaks of Dietrich Bonhoeffer, a German Lutheran pastor and theologian who was part of the German resistance during World War II and helped Jews escape to Switzerland. He died in a Nazi concentration camp in 1945. "I am so drawn to the life of this Christian German pastor, Dietrich Bonhoeffer, because in his actions he was neither a friend nor an enemy of Jews – he knew none," Pollack says. "In his actions, he was a serious Christian and accepted that his religion demanded that he say 'no' to acts that were wrong in religious terms and demanded that he act at his own risk, that he do things that were necessary in religious terms. In a country of one hundred million people, the Germans can't show you two more Bonhoeffers. So what he proves by his existence is it's possible – and it's very difficult – to live according to a religion."

At the center of Pollack's discussions with his students, at the seminary and elsewhere, is the idea that biology demonstrates that people have the freedom to make choices for themselves and that religion can provide guideposts for some of the most important of those decisions.

"Darwin's explanation, borne out by science, permits free will and therefore makes all ethical questions important rather than pre-determined," Pollack explains. "If you know that you act by your DNA, or if you know that you act by birth according to grace, then there are no choices left. But Jews have choices. And it's my understanding that nothing in founding Christian texts excludes choices either. In fact, I would say a religion by definition is an attempt to help with the burden of choices."

Pollack sees no contradiction between teaching divinity students at a seminary one day and biology students at Columbia the next. Nor does he see an inconsistency between his morning prayers at shul and his science classes. At Columbia, he says, "I say what I do know; [at shul] I say what I don't know." The two "are complementary parts of a whole life."

Science, he says, "does not have the capacity to say anything, except when cast in the form of a test that has the capacity to show the idea is false." So the atheist's argument that an all-powerful God would violate known laws of nature cannot be tested. "What is the test of the idea that Heaven can breach nature? How could one disprove the idea?" Pollack asks. But then he seems to take off his scientist's cap and put on his *kippah* to ask, "Who is a creation to measure its Creator's capacities anyway?"

. . .

By the early 1990s, Pollack had completed his tenure as dean and returned to running his lab at Columbia, but he was growing restless and was approaching another of those rocks in the river.

Something was missing in his life. Running a research lab at one of the world's top universities is a competitive business requiring raising money and being the first to make the next breakthrough. He was beginning to wonder if he ran the lab or the lab ran him.

At the same time Pollack felt he had been deprived of "an ancestral gift" and wanted to restore the connection with Judaism that his parents had severed. Yet he was plagued by the feeling that to be observant would be to disobey his parents, explaining, "I didn't have it in the past, my parents were nuts, I might put the shul at risk in some irrational way. Why would I be in shul? They basically raised me to be not Jewish, so why would I override them?"

Despite these feelings, the pull towards observance was strong. Some of his earliest memories were of the ID numbers tattooed on the arms of Holocaust survivors who had come to the U.S. after the war and, in his fifties now, he was struggling to come to terms with this tragedy that had killed many members of his family who had not emigrated.

The scope of his scientific knowledge also pushed him towards religion, as he describes in an interview with the website, Slate.com:

> I changed my mind about how I want to live in the world... my choice to become active in...Judaism was a choice driven by a closer appreciation of the facts of the world as I understood them through the data on natural selection...It is the meaninglessness and purposelessness and absence of directionality and absence of perfectibility in the mechanism of natural selection, which I find frankly unbearable...and so I felt freed by my free will...to behave irrationally and to accept the religion of my ancestors.

Still, even after the deaths of his parents, even after he became increasingly observant, and even after he decided to leave the lab to concentrate more on the connection between science and religion, he continued to struggle with the notion that in becoming more observant he was dishonoring his parents.

It was his good luck to meet Rabbi Adin Steinsaltz, a "once-in-a-millennium scholar," according to *Time* magazine, perhaps best known for his translation of and commentary on the Talmud. The two became unlikely friends while the rabbi was a visiting scholar at Columbia. Eventually, Pollack asked Steinsaltz "the biggest question I had, which was, 'How do I deal with my crazy parents?' I mentioned that my father was a Communist and a difficult person, not just not observant but actually hostile to the idea of Judaism. And I asked, 'How do I honor that and still feel comfortable as a Jew? How can you honor your mother and father when they are dishonorable?'"

His question was voiced not just to Steinsaltz, but was posed in front of five hundred guests at a fundraising dinner at which Steinsaltz was the star attraction. The answer had a profound effect on Pollack, who recalls Steinsaltz's reply: "The way you honor your parents is by being a serious Jew. And having other people say such a serious Jew must have had interesting parents. Forget the past, don't change it, don't convince them, don't argue with them, live a Jewish life, and that is how you honor them."

However, it wasn't Steinsaltz's answer alone that helped free Pollack to fully embrace Judaism. After Steinsaltz spoke, an old man at the dinner approached Pollack, hugged him, and said, "In 1941, I was with my father whom I adored, and we were taken to a camp and a German soldier said to me, 'Go that way' and said to my father, 'Go this way.' And my father said, 'No, come with me.' And I followed the commandant's instructions, instead of my father's and he's dead and I'm alive. From that moment until [I heard] the rabbi tonight I always felt guilty for not obeying my father."

When Pollack told Steinsaltz this story, the rabbi "looks at me and he doesn't skip a beat, he says, 'That's why we're here tonight. Not for you, not for me, but for him. The old man.'"

At that moment Pollack understood that "the measure of our success in Jewish terms" is that "together we could take a man who's suffered for sixty years and take it off him while he's still alive – and not knowing we're doing that. That's the point. The measure of good action in Jewish terms does not require knowing the outcome. It requires acting well and then finding out or not finding out. You don't wait for the answer," Pollack says.

By 1999, Pollack had established the CSSR and was completing work on *The Faith of Biology and the Biology of Faith*. "I said to myself as a husband, father, grandfather and Jew, what are the questions I want to study using the intellectual part of my life, the academic part of my life? And those are questions at the junction of science and religion," Pollack says. He also wanted to teach young people, by his own example, the importance of doing something for other people.

Underpinning these changes was a full-fledged, unapologetic commitment to Orthodox worship. "I couldn't have set up the CSSR if I wasn't going to shul myself. It wouldn't make any sense. Because what would I mean by religion if I had no religion myself?"

Though religious belief is not a prerequisite for those associated with the center, Pollack says there is no one there "for whom religion is a waste of time. I don't ask people to show me their religion at the door, but my sense is you wouldn't bother if you didn't think something about your own religious life as being important."

Pollack and his wife stopped working on the Sabbath and joined Congregation Ramath Orah, an Orthodox synagogue near Columbia, where he's a regular, active member. "I chose a place which links itself most completely to the history and the tradition of religious observance by Jews in the world, despite oppression. I chose the maximum link of continuity, despite my parents," he says. "I need to be Orthodox, I need not to negotiate whether this is too Jewish or not."

DENNIS PRAGER

by JANE ULMAN

At the age of eighteen, Dennis Prager knew exactly what he wanted to do. Sitting on his bed at his parents' home in Brooklyn, using a fountain pen filled with peacock blue ink, he wrote in his diary, "I want to devote my life to influencing people to the good."

Where did this mission come from? How would he accomplish such an enormous task? Prager didn't know. It wasn't until that moment, after a summer of earnestly imparting his ideas to his first girlfriend, that he had the confidence to write what has proved to be a life-long ambition.

Reflecting back, Prager says, "That is the ultimate motivation in my life. Always."

Just over forty years later, this tall, imposing man with a full head of silver hair hosts the *Dennis Prager Show*, a nationally syndicated daily radio talk show, and is a sought-after speaker, a gifted teacher of Torah, and the author of four influential books. He is a deeply committed Jew, identifying only as non-Orthodox, and a political conservative. In all these roles, he remains steadfastly committed to his teenage ambition of promoting goodness and reducing evil in the world.

How does one promote goodness? How can one reduce evil? Prager approaches the task not by appealing to people's emotions, but to their sense of what's rational, of what makes sense, by challenging people to ask "Why?" and "What is right?" and by holding them accountable for their actions.

David Woznica, currently a rabbi at Los Angeles' Stephen S. Wise Temple, credits Prager with being the first to raise the issue not of *how* to be Jewish but *why*, and of having a particular ability to engage Jews on the periphery on Judaism.

That description fits Woznica's younger self, who was in his early twenties when he first met Prager. "All of the sudden this then-twenty-eight-year-old guy was challenging me intellectually to take Judaism seriously," Woznica says. "He was talking about ethics, God, and how to conduct our personal lives in ways I had never heard before."

Prager estimates he has urged tens of thousands of Jews to take Judaism seriously – to get them to commit to the religion's three tenets of God, Torah and Israel. Not all, like Woznica, have gone on to become rabbis, but they have restructured their lives around Jewish values and a belief in God.

Allen Estrin, who has become Prager's radio producer, collaborator and close friend, says Prager was the first person to introduce him to a logical reason for a belief in God and a religious life. A formerly secular Jew who once celebrated only major Jewish holidays, Estrin now regularly attends minyan on Shabbat mornings. "Dennis showed me the path to a meaningful Jewish life," he says.

Prager is a convincing speaker, but perhaps the secret to his success is his charismatic personality. People view him as their trusted friend. He's not Mr. Prager, he's Dennis. They rush up to him after lectures, for photo ops, and for both personal and theological questions. Prager is always gracious.

Underlying Prager's mission, serving as both the foundation and the catalyst, is what he deems the most important book ever written, the Torah, which he likens to an instruction manual for life.

In lectures like "Answering the Hardest Questions In the Torah," which he delivered at the 2006 UJC/Federation General Assembly in Los Angeles, Prager provides the Torah's rational and relevant answers to questions such as why God destroyed the world and why stoning was the punishment for a rebellious child. He argues that the logic of the Torah is preferable to the emotion-based morality that so many people espouse today.

The heart, he says, is the worst guide for goodness that he knows. If he followed his heart, he would rescue his drowning dog over a drowning stranger. "But the Torah teaches me that animal life and human life are not equal."

In addition to his teaching and extensive speaking engagements within the Jewish community, Prager takes the universal values of the Torah out into the greater world through his radio work and writing, integrating these values into discussions about pressing social issues and breaking news stories. Besides influencing Jews, Prager suspects he has led an even greater number of non-Jews, many conflicted or atheist, to a belief in God and to take the issue of good and evil more seriously.

One of Prager's consistent themes is the troubling consequences of secularism, with the confusion created by moral relativism topping his list. He is careful to point out, however, that he champions secular government. "America has the best values ever devised in the history of the world," he says, attributing this to the country's strong Judeo-Christian foundation.

· · ·

Prager began broadcasting on radio in 1982 on KABC-AM's weekly *Religion on the Line* program, heard locally in Southern California. Every Sunday evening, he would host clergy of different faiths, an experience that made him realize that while Jews and Christians espouse different theologies, they share many of the same basic values.

In 1999, he began hosting his own show, broadcasting from KRLA-AM in Los Angeles, and he now reaches an estimated one million listeners in 120 cities. For three hours Monday through Friday mornings, he discusses a wide range of topics, including current events and culture, religion and relationships, parenting and politics. Woven through these subjects are Prager's values, his Torah-based beliefs – among others, that people are not basically good, that God judges everyone, and that justice and liberty trump equality, meaning that you can't favor a poor person only because of his diminished financial status. Prager presents these values clearly and rationally, with humor, patience and conviction.

"Buenos dias, buenos dias," Prager cheerily calls out as he hurries into the KRLA headquarters in Glendale, California, at the stroke of nine for his nine A.M. show. With one hand he maneuvers a rolling valise, in the other he holds a container of rice pudding. He's dressed professionally, as always when broadcasting, wearing a blue shirt, a yellow tie and khakis.

He quickly settles in the broadcast studio, donning earphones and tracking two computer monitors before him, and dives into the issues of the day, glancing only occasionally at a half-page of handwritten notes. His producer, Estrin, sits across from him, focused on his own laptop computer, reading breaking news stories and vetting callers.

Prager and Estrin are celebrating their fourth anniversary together on the radio show, but the two first worked together fifteen years earlier on Prager's three videos on values, *For Goodness Sake* I, II and III. Their most recent video production is the 2002 documentary, *Israel in a Time of Terror.*

Prager prefers to broadcast alone, free from distractions and able to concentrate completely on his listeners. When he interviews people, such as authors or political commentators, he does so by phone, which he says enables him to ask more penetrating questions. "I don't want to form a bond with my guests," he explains.

But he does want to form a bond with his listeners, ever challenging their thinking and behavior but never robbing them of dignity. "Dennis changes people's lives," says Estrin. While such transformation is hard to quantify, Prager believes the best proof lies in the hundreds of e-mails he receives every August 2, his birthday, when he invites listeners to tell him how he has impacted their lives. This past year, he received 714 responses.

"You let me know that it's okay to think and okay to speak up," wrote a woman from San Diego.

"You have helped make me both a better and happier person," a man e-mailed from Irvine, California.

"You make me happy and give me hope in a world that can be discouraging at times," a male listener from Louisville, Kentucky wrote.

Birthdays are important to him – he believes people should be honored on their birthdays. In fact, he pays tribute to his own father, Max Prager, every year on his birthday, July 18, by interviewing him for an hour.

"People love it," says Prager, who asks questions that allow his father to elaborate on historical and societal changes he has witnessed over his life and to expound on his philosophies.

"You must keep your sense of humor; that's number one," counseled the elder Prager on his most recent birthday. "You must have a wonderful attitude toward life and you have to keep busy."

. . .

Dennis Prager seems to have adopted his father's advice, as well as his penchant for giving counsel. But though he earns his living speaking, as a child Prager, who was born in 1948, was a late developer in terms of speech; he didn't begin to talk until he was three or four. He jokes that perhaps it was because he wasn't getting paid. But as long as he can remember, even before he began speaking, he was "always thinking and feeling deeply," and was especially affected by human suffering.

As a young child riding his tricycle near his Brooklyn home, he remembers watching a teenage neighbor carry a box of seltzer bottles up a steep stoop. When the boy dropped the box and cut open his leg, Prager "cried like crazy." He cried for days, inconsolable, until his mother visited the boy's family and ascertained that he was fine.

Growing up, Prager never liked school, finding it insufferably boring. He graduated from Brooklyn College where he majored in history and Middle Eastern Studies and then did graduate work at Columbia University at the Russian Institute and the Middle East Institute, but back in junior high and high school, he rarely did homework, despite parental pressure. He prides himself on having used only one notebook for all three years of high school.

He tells people he graduated in the top eighty percent of his senior class, pausing until they understand the significance. He is essentially self-taught, though he admits his yeshiva-based education gave him great grounding in studying Torah. "I got the tools, not the answers," he says.

Music, not academics, became his passion. He discovered music when, at age twelve, his parents limited his television watching to an hour each weekday. Prager thought taking up a musical instrument would fill the time, but knowing nothing about music, simply picked the first instrument listed in the Yellow Pages: accordion, under A. That's the instrument he plays to this day, as well as the piano.

He was captivated by music and eager to learn. Each afternoon, save Shabbat, he traveled from Brooklyn to Manhattan's cultural centers, especially the New York Philharmonic Library in Lincoln Center, where he studied the scores of Mozart, Haydn and other composers, teaching himself to conduct. When he turned fourteen, he had the opportunity to buy a one-dollar ticket for a chamber music concert at Carnegie Hall. "It was love at first hearing," he says. Soon he was skipping lunch and using that money to buy more concert tickets.

But music wasn't everything. Traveling back to Brooklyn one evening on the D Train, sitting back, his arms spanning the breadth of the bench, Prager, sixteen and in the throes of teenage angst, experienced a sudden and dramatic insight. He realized that being unhappy was taking the easy way out and that people have a moral obligation to be happy – not only does being happy help us realize our potential, it also improves the lives of those around us by making their environment more positive.

As he explains in his 1998 bestseller, *Happiness is a Serious Problem: A Human Nature Repair Manual*, "We owe it to our husband or wife, our fellow workers, our children, our friends, indeed to everyone who comes into our lives, to be as happy as we can be."

He has lectured on the subject worldwide, including debarking from a cruise ship in Antarctica to address an audience of penguins, the area's sole inhabitants. This fulfilled his goal of speaking on all seven continents, though the penguins' short attention spans limited his talk there to only five minutes. Prager currently devotes an hour a week on his radio show to happiness, which ties into his mission of reducing evil.

. . .

Prager traces another main turning point in his life, and his genesis as a speaker, to his being sent to the Soviet Union in 1969 on behalf of the Israeli government. At the time, Prager was spending his junior year at England's University of Leeds and had traveled to Israel during spring break. Kibbutznik friends gave his name to Israeli government officials who, because Russia had broken off diplomatic relations with Israel after the 1967 Six-Day War, needed non-Israelis to bring in Jewish items and smuggle out Jewish names. As someone who spoke Russian, Hebrew and English and was knowledgeable about Judaism, Prager appeared sent by central casting.

In Moscow, Leningrad and Baku, Azerbaijan, for three and a half weeks he met with Soviet Jews, climbing over walls and rendezvousing clandestinely in parks, "at the fourth tree," for example, where they would then walk to avoid being overheard. The *refuseniks* told him "make a lot of *shum*," or noise, about their plight, convinced that diplomacy was not effective.

The stories were staggering, and when he returned to the U.S., he found himself in demand as a speaker three and four times a week, in living rooms and synagogue sanctuaries, primarily in New York, Connecticut and New Jersey.

The experience jumpstarted a career that has made him a popular speaker on both Jewish and non-Jewish themes and led to the publication of his first book, the *Eight Questions People Ask about Judaism,* co-authored with his childhood friend Joseph Telushkin. Since its publication in 1975, it has been updated to *Nine Questions,* translated into Russian, Hebrew, Spanish and other languages, and is widely used in Introduction to Judaism classes.

Prager originally wrote the book to answer questions people invariably asked him after lectures. Writing has also helped him answer his own questions. When he doesn't understand something, he obsesses over it until he arrives at an answer – writing helps with this, he says, as does his innate ability to self-teach. "Writing is the mirror of the mind," he says, explaining that it is a crucial tool in clarifying his thinking.

That's essentially why he penned his second book (also with Telushkin), *Why the Jews? The Reason for Antisemitism,* published in 1983, as well as the seventeen-thousand-word essay "Judaism, Homosexuality and Civilization," originally published in 1990 in his *Ultimate Issues* newsletter.

The next step in Prager's budding career was in 1976, when he became director of the Brandeis Institute in Simi Valley, California. For two years previously, he had been a frequent guest lecturer at the Institute, a Jewish camp and conference center, later renamed the Brandeis-Bardin Institute and now part of American Jewish University. When the Institute's seventy-six-year-old founder, Shlomo Bardin, decided to step down, he handed over the Institute's reins to Prager, then only twenty-six, believing that Prager shared his non-denominational and morally charged approach to bringing Judaism to people. Bardin died the following week, and Prager remained as director until 1983, overseeing the collegiate and adult programming.

. . .

Though Prager is deeply religious, he abandoned Orthodoxy the day after his bar mitzvah. The reason? "*Yom Tov Sheini*," he tells people, referring to the second day added to most Jewish holidays in the Diaspora because of uncertainty over timing during biblical times. With modern calendars, he finds this illogical. "I cannot be an irrational believing Jew," he says, convinced that rabbinic law must change.

Shabbat has always been a "big deal" in the Prager home, a spiritually joyous celebration with family and friends, a time when Prager plays only Jewish music on his Clavinova, a modern digital piano, including the Chasidic *Moshiach* song. Prager celebrates Shabbat in a meaningful, albeit rational way, observing all Torah-based laws. He drives to synagogue and will use the telephone to wish someone "Shabbat Shalom," but he won't use the computer, watch television, or even read newspapers, as he equates them with work.

"It's not electricity. It's what electricity is used for," he has explained to his children. He's also told them that he doesn't care what Jewish denomination they each follow, only that they be serious Jews.

One Shabbat each month, Prager speaks at the Persian Nessah Synagogue in Beverly Hills. Even more frequently he teaches Torah – the only non-rabbi to do so – at the Mountaintop Minyan at Stephen S. Wise Temple. It's there that he stores his accordion, playing and leading *z'mirot*, or religious songs, after lunch.

Prager's career continues to encompass the radio show, frequent lectures and teaching, and a busy writing schedule. Looking forward, he plans for more of the same, with many goals still to be met.

For the past fifteen years, he has taught a Torah class at American Jewish University, formerly the University of Judaism, an academic and cultural institution founded in 1974, going verse by verse through all the books. His recorded lectures on the books – two hundred to date – are being edited into a printed commentary by friends and project coordinators Joel Alperson and Barry Wolfe, with eventual plans for publication. "It's accessible and it's compelling," says Alperson, referring to Prager's use of clear, understandable language and his ability not only to relate to people's modern lives but also to elevate them.

Prager's writing includes a weekly column for Creators Syndicate as well as less frequent columns for *Moment* magazine and other media. He is also working on several books simultaneously, including one making the rational case for belief in God and the superiority of Judeo-Christian values, and another explaining men's sexual nature, a topic he contends "men are embarrassed to talk about and women fear hearing about" – but his talks on the topic have saved many marriages, according to e-mails he has received.

These thankful e-mails are doubtless gratifying to Prager who, despite being twice divorced, believes that marriage is the ideal state. He sees this as ironic, though not contradictory, explaining that there are myriad reasons, not discernible by outsiders, why a marriage dissolves. "Divorce is terrible," he says, "but a bad marriage can be worse."

Someday he hopes to write an autobiography entitled *A Man, a Jew, an American,* which he considers his three identities. Being a father is another fundamental identity, and Prager is devoted to his three children. His younger son, Aaron, lives with him, and he remains in close contact with his older son, David, who resides in New York, and with his stepdaughter, Anya, whom he considers his daughter.

Prager, who hopes to live long enough to accomplish everything on his ever-growing mental to-do list, sees himself as intentionally doing Jewish work in all his endeavors. Despite his diverse audience and broad appeal, Jews in the know feel he is achieving this. "You do a *Kiddush Hashem* with your radio show," they write. "You sanctify God's name."

"That's the greatest *mitzvah* a Jew can do," Prager says.

NESSA RAPOPORT AND TOBI KAHN

by EVAN EISENBERG

Two years ago, Tobi Kahn and Nessa Rapoport broke down the wall of their apartment to set up an enormous table at which, every Shabbat afternoon, twenty or twenty-five guests gather to sit, converse, sing and consume the endless succession of dishes Kahn prepares in the still-tiny kitchen.

Traveler: If you seek a Jewish salon, seek no further. Here you will meet a molecular immunologist from the University of Pennsylvania; a renowned novelist and essayist for *The New Yorker*; an Israeli talk-show host; a Jesuit priest who curates a museum in St. Louis; an Obie-award-winning composer, playwright, and director of Broadway and off-Broadway shows. And you will meet your hosts: an editor, essayist, memoirist, poet, short story writer and novelist who was one of the first writers in English to drink deeply from the wellsprings of

Hebrew; and an artist who has reinvented American abstract landscape painting, created meditative spaces of rare beauty, and elevated the art of the Jewish ritual object.

Rapoport and Kahn, besides being creative artists of a high order, are pillars of the Jewish community on Manhattan's Upper West Side. "Their Sabbath lunches are legendary," says Carol Spinner, a frequent guest. "Jewish tradition isn't a thing apart with them. They make it vibrant and alive."

It's just as it was when Kahn was in his twenties and studying art at Hunter and the Pratt Institute, after spending four years in Israel. Back then, he was living in a brownstone apartment that was "basically one huge kitchen and a garden. I would have maybe twenty people on Friday nights and maybe again twenty on Shabbat," Kahn recalls. "I had very little money and a lot of potatoes and salads."

"He is responsible for our Shabbat table's food and ambience – and the mitzvah of *hachnasat orchim* (blessing of hospitality) is supremely important to him," says his wife fondly.

"I created a *chuppah* when we were married that was open on all four sides," Kahn says. Like the canopy, their home would be open to all.

The apartment Kahn and Rapoport live in with their three children is full of signs of the couple's rich cultural life. Cabinets cluttered with Kahn's flea-market booty – *netsuke* sages, tinplate *pushkas*, mugs with Dickensian faces – rub shoulders with paintings as uncluttered as any in the world. At once pure and earthy, abstract and jarringly real, they oscillate between macrocosm and microcosm, landscape and cellscape, and they are Kahn's. So are the ceremonial Jewish objects – kiddush cups, havdalah sets, menorahs, rich in beauty and meaning. These ceremonial objects are the heart of his 1999 solo exhibition *Avoda: Objects of the Spirit*, which originated at Hebrew Union College, New York and has traveled to a dozen museums around the country.

A painter and sculptor whose work has been shown in more than thirty solo exhibitions and over sixty museum and group shows, and is included in the permanent collections of the Guggenheim

Museum, the Houston Museum of Fine Art, the Minneapolis Institute of Arts and The Jewish Museum, among others, Kahn says, "Art transforms the way we think."

Kahn's sense of hospitality, of inclusiveness, is echoed by his wife of over twenty years. Rapoport came to the U.S. from Toronto at the age of twenty-one. "I moved to the Upper West Side in 1974, drawn by the unique possibility that one could be an artificially non-marginal Jew," she recalls. "New York could accommodate all the hyphens in my identity: observant-Jewish-feminist-working-woman-artist, and later, working mother, without my having to choose among them. I wanted a passionate worldly, authentic, unprovincial Jewishness. And I wanted to marry a man who could wear a kippah *and* go to a Rolling Stones concert!"

The Shabbatot she and her husband host continue the happy tradition in which she was raised. "My parents always had guests at our Shabbat table, as indeed most observant families do," she says.

When she moved to New York, she often spent Shabbat at the home of Rabbi Wolfe Kelman and his wife Jackie. Kelman served as executive vice president of the Rabbinical Assembly for more than forty years, and Rapoport recalls, "What was exhilarating about Wolfe and Jackie's table was the stunning range of accomplished, contributing people who appeared each week; you never knew whom you would meet, but you knew each one would be fascinating. The coffee table was piled to toppling with Jewish books so recently published that only their authors could have brought them, and the pre-Shabbat air was suffused with Chasidic or Ladino or Broadway music. Jackie was a superb cook and a scintillating partner to Wolfe's generosity, her wit complementing his stories.

"I met Chaim Grade at their house, I met Elie Wiesel, I met Heschel. And what it corresponded to was actually my own picture of the grandeur of Judaism, and the passion of it...And I made up my mind that that was the kind of Jewish life that was possible and that I wanted to be part of."

Rapoport's writing, like her life, is a table at which identities meet. Born in 1953, she was in her twenties when she wrote her first novel, *Preparing for Sabbath* (1981), the story of the awakening, in body and soul, of an observant young woman. "It was a Jewish story I hadn't yet read," she says, "and when I started playing with those sources in the novel – the *Song of Songs*, the *Ne'ilah* service of Yom Kippur – I was entranced by the prospects."

Preparing for Sabbath bespeaks "a rage of love, unquenchable. She would seal him into a tower, a jeweled wall, board him in cedar. A sea of light, she would wash him in light, anoint him with air, with water." The power is such that though the novel was published more than a quarter of a century ago, "I still hear about it once a week," Rapoport says.

. . .

Born in 1952, Kahn graduated from Manhattan Talmudic Academy, Yeshiva University's high school, then studied in Tel Aviv for four years before returning to New York at the age of twenty-two. He attended Hunter College then received his graduate degree from Pratt Institute.

He is proud to be Jewish and proud to be an artist, but don't call him a Jewish artist. "An artist is the entire, undivided person," he says. "I'm not only a Jewish artist or a male artist or a married artist or a father artist. Everything I am makes me the artist I am becoming."

Kahn has received several recent notable awards, including Pratt Institute's Alumni Achievement Award in 2000. He also received the Cultural Achievement Award for the Visual Arts from the National Foundation of Jewish Culture in 2004 and an honorary doctorate from the Jewish Theological Seminary in 2007. "I'm very proud of that," he says. Recent commissions include work for a synagogue in Milwaukee, the lobby of the JCC in New York, and he has an upcoming solo show at the Museum of Biblical Art, an interfaith museum.

The critics have named Kahn the heir to the Romantic tradition of American landscape painting. If he has to be pigeonholed, this is a hole he is fairly comfortable in. Though his canvasses can be large, his landscapes are done on what seems to be a cellular scale –

sperm and egg, seed and bud, embryo, dividing cell – all suddenly writ large. The paintings from his 2002 show *Tobi Kahn: Microcosmos*, based on the biblical narrative of creation and held at the Yeshiva University Museum, both magnify and shrink the world and in doing so, change the way you see.

In the catalogue for the exhibition, curator Reba Wulkan writes:

> Kahn has infused the visual elements of the biblical tradition with his own spirituality...Kahn has chosen to capture the paradoxes of nature, the seeming simplicity of its design and the infinite complexity of its structure, reducing them to minimal formations that reflect sky, land, water, molecules, cells, blood, and the nuclei of life itself. The names he has given his paintings suggest Divine acronyms that invoke passages from the text of Genesis and allude to Hebrew words. His paintings become metaphors for creation. This artist illustrates the beginnings of the universe with the sparest of means. In so doing, Tobi Kahn demands both interpretation and participation; his work becomes the vehicle through which we can reach our own sacredness.

"Taking people on a journey visually, that's what I want, but I want it to be a positive journey, one of contemplation and healing," says Kahn, who in 2001 created a meditative room for the HealthCare Chaplaincy of New York. The permanent installation consists of nine painted murals and sculptured furniture, all done in nature's palate of pale blues, soothing greens and rich, warm browns. "Art should take you to another place, a higher place."

The notion of Jewish art, of "Jewish artist" – the label that Kahn rejects – brings up clichés and misconceptions. Jews, it is said, are people of the book, and the book is not illustrated. Jews, it is thought, are verbal, not visual – another cliché, and one as entrenched as the hooked nose. Some blame this notion on the graven tablets that forbade all future graving, at least of a representational sort.

Kahn begs to differ. "I happen to believe in *Torah misinai.* Since for me God wrote the Torah, then God must think that the visual aspect of the world is really important," says Kahn. "And if you believe the Torah was written by many people, then all those people must have cared. It's not just the *mishkan* [the Sanctuary, whose decorations and appointments are spelled out to the last laver and curtain rod, the bane of *leyners* (Torah readers) everywhere], it's the garments of the High Priest and the flags of the Twelve Tribes, among so many other visual elements."

What happened? Jews were shut out, art was taken away, says Kahn. "During the Renaissance, we weren't allowed in the guilds. If you're not allowed in the guilds and you're not allowed to make things, you simply don't. But go through the contemporary wing at any major museum. You'll be amazed by the percentage of artists who are Jewish. We are a very visual people."

These notions, this historic turning away from the visual, has shut out many of those who, like Kahn, think visually. "Everything I learn is through seeing: color, shadow, light and their juxtaposition are a language, as illuminating as words. What interests me about the world is visual," he says. "I believe we [the Jews] are losing people who do not connect as easily to an ancient text without linking it to the visual world. By excluding their perspective from our understanding of Judaism, we are all poorer."

Kahn is acutely aware of the visual-verbal divide. Despite his gregariousness, despite being undeniably talkative, he contends that, "English is my second language. Knowing Nessa for twenty years has helped. I'm far more articulate than I was – but I'm still translating. This is coming to you from a camera in my brain."

One of Kahn's goals, then, is to invite visual Jews into the dialogue by giving them something to look at. He wants to create Jewish objects – Kiddush cups, havdalah sets – that are as rich in beauty and meaning as words. He did this in his exhibition, *Avoda: Objects of the Spirit,* which has traveled to nine museums with more to come. But in welcoming in the visual, Kahn doesn't want to exclude the verbal. That's why, for *Avoda*, he twisted Rapoport's arm (her words) to write "meditations" that would escort his objects on their travels, acting as their ambassadors to the verbal world. Here, for example, is Rapoport's meditation on the three high-backed chairs, teaming with shapes of sea, hills and sky, that Kahn designed for the *shalom bat* ritual with which their daughters were ushered into the world: "Leap into our lives, from the hidden places to the hills of spice, garden of pomegranate, apple of paradise, awakened by the perfume of your name, we sing you into our mothers' house and listen for your voice."

Similarly, this drive to open the discussion visually led Kahn to collaborate with Carol Brennglass Spinner to create Avoda Arts, a national nonprofit arts and education program that uses visual arts to foster creativity and communicate the lessons of Judaism to teens and young adults. They launched Avoda, which means both work and worship, in 1999. Since then, it has reached over forty-five thousand students through art exhibits, film, multimedia elements, academic courses and tutorials, many taught by Kahn himself, who serves as the organization's visual arts director.

. . .

Rapoport, of course, has a completely different relationship with language than does Kahn; her words become lyrical when describing what seems an almost physical relationship to language. "The moment I noticed our sacred texts flowing through me without cease," she writes in her essay "Body of Love" from *Who We Are: On Being (and Not Being) a Jewish American Writer* (2005), "was the moment I became a Jewish writer." And again: "My great-grandfather said: 'Yiddish is my mistress, but Hebrew is my wife.' I say: 'English is my mate, but Hebrew is my lover.'"

As with Kahn, her art is informed by her spirituality and commitment to tradition. "I am fascinated by the retrieval and rendering of our vast body of literature, commentary, law, ode, parable and praise into art," she says.

Rapoport's acute sense of ancestry, of legacy, flows through her memoir, *House on the River* (2004). The house in question belonged to her grandmother, Mattie Levi Rotenberg, a well-known commentator on CBC radio, and the first woman *and* the first Jew to earn a doctorate in physics from the University of Toronto. Her summer cottage in Bobcaygeon, Ontario is where Rapoport and her cousins spent the summer weekends of their youth, a place of golden memories.

"The house has lived within me all these years," Rapoport writes. In the summer of 1997, Rapoport, pregnant with their third child, rented a houseboat and with her two children, mother, aunt and uncle, floated along lakes and rivers to revisit the cottage and the memories it kindled. *House on the River* is notable not only for its sense of the intergenerational, complex currents, warm and cool, of an enviable family life, but also for its melding of sacred and secular Sabbaths.

Kahn, too, believes in the need for rejoicing and reflection in daily life. "That's why I create meditative spaces; that's why I'm so interested in ceremonial art," he says. Whether it's his miniature sacred spaces or the fourteen-foot granite *Shalev* (1991–1993), commissioned as an outdoor sculpture by the Jane Owen and Robert Lee Blaffer Trust, his painted wooden baby-naming chairs or his bronze ceremonial objects, Kahn integrates art into people's lives. "I want my art to be redemptive," he says.

. . .

In addition to her writing, Rapoport has held several day jobs. She first worked in publishing, where in the 1980s, she edited memoirs by Jimmy Carter, Geraldine Ferraro and the bestseller, *Iacocca: An Autobiography.*

She left publishing to work with foundations involved with the Jewish world. "I moved to the nonprofit world because of what my friend Reynold Levy [president of Lincoln Center for the Performing Arts] taught me: The task of the nonprofit sector is to step in where the for-profit world cannot," she explains.

She brought her organizational and editing skills to the

Mandel Foundation, where she has edited publications including *Visions of a Jewish Education* (2003), and to the Revson Foundation, where she is senior program officer.

"I began to work here [the Revson Foundation] at the beginning of 2005, because my brilliant friend, Lisa Goldberg, was president and brought me to the foundation as a consultant in the Jewish program area," says Rapoport. "She died in an instant on January 22, 2007 – and I honor her memory by trying to extend the work she had begun to teach me: to support talented people with original ideas, especially young people, women and others who may not have found a receptive ear."

Kahn, too, is "committed to giving back, especially through art. In my twenties, I developed art curricula for several Jewish high schools that had not previously had an art program. In addition to Avoda, I also cofounded the Artists' Beit Midrash at the Skirball Center in Manhattan with Rabbi Leon Morris. And I teach at the School of Visual Arts," he says, but doesn't mention that he has done so for twenty-five years.

This is all in addition to the sculpture and paintings Kahn creates in his five-thousand-foot studio, working on "between eight and ten projects at a time, including one or two museum shows, two or three installations and a gallery show." Fortunately, says Kahn, "I don't need a lot of down time."

Neither, apparently, does Rapoport, who often speaks about Judaism, culture and imagination and has led writing workshops, "especially in Jewish contexts," she says.

. . .

Kahn's desire to share, to communicate, to celebrate has an almost urgent sense to it, an urgency played out in his artwork. As he writes in the catalogue of *Tobi Kahn: Microcosmos*:

> I am continually aware of time's passing, of the possibility of loss, an abrupt reversal of safety. In the face of the world's instability, I want to reveal those elements that are transcen-

dent, not the evident reality but its essence, the inherent vitality that is possible. I want to transmute the darkness, salvage it for meditation without denying its power, revealing the spirit of our inner lives – mysterious, resonant, a sanctuary in a still struggling world.

Ancestry, expectations, family, responsibility – the obligations of history preoccupy and drive both Kahn and Rapoport.

"It's impossible," Rapoport says, "to overestimate the degree of responsibility that each of us feels, from different family narratives, to embody and fulfill the gifts we were given because of what our ancestors sacrificed for us. I have a cousin who, when he married, said at his wedding speech – I still remember this – 'Compared to our immigrant ancestors, we're pygmies.' He meant people like my paternal grandfather: an *ilui* [prodigy] in Talmud, he came to Canada and worked like a dog all his life – the store in the Depression that went under, and the milk delivery that was backbreaking. There isn't an elevator man or a doorman I pass in New York who does not make me think: that could have been my grandfather."

Kahn's feelings are similar: "Every day of my life I think about my uncle, my father's brother, for whom I'm named," says Kahn. (He is Tobi Aaron Kahn, named for his Uncle Arthur, or Aaron in Hebrew.) "My uncle, who was a medical student, was one of the first three Jews killed by Hitler in 1933 for protesting against the Nazis."

His other side of the family also gives rise to much thought. "The great rabbinic family is on my mother's side. When Nessa and I got married, one of our friends joked that we would have been a *shidduch* [a match] in Europe, because I'm from the Levush and she's a descendant of the Shach."

The Levush is Rabbi Mordecai Jaffe (1530–1612), a halachist, kabbalist, astronomer and philosopher, who was born in Prague, lived in Poland and authored an alternative to the *Shulchan Aruch*, Yosef Caro's great codification of Jewish law, called *Levush Malchut* (Royal Vestments). The Shach is Rabbi Shabbetai ben Meir HaKohen

(1621–1662), a Lithuanian scholar and poet who wrote the *Siftei Kohen*, a renowned commentary on the *Shulchan Aruch*, while living in Moravia as a refugee from the Chmielniki pogroms.

"I was amused," Rapoport says, "to find out how iconoclastic they both were. The Shach was fearless in his legal rulings. Yet the tradition came to accept him and his interpretations over others.'" Savoring her ancestor's glory, Nessa smiles. "The perfume of the past is intoxicating."

Rapoport is currently completing work on a new novel which, she says, "reflects my customary obsessions – Jewishness, memory, family, Canada, sisters, the allure of the past – and the quest for love." The themes that haunted her at the start of her career haunt her still. She reflects on her work in *House on the River*. "All of my work, I believe, is praise of my Creator," she writes. "Whatever I've done, and in whatever form it's taken, I see it as a form of service, an attempt to give back some of what was given to me."

Rapoport is also working on another collaboration with her husband. Commissioned by their friend, Rabbi Saul Berman, it is, explains Rapoport, "an English 'rendering' of *birkat hamazon*, the grace after meals." It is the perfect project for Kahn and Rapoport, a bringing together of ceremonial objects and lyrical, reflective prose, all to celebrate bounty, togetherness, joy and kinship at the table, to celebrate "the grandeur of Judaism," says Rapoport, "and the passion of it."

. . .

Sukkot is Kahn's favorite holiday. Rumpled, expansive, exuberant in a collarless linen shirt and a woolen vest, he circumambulates a table the length of a sixteen-wheeler, making sure his two dozen guests are well stocked with salads, potatoes, chicken, artichokes. But his attention, his focus, is not confined to this table – in a sense, he presides over all of the tables in this enormous *sukkah*, which seems extruded from the Lincoln Square Synagogue like the spiral of a chambered nautilus. Every year Kahn supervises the homeless people who build the sukkah and the children who decorate it.

"I'm a city person, which makes Sukkot particularly beautiful. To sit beneath the stars, if you're lucky enough to have access to a sukkah, is to be aware of yourself as a created being in the natural world, part of something much larger," he says. "I love a sukkah where you don't know everyone at the table and you don't have to talk to them, but they're there. To me it's like the beach. It's very open, everyone's on their own blanket, and you're just going around."

What interests Kahn is community in the true sense of the word, the co-mingling of souls. He has always invited people to the feast, whether it's a feast for the senses or the stomach – or both. While Kahn wanders through the sukkah greeting and offering sustenance, Nessa is still: seated, serene, communing with her near neighbors, her children, her thoughts, bringing to mind words she wrote a quarter of a century ago in *Preparing for Sabbath*; words that, like her entire body of work, communicate an awe about her own good fortune coupled with her sense of responsibility to those who have come before:

> Nothing but a series of becomings and extinctions, holiness certain to be profaned. Last night, bathed and rested, I feasted before the fast, and left to pray for emptiness. Now, as cleansed a vessel as I will be, when the moon begins to rise, ready to leave the earth I must return to it, to enter a door, to sit among cushions, peopled, at ease. The hammering together of sukkah beams, festival of fruition, ripeness of food and drink one degree from dust. After the holiday, chairs pushed back, sated, near sleep, the table strewn with peels, pits, half-eaten things, who will know that we stood empty and clean so recently. The manifold dyings implanted in our birth.

An image, lyrical as well as visual: Rapoport as the roots of the tree, seeking hidden waters, Kahn as the branches, reaching up, reaching out, embracing and sheltering. Together, a family tree, a tree of the Jewish people, even – if the Kabbalists are correct – the Tree of Life.

GARY ROSENBLATT

by BARBARA KESSEL

The offices of *The Jewish Week* (New York) are based in the Times Square area of Manhattan, the communications nerve center of the nation – an appropriate address for possibly the most influential Jewish newspaper outside Israel and certainly the largest, with a circulation of ninety thousand.

Gary Rosenblatt has been the editor and publisher of *The Jewish Week* since 1993. From his vantage point, Rosenblatt surveys the New York Jewish scene and beyond, reporting on everything from local community events to national and international trends, including groundbreaking reportage on highly sensitive topics.

Rosenblatt, who has spent almost all of his career writing for Jewish newspapers, has established a reputation as a master of balanced reporting who stands by his stories – even those that are controversial or portray the Jewish world in a negative light. A Pulitzer

Prize finalist who is involved in several initiatives aimed at strengthening both journalism and the Jewish community, Rosenblatt is an Orthodox Jew who is fiercely dedicated to the community, and a journalist who is just as determined to expose those stories that need exposure.

"Community is a huge benefit of being Jewish. There is so much *chesed* [kindness]," Rosenblatt says. "Part of the appeal of Jewish life is that it provides meaning. Why are we here? It gives a framework and historical context, a values set to grapple with."

Rosenblatt, born in 1947, spent his early years in Annapolis, Maryland, where his father was an Orthodox pulpit rabbi. "In the fifties, outside New York, if you wore a *yarmulke*, they didn't beat you up, but they thought you were an alien," he recalls. "I didn't know what my father's profession was. I just knew he visited the hospital and put a *mezuzah* on some guy's house and spoke in shul. I didn't know that was a job – I just thought he was being a nice guy."

Being the son of a rabbi may have been good training for becoming the editor of a highly visible newspaper. "I always felt it was tough to be a rabbi in a small town," Rosenblatt says. "You're the role model. And there is a stigma to being the rabbi's son: everyone knows everything about you. In later years, my father used to tease me when I got angry letters to the editor. He would say, 'I only have to worry about my *baale batim* [key members of the community]; you have to worry about everybody.'"

In a sense, Rosenblatt had a second set of parents – he lived with his maternal grandparents during the week from seventh through twelfth grade, when he attended the Talmudical Academy in Baltimore. "My *zaidy* was very short but very imposing. His daily routine was to get up at four A.M., learn downstairs in the shul until *shacharis* [morning prayers], have lunch, nap, learn, go to shul and go to sleep at ten or eleven," Rosenblatt recalls. "My grandmother was a real life force. She was a beautiful woman with a great voice, very loving, really funny. I have lots of *bubby* routines, all of them true. She liked to listen to the radio. When they gave the weather, they'd say, 'Here is the weather for Baltimore, Washington and vicinity.' I'd come into the kitchen and she'd ask me, '*Vu iz Vicinity?*' Where is Vicinity?"

With his grandmother's quick wit as inspiration and model, Rosenblatt once considered becoming a stand-up comedian, but turning down Friday night and Saturday gigs dead-ended that career path. Now, his main comedic outlet is the annual Purim issue of *The Jewish Week.*

Rosenblatt worked on the school paper all four years at Yeshiva College and found that he loved journalism. He went on to earn a graduate degree in journalism at the City University of New York. While still a student, working as a counselor in the summer of 1968 at Camp Hillel, Rosenblatt met his future wife, Judy, who was the drama counselor. His buddies ribbed him, "Rosenblatt, this is camp. You don't marry your summer girlfriend. It isn't done." But it was too late. "If I'd met her in camp at age eleven, I would have been married at twelve," he says. Rosenblatt and his wife are the parents of three children and grandparents of two.

After graduate school, Rosenblatt freelanced for almost a year. One of his first jobs was at TV *Guide.* "Working at TV *Guide* cured me of the notion that writing for a large audience is appealing in and of itself. I was writing mostly about sports, like getting the numbers right at the Rose Bowl."

He applied to *The Jewish Week* in 1972, looking for freelance work, but editor Philip Hochstein told him there was none to be had. "As I was leaving, he added, 'But would you be interested in a full-time job?'" Rosenblatt stayed for two years. Once he started at *The Jewish Week,* he realized he had found his vocation: Jewish journalism. "Joining *The Jewish Week* meant I could write about what mattered to me. It combined my two loves: Jewish life and writing."

In those days, *The Jewish Week* was a very different paper than it is today. It was small and privately owned. "I was about fifty years younger than the next youngest editor. These were seasoned guys who had covered World War II. I was probably the only one there who didn't have a prostate condition. I got to do every story that involved leaving the office. It was a great initiation in that sense." But it flew low on the journalism radar. "We had a scoop on Conservative women being counted in a minyan two weeks before the *New York Times* picked it up. When we ran the story – no reaction. They get hold of it and it's all over the world."

In 1974, when the paper shut down temporarily for financial reasons, the Rosenblatts moved to Baltimore for what was to have been a two-year stint at the *Baltimore Jewish Times*. It lasted almost two decades. Publisher Chuck Berger had boundless confidence in his protégé's ability. Because he owned the paper, he was able to let Rosenblatt run with any story he chose, without a bureaucracy to inhibit the process. Berger's criterion was he wanted a paper he could be proud of, and Rosenblatt delivered.

Ten years into Rosenblatt's stay, Berger bought the *Detroit Jewish News* and Rosenblatt started commuting to edit that paper as well. For nine years, he would fly out on Thursday mornings and return on Friday afternoons, armed with the mandate to give that paper a distinct vision and hire writers who could translate that vision into print.

As his career matured, Rosenblatt began taking on more complex topics, even when they challenged the Jewish establishment. A milestone in his career was his 1980 article "The Life and Death of a Dream" for the *Baltimore Jewish Times*, a lengthy investigative piece on the failure of the Institute for Jewish Life. The article, which garnered considerable attention, is still discussed in public forums such as the 2005 Limmud Conference.

The Institute was conceived in November 1969 at the annual General Assembly of the Council of Jewish Federations (CJF) by two unlikely parents who subsequently separated: the Concerned Jewish Students, an activist organization, and the CJF. It was to have been a one hundred-million-dollar, five-year laboratory for innovative projects that would engage disenchanted Jewish youth and their families, and ensure the future of the Jewish community.

The Institute officially began operations on May 15, 1972 and ran into difficulties almost immediately, some of them budgetary. "At the end of the first year, the official deficit for the Institute was $81,000, and money – or the lack of it – had become an issue of bitter contention," Rosenblatt wrote. Financing alone, however, was not the critical issue. The Institute was ultimately paralyzed by tensions between the young independents seeking alternative ways to bolster Jewish identity and the establishment that was invested in the status quo. Rosenblatt was able to unearth and articulate these conflicts by conducting insightful interviews with individuals central to the Institute's development and, ultimately, its dissolution.

He saw in the demise of the Institute a story larger than just the unraveling of one initiative. As he put it in the article, "The problems the Institute for Jewish Life faced are still with us today and shed light on the dynamics of power, on how funds are raised and priorities set, how local and national Jewish goals differ and are resolved, and how the Jewish community responds to creativity and challenge."

Rosenblatt's article chronicling the Institute's decline was emblematic of the kind of thoughtful, balanced investigative journalism at which he would excel. It was no small thing to take on the Jewish establishment by tackling a project it had funded and nurtured, but Rosenblatt did not shy away because he sensed that it spoke to a central theme in American Jewish life. This was to become his *modus operandi.*

Rosenblatt was not simply building a career, but working to move the paper to a new level. "We were trying to make a national reputation for the paper. I went to Israel once a year and wrote about it. I went to conferences in New York or elsewhere that normally only the local paper would cover, if at all. We were looking for broader content, like the 1977 Nazi march in Skokie. Our goal was, you didn't have to live in Baltimore to read the *Baltimore Jewish Times*," he explains.

A piece Rosenblatt wrote in 1984 for the *Baltimore Jewish Times* was a Pulitzer Prize finalist – one of two finalists in the category of Special Reporting. "The Simon Wiesenthal Center: State-of-the-Art Activism or Hollywood Hype?" is an incisive article about the phenomenally successful Holocaust Center in Los Angeles and the differences in style and goals between its publicity-savvy director, Rabbi

Marvin Hier, and its down-to-earth namesake, Simon Wiesenthal. Addressing the question of whether the Center capitalizes on Jewish suffering, the piece closes by remarking that, "If...the Center is keeping the memory of the Holocaust alive to prevent its recurrence, it will fulfill its mandate – to transform the ashes of tragedy into the fire of commitment."

Being a Pulitzer finalist was a first for an article in a Jewish publication and a serious accolade for Rosenblatt, but it did not spur him to seek a different type of job. "My friends asked me, if I had won, would I have gone to work at the *Washington Post* or the *New York Times*, but by then I was a great believer in Jewish journalism," he says.

The article that far and away has drawn the most attention in his career to date is "Stolen Innocence," Rosenblatt's exposé of allegations of child sexual abuse by Rabbi Baruch Lanner, an educator in the Union of Orthodox Jewish Congregations, and the organizational awareness and denial that protected the rabbi for years. With a supportive board of directors in his corner, Rosenblatt published "Stolen Innocence" in *The Jewish Week* on June 23, 2000, and blew the lid off the topic of sexual abuse of children in the Orthodox community with a force that continues to reverberate.

The decision to print the article was difficult but, Rosenblatt felt, inevitable as the evidence mounted. Rosenblatt did not make his decision lightly. Sensitive to the Jewish prohibition against *lashon hara* (malicious gossip) and under pressure from the Orthodox Union to keep the story quiet, Rosenblatt consulted a rabbinic authority. The rabbi's ruling: If this article will prevent future abuse, one is not only permitted to print it but one is so obligated. "To show you how clueless I was, I said to Judy when it was finished, 'Well, that's the end of that story,'" Rosenblatt recalls. Instead, to his astonishment, it provoked an explosive reaction. Letters to the editor began streaming in. "Destroying a person as you have is not merely distasteful but against Torah teachings." "At what point did *The Jewish Week* assume the role of criminal investigator, district attorney, judge and jury?" "I will only say this once: If the article on your Web site is not removed, you will lose at least fifteen ads per week, forever."

There were positive responses as well. *The Jewish Week* received over a thousand letters, e-mails and phone calls, with the vast majority thanking Rosenblatt for bringing this problem to light. "The support from *amcha* [the general public] was overwhelming, but I found it galling that institutions and rabbis were accusing me of lashon hara. It was topsy turvy," Rosenblatt says.

A month later, on July 20, Rosenblatt followed up with an article entitled, "Lessons from the Lanner Case," in which he urged the Jewish community not to "ignore, dismiss or cover up potentially embarrassing problems...They won't go away on their own, and by pretending they don't exist, we only erode our values and endanger our children."

The fact that the rabbi was convicted and sentenced to seven years in prison was a vindication of the decision to print the story. Ultimately, "Stolen Innocence" was a watershed that went beyond the individual incident. "Different standards have been set about how to deal with these things. It makes it easier incrementally to take on tough issues," Rosenblatt says.

Stories of rabbinic sexual abuse of children and adults have come out since "Stolen Innocence," and Rosenblatt has had the support of his board of directors, which he apprises of sensitive stories before they appear in print. Mark Charendoff, *Jewish Week* board member and president of the Jewish Funders Network, credits Rosenblatt with tackling difficult subjects. "I think there is an enormous amount of frustration in certain areas of the Jewish world about the lack of opportunity for honest dialogue. Rosenblatt does it out of a genuine dedication to the Jewish people and to using his vocation to do good. That can be a hard and lonely thing to do. It's very easy to be brave if there's no consequence to what you're writing, but he's writing in the largest Jewish weekly in North America to a very affluent audience. With all of that, to have the courage to take on decidedly unpopular issues because they need to be taken on, and not become cynical and not become irresponsible is difficult. He really pulls it off with grace."

Rosenblatt himself says that while he tries not to sound self-righteous, there are topics that need to be aired, including further exposure of sexual abuse. "It's still a problem, still being swept under the rug," he says, "but I think the community is starting to deal with this stuff. There is more awareness and other rabbis have written about it. It's out there and people can find out about them [educators accused of abuse]."

Despite his convictions, it is still painful for him to be vilified in his own community – some in the Orthodox world accuse Rosenblatt of conducting witch hunts against his peers. "It's such a nuanced issue," he says. "The Orthodox community is a geographic neighborhood. People are vested because they're visible. They are scrutinized more closely and hold themselves to a higher standard. So when there's abuse, it's more of a story. And people have selective memories. They remember the one negative story instead of the five positive ones."

Being enmeshed in the community one writes about has other challenges as well. People in his hometown of Teaneck, New Jersey know who Rosenblatt is. "Writing about the community you live in heightens expectations. I get people calling me at home telling me they didn't get the paper. 'I've had a prescription [*sic*] for twenty-three years!' 'Should I bring it to you?'" Rosenblatt remarks that there is little separation between his personal and professional life. "If people don't *hock* [pester] you in shul, you worry they're not reading it…Sometimes they give you 'the look.' 'Aren't you…? You look so much bigger in person than your picture.' They must think I'm six inches tall."

．　．　．

These days, much of Rosenblatt's writing is in his weekly column, which ranges from the introspective to the political to the personal. He is as likely to write about his participation in the June 2005 World Jewish Forum in Israel as he is about the death of his father in a hit-and-run accident over twenty years ago. The fact that the driver was acquitted has caused Rosenblatt to struggle "with a sense of existential injustice and with the legal system," he says.

In addition to writing and assigning editorials, Rosenblatt holds a staff meeting every Monday morning at which *The Jewish Week* writers bat around story ideas, talking through "front-burner" topics to find a fresh angle. He also chooses the letters to the editor, which takes time and judgment, according to Rosenblatt. "How long do you let a story simmer? How many letters do you print on a given subject? How do you avoid being nasty to others?"

Because his managing editor, Rob Goldblum, undertakes the nuts-and-bolts of getting the paper out each week, Rosenblatt has the opportunity to pursue the special initiatives that reflect his commitment to professionalizing Jewish journalism. Nine years ago, he helped found the Gralla Fellows Program, through which young journalists spend the better part of a week at Brandeis University taking courses in Judaism and journalism, and examining where the two intersect. He is chairman of the Fund for Jewish Investigative Journalism, which has made possible articles on Jonathan Pollard, French anti-Semitism, and why Israel is losing the media war. In keeping with his concern for both Jewish youth and Israel, he founded and directs "Write On for Israel," a *Jewish Week*-sponsored advocacy journalism program for high school students, in addition to "Fresh Ink," a student-written supplement to the paper.

Rosenblatt's communal involvement is not restricted to journalism. He is undertaking a proactive role in helping "define the agenda for American Jewry." One of the most exciting ventures he has conceived is The Conversation: Jewish in America, an annual three-day retreat that began in the fall of 2005, hosting about sixty-five participants each year that brings together Jewish professionals who are prominent in their fields.

Writers, filmmakers, academics, philanthropists, comedians and musicians are invited to each retreat. "We had no planned outcome but we encouraged people to network and let us know what, if anything, tangible came of their being there. What they loved the most was the mix of people and that it was a totally level playing field with no panels. You weren't being lectured to. A couple of projects have started from it," Rosenblatt explains.

A sought-after speaker on campus, in high schools, at Jewish community centers and organization meetings, Rosenblatt's lecture topics reflect his primary interests and include: "Seeing Ourselves in the Mirror: Jews and the Media," "Doing the Right Things: Ethics and Jewish Journalism," "Israel and American Jewry: Is the Gap Widening?" and "Can We Still be One? Advocating Unity in a Divided Community." He finds that speaking throughout the country gives him an opportunity to take the pulse of the many host cities he visits.

While not the oldest editor in American Jewish journalism, Rosenblatt is certainly the most senior, having spent more than half his life in the profession. After his Pulitzer Prize nomination, Rosenblatt was asked where he wanted to go in his career. His reply is the same today as it was then – "I consider myself fortunate to be right where I am, doing what I love."

SUSAN WEIDMAN SCHNEIDER

by DENISE COUTURE

Susan Weidman Schneider, founder, editor and publisher of *Lilith*, a magazine devoted to Jewish feminism, has ruffled the feathers of more than a few readers in the magazine's thirty-plus-year history, and has no plans to stop anytime soon. Reflecting on the magazine's legacy, she says, "I think we have effected change by naming problems, by allowing women to speak their own truths. It's very important that we hear those voices."

Hearing those voices – being receptive and being inclusive – is of paramount importance to Weidman Schneider, who has been at the helm of *Lilith* for more than three decades. With wide-open arms, she embraces diversity of opinion and experience, especially among Jewish women.

In discussions at both the magazine's cramped and cluttered headquarters in midtown Manhattan and at her home in Washington's Georgetown neighborhood, Weidman Schneider, who is neither grandmotherly nor glamorous but somewhere in between, repeatedly expressed her desire to understand perspectives outside her own, and, in *Lilith*, to create and nurture a compassionate forum for expressing those views.

Lilith was born in 1976, partly out of a desire to examine and share with others the perspectives of Jewish women who at the time felt excluded from both Judaism and the burgeoning women's movement. To Weidman Schneider, these twin exclusions "seemed unjust and in lots of ways harmful to individual women and to the Jewish polity as a whole." Jewish women in general, she says, were considered too privileged to need the kind of economic and social support the women's movement sought to foster in America. As for Judaism, Weidman Schneider recalls that this was an era when women couldn't read from the Torah in synagogue, couldn't count for a minyan, and Reform Judaism had only just ordained its first female rabbi, Sally Priesand, in 1972. Almost as scarce were baby-naming ceremonies for girls as we know them today. And, Weidman Schneider says, all of the Jewish magazines were edited by men.

Some feminists at the time were asking, "Why would Jewish women care about a parochial, patriarchal religion that puts women down? Why don't you throw out the baby with the bathwater?" says Weidman Schneider. But that approach was untenable to her – she identifies herself strongly as a Conservative Jew, though her level of observance has admittedly waxed and waned over the years. "Judaism is a kind of ineluctable part of who I am," says Weidman Schneider. "It's a tradition with a great deal to offer women as well as men, and I felt what's needed is some retooling, perhaps, but certainly not anything that comes close to outright rejection."

Having had their consciousness raised during the 1960s, American Jewish women were radically rethinking gender politics and seriously questioning Judaism's ability to adapt to social change. It was during this era, which crackled with activist excitement, that Weidman Schneider and a small group of like-minded women writers gave birth to *Lilith*. They recognized that there was an alternative perspective, one that was true to Judaism yet could help propel the much-needed reform they believed was essential if Judaism were to remain a viable religion for a politically awakened generation of women.

The very name chosen for the magazine promised a refreshingly bold take on familiar subjects. Lilith, according to the *midrash*, was Adam's first companion in the Garden of Eden. She was Adam's equal, but she left him when he tried to make her submit to his authority. The more compliant Eve took Lilith's place. Weidman Schneider says the magazine's name came about naturally, almost accidentally, at an early planning meeting. She and the magazine's other founding mothers sat around someone's kitchen table over sandwiches. One of them simply said, "Of course, we have to call the magazine *Lilith*." Everyone agreed.

Lilith appealed not just to radical feminists but to women who, in *Lilith*'s first few issues, saw many of their seldom-discussed concerns blazoned across the publication's cover. In *Lilith*'s second issue, the cover line was "Beyond the Stereotypes: How Ten Jewish Women Changed Their Lives." In it, one writer came out as a lesbian and another wrote about feeling excluded from Jewish life when she was not allowed to say *Kaddish*, the mourner's prayer, for her grandmother. A third writer, recalls Weidman Schneider, described feeling as if she were slipping through the cracks. "She was somebody who cared very much about Orthodox Judaism and at the same time cared very much for feminism. Where was her place? Now there's something called the Jewish Orthodox Feminist Alliance. If you had said at *Lilith*'s inception that the words 'Orthodox' and 'feminist' would be in the same title, someone would have said, 'What are you smoking?'"

Today *Lilith* is a nonprofit quarterly with a circulation of about ten thousand and an estimated readership of twenty-five thousand. *Lilith* is credited with being the first to publish women's Holocaust memories and women's accounts of domestic violence and incest in their Jewish families. *Lilith*, says its editor, was also the first to advocate strongly against the Jewish American Princess stereotype.

And it was probably the first publication to devote nearly an entire issue to Jewish hair.

Along the way, Weidman Schneider emerged as a major voice in Jewish feminism. She has commented on issues affecting contemporary Jewish women on *The Oprah Winfrey Show, Good Morning America* and CNN and in the *New York Times* and *Newsweek.* Cementing her status are the three books she authored, including *Jewish and Female: Choices and Changes in Our Lives Today,* first published by Simon and Schuster in 1984. In 2000, Weidman Schneider was awarded the Joseph Polakoff Award for distinguished service to Jewish journalism. She has also received Hadassah's Golden Wreath Award and the American Jewish Congress's Woman Who Made a Difference award.

"I think she's had a great influence on Jewish feminism – an influence on women and men," notes Blu Greenberg, who cofounded the Jewish Orthodox Feminist Alliance (JOFA) in 1997, more than two decades after *Lilith*'s arrival. (Interestingly, like *Lilith*, JOFA was conceived by a group of women at a kitchen table.) Greenberg, a widely published Orthodox feminist writer who has served on *Lilith's* advisory board, says the magazine is "the only feminist publication that actually reaches the masses in the community." She credits Weidman Schneider's "special," "compassionate," "*neshama*" (soulful) personality with enabling her to reach the Jewish establishment. "She made Jewish feminism accessible to all sectors of the community." Moreover, notes Greenberg, Weidman Schneider "has dedicated herself to this publication. For many years she worked without a salary."

Weidman Schneider was born in 1946 and reared in Winnipeg, the capital of Canada's Manitoba province and home to a sizable population of Russian immigrants. "Winnipeg was a very comfortable place to be Jewish," says Weidman Schneider. "It had a very active, lively Jewish intellectual tradition – everything from free thinkers who didn't believe in marriage and didn't believe in religion but felt they were culturally Jews or politically Jews, to more traditionally religiously observant people."

Her early Jewish education was remarkably non-sexist,

especially given the era, and likely was a key factor in Weidman Schneider's taking on a leadership role as a feminist activist in Judaism. "I was part of a Conservative synagogue's junior congregation where girls had completely equal participation with boys," she recalls. "I was very comfortable at the age of ten or eleven leading services along with the guys. There were two Israeli men who ran this junior congregation. They were very progressive educators."

Her identification with Judaism was reinforced at home – her Winnipeg kin were "very Zionistic," she says. "I certainly learned to sing 'Hatikva' long before I learned to sing 'O, Canada.'"

Her mother, who was born in 1904, was active in Yiddish theater and taught Weidman Schneider that being different didn't necessarily mean being wrong. "Given the era in which she grew up, she probably was somewhat unconventional." Although her mother was much more interested in the arts than in politics, she "lived as much of an intellectual life as the women of her generation were permitted or expected to live," says Weidman Schneider. "She had a coterie of friends with whom she gathered once a week for about forty years. And they read all the Bible, then all of Shakespeare, then all of James Joyce, then all of Anaïs Nin. They were thoughtful, smart women. Whether they bared their souls to one another and tried to make a dramatic change in the universe...I suspect not. They were intrigued by ideas."

Typical of her own generation, Weidman Schneider married in her twenties and began having children relatively soon thereafter. She had met her husband, endocrinologist Bruce Schneider, while at Brandeis University, and reared their three children – a son, Benjamin, and two daughters, Rachel and Yael – in the various places Schneider's work took him. These days Weidman Schneider commutes weekly to *Lilith*'s office in New York from their home in Washington, D.C. "People ask, 'How'd you end up in Washington?' And I say, 'A good feminist answer: My husband took a job there,'" she jokes.

Shortly after their marriage, the Schneiders lived for a time in South Dakota, where Schneider was assigned to a Bureau of Indian Affairs hospital – and where Weidman Schneider, with a manual typewriter on her lap, wrote freelance articles on parenting and other topics for American newspapers while sitting inside her young son's large playpen with him. She had had an interest in writing from a very young age. As a teenager in Canada, she edited the newsletter *B'nai Brith Girls* and worked for her high school newspaper. Before that, when she was just eight years old, she worked on a newspaper at summer camp in Gimli, an Icelandic fishing village in Manitoba.

Not long after her husband's tour of duty in South Dakota, he signed on for a six-month stint at a Jerusalem hospital. Weidman Schneider recalls that it was "thrilling" to find herself living in Israel. When she was about four years old, her paternal grandfather had given her a small bronze key ring decorated with Israel's statehood symbol. "I couldn't understand why they were making a fuss that there was a State of Israel – like, of course there's a State of Israel. Wasn't it always there?"

In some ways, Weidman Schneider's transition from trailing spouse to trailblazing feminist seems unlikely. But upon her return to the U.S., Jewish groups began inviting her to speak about her experiences in Israel, where she had been struck by the paradoxes in a society that had plentiful childcare because it was expected that women would have a work life, but also so many impediments to women's career advancement. Weidman Schneider, who insisted that onsite childcare be provided during her appearances so as not to exclude women with small children, found she was good at expressing in public what she had witnessed in private as a young wife and mother living in Jerusalem.

"I think I'm a convincing public speaker in part because I'm able to temper the message with a personal approach, personal anecdote, humor, wherever possible," says Weidman Schneider. "Maybe it has to do with my Canadian background and a certain kind of Anglophilia." She has a strong sensibility about what is and isn't appropriate, she says, adding that after more than forty years in America, she is still uncomfortable if people argue at the dinner table. "It's okay to have political differences, but you always hear the other person out. That's not necessarily the New York Jewish way of expressing things."

While Weidman Schneider is loath to argue forcefully at home, she has had no such reservations about using her voice to fight for justice and equality through her magazine. Sometimes, she admits, it has taken a good deal of courage to publish certain stories, such as ones that shine an unflattering light on a Jew. "We often hear people say, 'So many people don't like the Jews anyway, why do you talk about domestic violence?'" Weidman Schneider responds, "We need to, of course, be worried about protecting Jews and this is why I'm concerned about violence in Jewish homes. Where does this leave the victim if what we're worried about is the reputation of the Jews as a whole?"

The *Lilith* article that garnered the most controversy was a 1998 story covering the sexual misconduct of Rabbi Shlomo Carlebach. Prior to publication, the magazine received warnings from people trying to dissuade Weidman Schneider from running the article. "It was not a comfortable time for us," she says. Before she made a final decision, she turned to others for guidance. It was her husband's words that struck the strongest chord. "He said, 'This is a terrible experience that these women went through and you have an obligation to the truth,'" recalls Weidman Schneider. "We ran the article."

For many of the magazine's readers, like twenty-two-year-old Melanie Weiss, a college senior and *Lilith* intern, Weidman Schneider's courage to live up to the magazine's subtitle – *Independent, Jewish & Frankly Feminist* – has made an enormous difference. An avid reader of the magazine for years, she believes it is as relevant to her generation as it was to young women three decades ago. *Lilith* tackles articles on topics "not being published anywhere else," says Weiss, noting that it meant a lot to her to learn that "there are alternative voices inside the Jewish community."

Weiss says she appreciates the willingness of the editorial staff to seriously consider any subject that could be interesting or useful to readers. "It all emanates from Susan. Working here has been the best thing that could have happened to me."

Former intern Ilana Kramer, now a PhD candidate in clinical psychology with a focus on gender violence, has fond memories of sitting around the table at *Lilith*'s New York office, eating apples, honey, hummus and pita, and discussing article ideas. "When you have someone as successful and respected as Susan telling you that you can write, it's a powerful thing."

Weidman Schneider takes her interns seriously, and perhaps her receptiveness to the younger generation has helped to keep the magazine relevant. *Lilith*'s interns – more than one hundred over the years – have been "fabulous, smart and stimulating" and "we learn a lot from them," Weidman Schneider says. "We've provided a very safe and supportive place for people who are looking for ways to merge their Judaism and their feminism and their interests in changing the world through words."

Weidman Schneider, however, isn't ready to turn her life's work over to a new generation just yet. She is too busy ushering *Lilith* firmly into the twenty-first century – with podcasts, blogs and digitizing *Lilith*'s back articles for web postings – and overseeing a network of salons, or discussion groups, around the country where women meet face-to-face to explore issues raised in the magazine.

"I was recently at a *Lilith* salon that [Weidman Schneider] hosted and she's really wonderful at bringing together different generations of *Lilith* readers," says Rahel Lerner, twenty-nine, a New York book editor and occasional contributor to the magazine. "She's lovely. Very enthusiastic. Very welcoming of new ideas." Adds Lerner, "I grew up in a Jewish feminist household and *Lilith* was always around."

Weidman Schneider recognizes there are many fights yet to be won – for instance, redressing the inequities suffered by female rabbis, who are often paid only seventy-five percent of what their male counterparts earn, she says.

But the tone of her voice is softer now, perhaps the effect of looking at so many tough issues over the years from a multitude of perspectives. The cover of a recent issue of *Lilith* features a photograph of an Israeli woman, rifle slung over one shoulder, the young child she carries looking over the other. It illustrates the issue's main feature, "A Different Lens on the News? Women Reporting from Israel." Provocative, but not shocking, as some of the early covers were.

"I think it's useful to take a more nuanced look at what's going on than you are able to do when blinded by anger," says Weidman Schneider. "The people who are involved with *Lilith* as writers and as editors tend to be able to see complexity. I like that, and clearly our readers do, too. I think you get a much richer view of the world."

ALICE SHALVI

by STEPHEN HAZAN ARNOFF

Seated in the living room of her Jerusalem home – every flat
surface but the floor covered by neat stacks of papers and
books, the room lit softly by small lamps, and a breeze blowing gen-
tly through open windows facing gardens she loves to tend – Alice
Shalvi explains making peace with the conflict between her love for
and observance of traditional Judaism and her objections to gender
discrimination in many areas of Jewish life.

Shalvi looks at the ceiling for a moment, the fingertips and
palms of her hands resting lightly upon each other as she pauses to
think. Then she lowers her hands, smiles, and says, "The time has
come for someone to do an *Ethics of the Mothers.*"

For more than half a century, Shalvi has confronted contemporary challenges to women, serving in prominent leadership roles
in an array of major Israeli institutions – forty years as a professor of

English Literature at the Hebrew University, fifteen years as principal of the Pelech Religious Experimental High School for Girls in Jerusalem, sixteen years as the chair of the Israel Women's Network, and seven years successively as rector, president, and then chair of the executive committee at the Schechter Institute of Jewish Studies, the Conservative movement's academic center in Israel.

Having juggled the equivalent of two, if not three, full-time jobs at every stage of her career, Shalvi, now semi-retired as an institution builder and leader but still working full-time on her own writing, was awarded the Israel Prize for Lifetime Achievement and Special Contribution to Society and the State of Israel in 2007, the nation's highest academic honor.

Immersed for so long in the often onerous tasks of navigating, restructuring and enlivening Israeli and Jewish trends that resisted the expansion of women's roles, Shalvi notes a reflective spiritual creed that naturally supports her activism: "The Jewish enterprise," she says, "lies in the social, human application in our everyday lives of divine, spiritual inspiration."

Yet the resistance Shalvi has encountered while seeking to empower women has deep roots in ancient Jewish divisions between the sexes. "When a man speaks often with women he brings evil upon himself, neglects the study of the Torah, [and] winds up in Gehennom [Hell]," says Yossi ben Yochanan in the Mishnah's *Ethics of the Fathers* 1:5, a text believed to be the first fully recorded in written form in the second or third century. The Mishnah continues: "And don't talk too much with the wife."

Formal Jewish study "just wasn't available to me," says Shalvi. "What I learned was from home." Learning from home meant a mixture of religious Zionism and humanism, represented most strongly by her father, whom Shalvi considers the key teacher in her life.

Born in Essen, Germany in 1926, Shalvi was eight when she and her family moved to England in 1934. She describes her mother as a "typical Jewish mother and homemaker," distinguished by her commitment to taking care of guests and giving charity despite financial difficulties during and after the Depression. When beggars knocked on the family's door, "I don't recall an instance when my mother didn't invite them into the house. If she had anything that she could give she would do it" – food, clothing, linen, whatever she could find. "No one ever left empty-handed." Shalvi's father represented a figure of immense wisdom to his daughter – compassionate, a resource of information and advice for neighbors, family and friends, and a committed Jew.

Restricted from directing her intellect and curiosity towards Jewish academic subjects, Shalvi invested herself in receiving both a B.A. (1947) and an M.A. (1950) in English from Cambridge University as well as a Postgraduate Diploma in Social Work from the London School of Economics.

She made aliyah in 1949, a decision driven by a combination of Zionism and lack of available Jewish learning opportunities, and a move she says she had an inkling of from the age of six. "The matter was clinched," she says, "when I first visited the country in December 1947." Shalvi moved to Israel alone, traveling by boat from Italy. In 1950, she joined the Department of English Literature at the Hebrew University of Jerusalem, where she earned her PhD in 1962 with a dissertation later published in book form as *Renaissance Concepts of Honour in Shakespeare's Problem Plays*. She has co-authored Hebrew and English editions of *The World and Art of Shakespeare*, as well as a range of articles in the fields of literature and theater.

Though she has written extensively on feminism and the Hebrew Bible, it is Shakespeare's canon that girds her intellectual foundation, playfulness and sense of wonder. Her husband, children and grandchildren, with whom she holds informal Shakespeare study sessions, are known to stop her in the middle of day-to-day conversations, reminding her that she is quoting "him" again. More than mastering a subject of academic discourse, Shalvi has applied Shakespeare to access the channels of spirit, inspiration and wisdom that have animated her life as a Jewish leader.

Shalvi says Shakespeare's plays are filled with *hochmat hayyim*, "the wisdom of life." Employing the language of the Jews to explain the impact of Shakespeare illustrates one of Shalvi's core beliefs about the life of the spirit. "Great art can, I think, be inspiring and elevating. Great art can bring us closer to God, as can nature. For me the greatest sources of spiritual elation come from nature on the one hand and great art on the other," she says. "Is a belief in some superhuman force necessary in order to be a good human being? No. The proof is nature and art." Spiritual inspiration encountered in Shakespeare or Mozart (another one of her favorites) or sitting in the garden meditating – increasingly Shalvi's practice on Shabbat and Jewish holidays – need not be definitively Jewish at its source. Jewish spirituality emerges when a person filled with what Shalvi calls "the essence and spirit of the divine" gives this emotion a Jewish context through Jewish learning and action.

While her work choices and opportunities over the years guided her into public positions as a Jewish professional and role model, her transitions between Jewish and non-Jewish content, inspiration and expression have always been fluid and open.

Hamlet and *King Lear* are Shalvi's most constant sources of raw wisdom ultimately refined by practice. Reflecting on the lessons in moral leadership these plays granted her before she even knew that she would inhabit such roles in the Jewish world, Shalvi describes *Hamlet* as "the prime example of the dilemmas that are involved in seeking to combat evil in life without employing the weapons that evil itself employs." She calls *King Lear* a play that "powerfully and painfully encapsulates the tragic misunderstanding of the failure to express our feelings – particularly of love for each other."

The applications of these lessons to Shalvi's Jewish feminist practice are clear: Just as Hamlet, her favorite Shakespearean character, is challenged to avoid becoming the shadow of his own enemy, Jewish feminists must create practices that filter out the oppression they have absorbed from society, lest they project this pain and negativity back on themselves and others. And just as *King Lear*'s Cordelia sparks tragedy because she cannot express love for her father – the symbol of her roots and the ultimate bearer of her past – Jewish feminists must create identities that embrace the constructive elements of Jewish tradition while disposing of elements deemed obsolete or damaging.

Even while serving solely as an academic, Shalvi developed a pedagogical style that supported teaching the "wisdom of life," emphasizing "the interaction between life experience and text that is where, dare I say, women are better than men," she says. Shalvi encouraged all of her students – men and women – to "bring one's own life experience to bear on the text."

Holding that any process of learning must not only connect students with new knowledge but also guide them towards forms of expression and wisdom demanding *tikkun olam* – the repairing of the world – Shalvi modeled this lesson herself late in her career. After decades as perhaps the most widely known modern Orthodox feminist in Israel, Shalvi lost patience with teaching about innovation within tradition, not only identifying personally with the Conservative movement's more liberal approach to *Halacha* – Jewish law – with regard to women, but taking on key leadership roles at the Schechter Institute of Jewish Studies, the movement's flagship institution in Israel.

Shalvi's teaching, her example, and even her presence had an impact that still resonates for many of her students. Tami Biton, an Israeli educator and activist who studied at Pelech High School in the 1980s while Shalvi was principal, recalls a morning when one of her classmates jokingly sang a traditional Israeli children's song during recess in which a girl winds up crying. "The song stopped when Alice came into the classroom," she says. "So did the class. Alice lectured for forty-five minutes about how a simple song – a text you would never even think twice about – could teach young women to hold themselves back. None of us ever forgot that."

Another former student at Pelech, Tamar Eyni-Lehman, recalls the confidence Shalvi imparted to the young women around her. "She was probably too busy to teach as much as she wanted by the time I was there, but we knew she believed so much that our education mattered. And as girls in a religious high school that was pretty different than the others around us at the time, that really meant something. She made us feel like we were part of something important."

"Only God could create a Shakespeare," Shalvi enjoys telling students. "But he was a self-made person!" It is no wonder that Shalvi's Jewish value holding that learning leads to action – famously discussed by Rabbi Akiva and Rabbi Tarfon in the Babylonian Talmud Tractate *Kiddushin* 40b – found an intellectual, inspirational home in the work of Shakespeare.

Shalvi's "self-made" Jewish feminist activism emerged publicly at an unexpected turning point in her life. She jokes that it has always been "providence and chance" rather than careful plans that have led her to major life changes. She met her husband Moshe, a translator and writer, at a Hebrew University event. "On my part, it was love at first sight!" she says. They married in 1950 and Shalvi is currently collaborating with her husband on his magnum opus, a reference tool entitled *Jewish Women: A Comprehensive Historical Encyclopedia*.

Unexpected circumstances also helped form her commitment to feminism. "In the 1970s," she says, "I became increasingly aware of discrimination against women in Judaism and began to study that particular area more." At the same time, Shalvi was passed over for a dean's position at Ben-Gurion University because she was a woman. "In fact," she remembers, "all four of the men who had to decide on the appointment specifically mentioned this. It was an eye-opener for me, since I'd always believed that there was gender parity at the universities."

This incident in particular pushed Shalvi to translate her literary and educational ideas into the realm of activism. Yet a tangible, teachable Jewish feminism had to be created from scratch. Shalvi recognized that the traditional Jewish world offered very few clear resources or role models for the first wave of modern Orthodox feminists. "In my working with other Jewish women – feminists, particularly modern Orthodox women like myself – I learned a great deal. We all learned together. It was a process. A common development for all of us." Acting out of the necessities of her own personal challenges and the needs of others, Shalvi pushed ahead.

And it was chance, she says, that led to the offers to take on leadership roles at all of the institutions where she has served. Her first real role as a Jewish feminist leader became her "day job" when in 1975 she volunteered to take over administration of Pelech High School – an Orthodox all-girls school where two of her daughters were studying – when a new principal was needed. "I was on the parents' committee and when we proved unable to find a suitable candidate I volunteered to fill the gap temporarily." Shalvi pauses. "That lasted for fifteen years."

Focusing on a curriculum and pedagogical style different from most other religious schools for girls in Israel at the time, Shalvi "preferred to take on totally inexperienced younger people [as teachers] and then I encouraged them to do new things." This included giving young women opportunities to study Talmud, traditionally a male-only pursuit. Shalvi's passion for proactive text experiences charged Pelech-style learning with a unique spirit.

"Text study is for me the core of any learning," she says. "Joint learning – listening to each other and using the text as a basis to learn to comment, with everybody giving equal respect and attention to everyone else in the group – became a model of study for the women." The result of what was once considered Pelech's avant-garde approach, which has now become accepted by many other institutions, is a large and heterogeneous cohort of Israeli women alumni – academics, educators, artists, activists and more – with roots and skills in Jewish studies that often surpass those of their male counterparts.

While recognizing an ultimate goal of integrating young women fully into general society, Shalvi affirmed at Pelech that separate gender education makes the most sense for young people until the end of high school. When studying with boys, Shalvi says, "Girls will hold back from demonstrating their own capacities. Women tend to bring their own life experiences" to study and this is much more threatening in a coeducational environment. Still, she says, "Separate gender study is not ideal forever," pausing for a moment and smiling. "Just until we change society as a whole, you know."

While former high school students who participated in the literature classes that made up much of Shalvi's formal classroom time at Pelech describe courses at times overwhelming, the young women digging into material suitable for an undergraduate or graduate students, all recall Shalvi's uncanny ability to guide and shape lives. "She was just this incredible presence for us," says Biton. "We learned about character."

Shalvi traveled often, fundraising, planning and advocating for the school, delegating teaching responsibilities for a dynamic curriculum to her staff. "She was always about leadership and example," says Shalvi's daughter Peninah, a Pelech graduate who recalls sitting on her mother's lap when Shalvi decided to take over leadership of the school. "We kids always knew how hard she was working for what she believed in and we loved it."

During her sixteen-year tenure as chair of the Israel Women's Network – a trans-ethnic, class and religious Israeli advocacy group promoting social, legal and religious support for women's encounters with the workplace, politics, family, violence, sexual harassment, education, health, the military and sports that she helped found – Shalvi claims to have seen "a total turnaround" in the status of women in Israel. Women's issues are now a standard plank on the Israeli national agenda, but Shalvi wants more. She supports expansion of women's roles in Israel not just in order to improve the health and well-being of women, but as a way of benefiting the world as a whole in many areas of gravest concern and sensitivity.

"Having no woman on the peace negotiating teams is a disgrace. The same is true of the teams that craft social policy, which are almost exclusively male," she says. Shalvi believes that life experience makes women "more receptive" to suffering and the needs of others and that they can help establish policies that "make the workplace more human – both for men and women, mothers and fathers, husbands and wives." In the broadest sense, Shalvi holds that "feminist practice teaches society what it could and should be."

As she enters a period when her responsibilities to major institutions fade after the equivalent of four full careers, Shalvi spends much of her time reading, studying, listening to music and being with her family. Though often asked to speak or write in areas of her expertise, she is attempting to concentrate her creative energies on a memoir she describes as "a midrash on myself" – a project interrupted during her first retirement in the 1990s when Machon Schechter required her leadership.

Reminded that she had begun by saying that the Jewish world required a handbook of ethical practice compiled by wise women – an *Ethics of the Mothers* – Shalvi says that more than anything she could write, the most eloquent expressions of her impact on the world are the living acts of wisdom she and the people she has inspired and trained have institutionalized, taught and lived. Her greatest joy is watching the many young women she has taught and counseled emerge as leaders in their own right.

"It's amazing what you can achieve if you know what your aims are – what ideal you are striving for – if you succeed in enlisting as many other people as you can to join you in the act, in the struggle to bring about the changes," she says.

MICHAEL STEINHARDT

by DANIEL TREIMAN

M ichael Steinhardt, the mega-donor who spearheaded the revolutionary Birthright Israel program and a host of other ambitious projects aimed at revitalizing American Jewry, sits erect behind
a giant, curving desk in his midtown Manhattan office. To his left,
a computer screen provides up-to-date financial information, a reminder of his days as a pioneering hedge fund operator. He doesn't
waste time getting down to business.

"Are you Jewish?" Steinhardt asks within little more than a
minute of meeting a visitor. Receiving an affirmative reply, Steinhardt's questions come in quick succession: "How old are you?" "I've
got some Jewish girl coming up in a while, who's thirty-one, lives in
Los Angeles. Are you single?" "Are you looking for the woman of
your dreams?" "Okay, we'll see if we can marry you off to this woman."

It is vintage Steinhardt. His philanthropy is focused on grand projects to get young Jews to connect to and engage with their Jewish identities, and Steinhardt, ever the hands-on donor, has taken a very personal interest in getting young Jews to connect with, get engaged to – and, ideally, marry – one another. "Take phone numbers. Flirt, meet, breed, do whatever is necessary," he implored at a 2004 conference for young Jewish professionals.

"Two people – he'll run around introducing them, and they really have nothing in common, but he's all ready to fix them up," says Lynn Schusterman, a Tulsa-based philanthropist who works closely with Steinhardt on Birthright and other projects and considers him a close friend. As an added matrimonial incentive, Steinhardt occasionally offers the use of his house in Anguilla as a honeymoon spot for couples who meet on Birthright.

The philanthropist may play matchmaker with puckish enthusiasm, but there is also an underlying urgency to his Jewish-cupid routine. "It's very difficult to overcome the fact that the next generation of Jews, by almost every measure, has less Jewish intensity, less Jewish education, less Jewish commitment – and there are less Jews!" he laments. His philanthropy, accordingly, has ambitious aims: It's a bid to save the nation's Jews – or at least the ninety percent who aren't Orthodox – from assimilating amid the unprecedented opportunities of contemporary America.

Steinhardt is certainly one of the more colorful figures on the Jewish communal landscape. Bald, with a fringe of white hair, a bushy moustache, wire-rim glasses, a ruddy complexion, and a belly that testifies to his not-entirely-healthy appetite for fine foods, he bears a passing resemblance to the actor Wilford Brimley. An avowed atheist with a nevertheless active interest in religion, his broadsides against the Jewish establishment and jeremiads about American Jewry's future are legendary.

He also happens to be one of the Jewish world's most important figures. Steinhardt arguably has done as much as any one person to refocus the Jewish communal agenda around the issue of continuity. In addition to Birthright Israel – his best-known project, which, since 1999, has sent tens of thousands of young Diaspora

Jews on all-expenses-paid trips to Israel – Steinhardt is behind a slew of hugely influential initiatives.

Two years prior to Birthright Israel, he launched the Partnership for Excellence in Jewish Education, an organization that has helped spur the rapid expansion of Jewish day schools nationwide. In 1999, he opened Makor, a popular Manhattan venue for music, film and learning where Jews in their twenties and thirties can meet, mingle, and maybe even find a mate. Through Hillel: The Foundation for Jewish Campus Life, he initiated the Steinhardt Jewish Campus Service Corps, which has put hundreds of recent college graduates to work doing campus outreach and developing Jewish programming for their peers.

"The common thread in my philanthropy is the effort to create a renaissance in the next generations of non-Orthodox Diaspora Jews," Steinhardt says. "The objective is to create a Judaism that will be far more appealing and accommodating and welcoming and exciting than the Judaism that exists for the non-Orthodox cohort in North America today."

All told, Steinhardt has given some $120 million to Jewish causes through his foundation, the Jewish Life Network, since its launch in 1994. But his contribution can't be measured in dollars alone. "There are a lot of people who are spending a lot more money than Michael on Jewish philanthropic causes," says Mark Charendoff, president of the Jewish Funders Network, "but they're having nowhere near his impact."

Back in his Wall Street days, Steinhardt was renowned for his temper. In his 2001 autobiography, *No Bull: My Life In and Out of Markets*, he readily admitted that his nine-to-five personality was not entirely pleasant: "I would be scowling and fuming, shouting over the intercom, storming in and out of the trading room."

In contrast, Steinhardt remains calm as he discusses his new professional focus, the Jewish world. But while he speaks softly, what he says is withering: Contemporary Jewish life is "fraught with weakness, fraught, frankly, with failure." Non-Orthodox religious movements in America, such as Conservative and Reform Judaism, "are finished, but they're going to take a long time to die." Jewish leaders "don't exist anymore."

Does Steinhardt consider himself a Jewish leader? "I don't know," Steinhardt sighs. "I don't aspire to be a Jewish leader if being a Jewish leader is relating to the broad constituency of Jews and persuading them that I should be their leader," he explains. "If a Jewish leader means having a vision and taking steps that are meaningfully different and perhaps meaningfully ahead of that which exists in the community, of taking real chances of failing, perhaps, at some of them, but of moving the community forward, whether it be recognized or not, if that's the definition, I think I'm a Jewish leader, and I'm proud of that."

If Steinhardt is a Jewish leader, it is because he has chosen to be one. Unlike his fellow mega-donors and frequent philanthropic partners, Charles and Edgar Bronfman, heirs to the Seagram liquor fortune, Steinhardt is no scion of Jewish nobility. Nothing about his life's path was preordained.

Born in 1940, Steinhardt grew up in Bensonhurst, a working-class neighborhood of Jews and Italians in southern Brooklyn. His parents' brief marriage ended in divorce before his first birthday. He was raised by his mother, a bookkeeper whom Steinhardt credits with providing him with a happy childhood. Steinhardt's father, a tough-guy jeweler and chronic gambler who was friendly with various high-profile underworld figures, flitted in and out of his son's life.

Though his mother was not particularly observant, Steinhardt grew up in a kosher home, and his family celebrated the major Jewish holidays. He attended Hebrew school at an Orthodox synagogue, which he remembers as joyless and largely irrelevant to modern American life. While he had more positive experiences attending a small, homey basement shul, by his teens he drifted toward atheism, an intellectual trajectory that was reinforced by his secular education. This is not to say that he became disconnected from the Jewish experience. Seeing tattooed and disfigured Holocaust survivors walking the streets of his youth, Steinhardt says, gave him an "early sense...of the Jewish experience in the twentieth century and how terrible it was." And then, he adds, there was "the war related to the birth of the State of Israel and how exciting that was."

"I remember when we were first married, and it was the Six-Day War, he wanted to just pack up and enlist," recounts Steinhardt's wife, Judy, with whom he has three grown children and seven grandchildren. "I think that if he hadn't had a business already established, because those were the first years of his hedge fund, that he probably would have done that if he had been free. And so where did that come from? It must have come from growing up in Brooklyn surrounded by lower-middle-class Jews."

But even as a youth, Steinhardt also gazed outward, beyond Bensonhurst and beyond his boyhood Jewish milieu – in particular, across the East River toward Wall Street. Steinhardt had been fascinated with the stock market ever since his father gave him some shares as a bar mitzvah gift. Soon the Brooklyn teen was hanging out at brokerage houses after school. Upon graduating from the University of Pennsylvania at the age of twenty – a school he was able to attend thanks to his father's prodding and funding – Steinhardt returned to New York and landed an entry-level job with a mutual fund. Six years later, he started his own hedge fund with a pair of young partners.

Steinhardt was an aggressive trader, buying, selling, betting on the markets, often changing course dramatically, sometimes within the space of a few hours. He had tremendous confidence in his instincts, stressed the importance of good research and demanded results. His brash style paid off. Year after year, his fund beat the markets – usually by a wide margin. A dollar invested with Steinhardt in 1967 would have been worth $481 twenty-eight years later. One of his early clients noted that an initial investment with Steinhardt of $500,000 grew to more than $100 million.

But Steinhardt's personal investment in his work took a toll. Although he consistently enriched his clients, fluctuations in his fund's fortunes had the power to shake his very sense of self-worth. In 1994, Steinhardt overextended himself, investing heavily in exotic markets with which he wasn't very familiar. Amid a global bond sell-off, the value of Steinhardt's fund plummeted, losing nearly a third of its value. He sank into despair.

Steinhardt managed to recoup his fund's losses the following year, but by then he had had enough. He decided to kick his trading addiction. In 1995, he closed his firm.

Steinhardt certainly had no shortage of enthusiasms to take the place of work: horticulture (he has created extensive orchards and gardens on his Westchester estate), zoology (he maintains a private menagerie stocked with zebras, kangaroos and other exotic creatures), art (he is an avid collector of Judaica and ancient art), media (he once owned a fifty percent stake in the English-language *Forward* newspaper, was for a time a major investor in the neo-liberal *New Republic*, and was a key backer of the now defunct, neo-conservative *New York Sun*), Hollywood (he has helped finance several motion pictures, including *The Addams Family* and *Hotel Terminus*, an Academy Award-winning documentary about Nazi war criminal Klaus Barbie), and politics (he is a former chairman of the centrist Democratic Leadership Council and talked up the presidential prospects of fellow tycoon, New York City Mayor Michael Bloomberg).

Jewish philanthropy, though, is his new vocation, and he has brought to it the habits of his old one. "He's not the committee, process-it-to-death type. He's very much, 'Let's get this done.' He sees things quickly; he jumps, in a brilliant way. He'll see things whole in the first thirty seconds, and he's ready to start carrying it out," says Rabbi Irving "Yitz" Greenberg, the renowned and unorthodox Orthodox theologian who headed Steinhardt's foundation from 1995–2007. "I often joke, it's like his investing style: he would concentrate, make quick bets. He was always looking for the out-of-the-box advantage. He was ready to make a quick decision. He was ready to make a quick reverse decision."

The concluding chapter of Steinhardt's autobiography is titled "Two Rivers," a reference to the two currents he describes as having powerfully shaped his life and values: "the age-old river of Judaism, the people and the tradition, and the river of secularized

America." While Steinhardt navigated these two rivers successfully, this has proven more difficult, he noted, for many younger Jews, as the currents of contemporary American life have pulled them far from their Jewish moorings.

Steinhardt devoted much of the chapter to his experience launching Birthright Israel, the program that set out to make a free, ten-day trip to Israel the "birthright" of every young Diaspora Jew, from the age of eighteen to twenty-six. Birthright sent its first participants, six thousand of them, to Israel in December 1999. The trip represented the fruition of two years of dogged work by Steinhardt and Birthright co-founder Charles Bronfman to mobilize the Jewish world behind this revolutionary and unprecedented undertaking, which, in its first five years alone, involved a commitment of $210 million from individual philanthropists, the Israeli government and local Jewish communities.

At the conclusion of that historic first trip, thousands of Birthright participants assembled in a Jerusalem auditorium for a pep rally of sorts. Steinhardt delivered a speech not-so-loosely based upon Lincoln's Gettysburg Address: "We here must firmly resolve that all those who lived and died for Jewry shall not have lived and died in vain. We must promise that this people, in partnership with the living and the dead, with God and humanity, shall have a new birth of freedom. We must live our lives as witnesses, as teachers, as builders, so the Torah of the Jewish people, the teaching by the Jewish people, the concern for the Jewish people, shall flourish again on this earth."

He received a standing ovation, after which participants came up to Steinhardt to thank him. Steinhardt recounted how one young man, tears streaming down his face, approached him and said, "I feel a connection to the Jews who have come before me that I didn't even know existed."

"I will take the image of that young man's face, streaked with tears, with me for the rest of my life," Steinhardt wrote to close his book. "I believe those tears represented the strong reunion of the two rivers of my life: a reinvigorated American Judaism."

In 2006, Birthright sent its 100,000th participant to Israel. Critics, who initially saw the program as a waste of money or questioned its worth, now call it one of the Jewish community's great success stories.

Yet the Steinhardt of today sounds far less optimistic than the one who saw in that young man's tears American Jewry's rebirth. It's not that Steinhardt doesn't think Birthright has been a success – indeed, he calls it "the shining light in an otherwise miserable Jewish institutional world." Rather, sparking a Jewish renaissance has proven even more difficult than he – no Pollyanna to begin with – had imagined.

"When I started, I was more optimistic about bringing the unaffiliated world closer to the affiliated world, and that that would solve our problem," he says. Since then, he confesses, he has "become disaffected with that view." Now he believes that American Jewry's problems go much deeper, that existing expressions of Jewish religion and community are out of date and have lost their ability to speak to young Jews.

It is a situation that calls for more radical remedies than simply trying to get more Jews enrolling in day schools or participating in Hillel activities, he believes. "I think what we need is a new Jewish spirituality that will be far more compelling than anything that exists today," he says. "And I call that 'common Judaism.'"

Steinhardt's "common Judaism" remains a work in progress. The term is, as much as anything, a rebuke of what he sees as the stale and stultifying denominationalism that defines American Jewish life. As a small example of the need for a new direction, Steinhardt notes that on an average Friday night only two to five percent of non-Orthodox Jewish college students show up at their campus Hillel. To remedy this, he has convened meetings of rabbis, Jewish campus professionals and musicians "with the idea of creating a new Sabbath service that will be resonant, exciting, that will have music and dance, that will be fulfilling in a way that present services are not fulfilling."

In his effort to build a better campus Sabbath service, there are echoes of Steinhardt's own search for Jewish contexts that he finds appealing. Steinhardt has tried a number of different synagogues, but he has yet to find the perfect fit. He raves about the Upper West Side's nondenominational Congregation B'nai Jeshurun, famed for its instrumental music and dancing, calling its Friday-night service "magical" – "It really did something for me, like nothing else!" – but he then goes on to complain that it's "a mile wide and an inch deep," citing the poor quality of the rabbis' sermons. For an atheist, Steinhardt is quite the seeker.

"I work very hard on thinking about what it is that makes me care so much about my Judaism," he says. "Most people who care a lot about their Judaism at least ostensibly or overtly are believers in God, and I'm not. But I feel very comfortable now, having been very uncomfortable for much of my Jewish life in being an atheist."

He attributes this newfound comfort to an intellectual epiphany about the nature of Jewish identity. "It's not our being a chosen people, it's not social Darwinism, it's not DNA," he says. "It's only because of our values, which have endured for three or four or five thousand years and have evolved to some degree during that period, and which make us a special people."

But Steinhardt, no fan of vague, feel-good rhetoric, says that these values need to be "carefully and thoughtfully sifted out and articulated." Indeed, he has identified precisely four Jewish values, which he eagerly and authoritatively lists: "Education – Jews put more time, energy, money into education than any other people." "*Tzedakah* – We feel a responsibility for helping those in need." "Meritocracy – Jews only do well in those societies that are meritocratic." "Fourth Jewish value – and I'm having a hard time articulating this clearly – is being the outsider. Jews have been the outsider in so many different places. And we function very, very well as an outsider and maybe not so well as an insider."

But couldn't Jews hold onto these values while leaving Jewish identity itself by the wayside? "Well, Jewish identity is an issue: Can you have Jewish values without Jewish identity? Maybe you can," he says, sounding resigned to a possibility that he does not entirely like.

"I've said that the best of American values and Jewish values have really begun to merge. Don't you sense that? Social net, great emphasis on education…" He trails off.

Steinhardt is fond of boasting of what he sees as his keen grasp of the contemporary American Jewish situation. Yet when asked why being Jewish means so much to him, he confesses: "I'm not sure I've ever totally grasped it." But these two things are not necessarily inconsistent.

"Michael has increasingly felt that he's the only one who was sort of feeling the full intensity of the people who are drifting away," Greenberg says. If Steinhardt understands them, perhaps it is because he in some ways identifies with them.

Modern-day America has given Jews unprecedented opportunities. But it also has shaken old certainties and given us in their place new questions: How does our ancient faith fit into our modern American lives? Can we reconcile Judaism and disbelief? What is the right balance between spirituality and reason? What is it that makes the Jewish people so special, and so worth preserving? At a most basic level, what does it mean to be Jewish?

Steinhardt viscerally grasps the importance of these questions, because he has wrestled with them himself his entire life. And for the past dozen years, he has been wrestling with them for the rest of us as well. "I feel I understand the contemporary Jewish world as well and perhaps better than any other lay person alive," Steinhardt says. "I know that's a presumptuous statement, but I believe that."

ADIN STEINSALTZ

by ILENE R. PRUSHER

When Adin Steinsaltz was a boy of five, he was playing with a few of his cousins on a kibbutz in the countryside. They had corralled a donkey, linked it up to a makeshift carriage, and told him to climb in for a ride.

He refused, telling them he could not do such a thing on the Sabbath because he was a Jew. One cousin laughed at him and said, "So? We're all Jews here!"

"I was slightly precocious," Steinsaltz recalls somewhat sheepishly. "I said, 'I am more of a Jew than all of you!'"

Today, in his early seventies, Rabbi Adin (Har-Even) Steinsaltz views with bemusement that memory of his young self, a boy growing up in a secular Jerusalem family who was somehow drawn to a pious life from a very early age. Even more striking is that the distinction – as expressed by the pint-sized Adin – flies in the face of what he ultimately came to believe and what his life's work is about.

"These differences we draw between religious and secular people are not a true picture at all. It's really more like a mosaic; you have all kinds of combinations," the white-bearded, slightly stoop-necked, bespectacled rabbi says in a conversation in his modest but ultra-modern Jerusalem office. Just outside his door, an array of men and women who come to learn in the rabbi's evening *shiurim* (classes), scheduled to begin in an hour, are already assembling, seeking a good seat. Others, his long-distance learners, will join by teleconference.

That Steinsaltz grew up in a non-observant home is a fact that many people find fascinating. Born in 1937, he has become a Torah luminary of his generation and is celebrated for his ongoing work of translating the Talmud into modern Hebrew, making it accessible to a huge portion of the Jewish population for whom the Talmud's esoteric, arcane Aramaic and classical Hebrew make the core texts of Jewish study unapproachable.

When asked about the rarity of having been reared in a secular home and becoming a world-renowned Orthodox rabbi – his father was a Communist and "one of the few Palestinians to volunteer for the civil war in Spain" – Steinsaltz recalls that he nonetheless grew up in a home steeped in Jewish values. "I am far more observant than my father, but my father is far more Jewish than me," he explains.

On some level, this view fits with Steinsaltz's vision of education in general and Jewish learning in particular. A person isn't born a Torah scholar or a scientist, he says. Learning is more of an acquired taste than it is an inherited one.

"Most of our abilities don't come to us naturally. We have to learn them," says Steinsaltz, as he packs a deep-curved pipe, which he loves to smoke in his rare leisure hours, with a pinch of Captain Black Royal tobacco. "You may be born Jewish, which means you have it in your genes, in your brain in some form, but it won't express itself naturally, except in extraordinary places. When I teach people, it's like teaching them to talk, to walk. I'm teaching them to get to their potential."

· · ·

Called a "once-in-a-millennium scholar" by *Time* magazine and a recipient of the Israel Prize, the country's highest honor, Steinsaltz has authored more than sixty books on a staggering range of subjects – theology, of course, but also zoology, social commentary and even a detective novel. The most well-known among them is *The Thirteen Petalled Rose*, his classic work on Kabbalah, which was published in 1980 and has been translated into eight languages.

"In a way, I'm a very slow writer," Steinsaltz shrugs, exhibiting his streak of self-deprecating humor. Since graduating from the Hebrew University, where he studied physics and chemistry, he has averaged over a book a year, and that's in addition to all of his other endeavors, which includes an extensive commitment to education – he has established a network of schools and educational institutes in both Israel and the former Soviet Union. His involvement in education began early in his career, when he founded several experimental schools and became Israel's youngest school principal at the age of twenty-four.

But of all his life's work, the books he has written, the many schools he has established, the countless lectures he has delivered, Steinsaltz's crowning achievement is his translation of the Talmud, opening the texts at the very heart of the Jewish tradition to people for whom they were closed books. He began this work in 1965 and so far, he has published thirty-eight of an anticipated forty-six volumes. The work has been translated into several languages including English, French, Russian and Spanish.

The significance of the translation is far-reaching. "It's a translation and a commentary," explains Arthur Kurzweil, author of the book *On the Road with Rabbi Steinsaltz: 25 Years of Pre-Dawn Car Trips, Mind-Blowing Encounters, and Inspiring Conversations with a Man of Wisdom* (2006), and Steinsaltz's chauffeur when the rabbi is in New York. "He takes you by the hand to show you what's happening on the page. As Rabbi Steinsaltz says, the Talmud was never supposed to be an elitist document, but it became that. Many students are spending most of their time trying to figure out what the darn thing means. Rabbi Steinsaltz says, 'If you're going to spend three-quarters of your life just trying to crack the text without engaging with what it means, what's the point?'"

Steinsaltz's translation has made possible a profound change in the way Talmud can be learned – and by whom. "It means that if you're a Hebrew speaker, he does the job of translation, and that's tremendous," explains Avital Hochstein, a preeminent teacher of Talmud at leading Jewish learning centers such as Pardes Institute of Jewish Studies and the Shalom Hartman Institute, and co-author of the book, *Women Out, Women In: The Place of Women in Midrash* (2008).

One has to turn the clock back nearly a thousand years to find a scholar who undertook something as far-reaching as Steinsaltz's opus. Rashi, who was born in eleventh-century France and is considered the most prolific of all Jewish commentators, writing on both the Torah and Talmud, took on a similar project to Steinsaltz's.

Not only has Steinsaltz opened the door for secular Israelis to learn Talmud, but Hochstein points out that while Steinsaltz did not set out to make a feminist statement, his translations opened the door for many women to study Talmud. Traditionally, throughout the Orthodox world, girls were not taught Gemara. By the 1980s, that began to change, and a few modern-Orthodox schools such as Pelech High School in Jerusalem were teaching girls Talmud.

Steinsaltz's text includes introductions, commentaries and marginal notes that help guide the reader through the text and make it more accessible. Hochstein explains the end result: "It really allows me to stand in front of the text. That's the highest level of generosity a teacher can give, to allow you to learn on your own."

Kurzweil echoes this: "I roll up my sleeves, and with Rabbi Steinsaltz's direction, I can start engaging with the text and ask the big questions. I'm not just spending all that time trying to understand what the darn words are saying."

That in fact, comes pretty close to precisely what Steinsaltz was aiming for when he began the project more than forty years ago. The ultimate goal was to make more space at the table of Jewish thought by enabling people to tune in to the complex, intergenerational conversation taking place on the pages of the Talmud.

"Talmud study is basically an oral teaching," Steinsaltz explains. "It is not a systematic book by any means. You're always in the middle and you never have an entry point. It begins in the middle and goes in all directions. It always assumes that you have a previous knowledge." He knew well what it was like to be coming in from the outside, without as much of the "backstory" as he would have liked.

"Most Jews don't have access to our texts. If you're an outsider, it's like hearing other people have a conversation you can't follow," he says. "What I did was to try to make a portable teacher, because the teacher is not always nearby and not always so available."

Some say this is the equivalent to democratizing Jewish learning, making it a possibility for people to study without being dependent on a rabbi or school of thought. Steinsaltz pokes fun at such claims, saying that such an achievement sounds a bit like "democratizing chess," adding playfully: "If you're not into it, it's not very amusing."

Of course, creating a "portable teacher" is not equivalent to making a teacher irrelevant. As Hochstein points out, "If you don't know Talmud at all, you won't necessarily be able to pick it up and understand. Something that is difficult to understand in the text will remain difficult. But the unmediated connection with the text is amazing. He doesn't give you his opinion. That's its greatness."

But still, the controversy remains. The fact that Steinsaltz has enabled untold numbers of Jews to have direct access to the debates of their forefathers is a particularly interesting position for someone who, having been quite close to the late Lubavitch Rabbi Menachem Mendel Schneerson, is viewed by many Jews to be part of Chabad, with its accompanying emphasis on the revered place of the Rebbe. Steinsaltz acknowledges that Schneerson was a beloved friend and an inspiration, and that he even worked in the Soviet Union to assist

Chabad's network of *shluchim* (emissaries) there. For many years, Steinsaltz traveled to the region each month. In 1990, he founded the Free Jewish University in Moscow, and in 1994, the Institute for Jewish Leadership Training in the Commonwealth of Independent States.

Clearly, though, Steinsaltz through his actions – the schools he has founded, the students he teaches, the lectures he delivers – does not believe in making the teacher irrelevant. He does, however, believe in questioning, in skepticism.

As Kurzweil puts it, Steinsaltz is both "a man of faith and a huge skeptic." He recalls a talk Steinsaltz gave at a religious high school. "He said, 'Look, I don't know that much about many things, but I know a little bit about Torah study. Make the lives of your Torah teachers as miserable as you can. Try to trip them up and find contradictions in what they say. Ask them the most difficult questions you can think of.' When he was leaving the principal got up and told the students, 'Don't take him too literally.' At which point, Steinsaltz goes and takes the microphone back and says, 'My message to you today is: Make the lives of your teachers as miserable as you possibly can.' And then he walked off the stage."

. . .

Rabbi Menachem Even-Israel, or Meni, is one of Steinsaltz's three children and his father's right-hand man. In his early thirties, he manages the newly designed Steinsaltz Center in the colorful Jerusalem neighborhood of Nahlaot, a diverse and dense district where hip young artists cross paths with some of the city's more pious personages. He constantly checks on his father, managing a round-the-clock schedule of lectures and travels that seems appropriate for a man half his father's age. Steinsaltz usually teaches each night until 10:30 P.M., and will often get home between 1 and 2 A.M. His only break is his afternoon nap, which is "almost holy," Meni says.

"His pace? I think he's remarkable," he says. But this is the way he remembers his father always having been: learning constantly, sleeping sparingly. "I always saw him with a book ranging from

Talmud to science fiction, and not necessarily at different times," Meni recalls. "I'd wake up from a nightmare and he was up, sitting on the couch, reading a book."

At some point, his family tried to rein in his schedule. Steinsaltz, who has the metabolic disorder Gaucher's disease, is not in the best of health. But instead of slowing him down, the opposite seems to have happened. "The thought that his time was limited, that made him work especially hard," Meni explains.

When he was younger, having a father constantly on the go and increasingly in the public eyes sometimes meant he was not around as much as his children wished. "Once you make a decision to give your life to the public," Meni says, "often your family suffers." To make up for it, they often skipped having Shabbat guests, because Fridays and Saturday were for family only.

"The moral of the house was that knowledge comes before all else," recalls Meni, quoting the gist of a maxim his father taught him: "It is better to be a heretic than an ignoramus." At the same time, he says, though Steinsaltz sits firmly in the Orthodox world, he has actively engaged with and accepted leaders of different streams of Judaism. "In our house we've had Reform rabbis, Conservative rabbis," Meni recalls. "We understood that they are a part of the conversation. They are all part of one big thing. I think his mission in life is something we as a family will carry forward."

. . .

While not aligned with any party, Steinsaltz has sometimes taken positions that have propelled him into the political fray. Following the Six Day War in 1967, in which Israel occupied the West Bank, east Jerusalem, the Gaza Strip and the Golan Heights, Steinsaltz was one of those rabbinic voices suggesting that, were it a means to saving lives (*pikuach nefesh*), a land-for-peace compromise with Israel's Arab neighbors was conceivable. This position ran counter to those of other influential rabbis who said it was forbidden that a Jewish state, once in control of any part of the Land of Israel, would willingly forfeit it to another people.

This theoretical flexibility aside, Steinsaltz has been supportive of controversial West Bank settlements, founding a boys' high school in the settlement of Kfar Etzion and a *hesder yeshiva* – a seminary that combines religious study with military service – in the settlement of Tekoa. "Halachicly speaking, it would have been permissible to make territorial concessions...However, at this point in time the question should not be asked, since in the current situation there is no room to talk about peace," Steinsaltz said in a speech in April 1970. Published in a collection of his speeches and articles, his point sounds like a quote any major figure on the Israeli Right might have given to a newspaper reporter only yesterday.

Abroad, Steinsaltz is better known for his books and for educational outreach through organizations such as the Aleph Society, which he established in 1988. It has centers in New York, London, Melbourne and Israel. The organization is aimed at giving Jews "access to fundamental texts, the skills with which to understand those texts, the motivation to study, and an appreciation for the contributions of fellow Jews of all backgrounds," its mission statement says. The Aleph Society's website features, among other things, a user-friendly commentary on the *daf yomi* (daily page of Talmud), which is studied the world over until each tractate of the Talmud is completed – a cycle that takes about seven-and-a-half years.

Recently, Steinsaltz stirred more than a little controversy when he joined a movement of rabbis to restore the Sanhedrin. The highest court in the Jewish tradition and a body that once commanded universal authority over the entire Jewish people, the Sanhedrin was last functional in the year 358, although some say it was in power until 425, when the rabbinic patriarchate was abolished. The medieval scholar Maimonides (Rambam) was keen on reviving the Sanhedrin and, with his plan in hand, several rabbis met in 2004 in Tiberius to work toward re-establishing the body according to Maimonides' proposal. The group elected Steinsaltz as their president, and they continue to meet every month.

Ask two Jews, the saying goes, get three opinions. The prospect of one body to oversee Jewish affairs raises worried eyebrows for many, including those within the Orthodox world. Steinsaltz has worked to allay fears, saying he understands why the concept is off-putting.

"It's no wonder that these things frighten people," he said in his acceptance speech in 2004, according to the *Haaretz* newspaper. "There are people who are concerned about what is emerging here. And where is it headed?" He answered his own question by saying that restarting the Sanhedrin was a process that could take generations to complete, and that there was no rush to set up a body that could be seen as a threat to existing institutions, from the Supreme Court to the Israeli Rabbinate.

"We will do things with an eye toward future generations, not with a stopwatch and an annual calendar. The Jewish calendar is a calendar of thousands of years. A lot of patience and a lot of work are needed. I'd be happy if in another few years these chairs are filled by scholars who are greater than us and we can say: 'I kept the chairs warm for you.'"

Steinsaltz also said at the time that a rabbi has a right to engage in public issues, but to do so he has to have all the appropriate material before him, whether he is "dealing with the kosher status of a chicken or the disengagement."

The rabbi can be as enigmatic as he is witty. While he still believes in the idea of re-establishing the Sanhedrin (Meni insists it's just his father's "hobby"), Steinsaltz has also spoken out against what he calls "religious atavism," criticizing the tendency in the *haredi* (ultra-Orthodox) world to assume that turning the clock back is a route to redemption.

What's important, he says, is to keep asking questions.

"When I ask God questions, I can only hope for limited answers," he told an audience in Miami in 2005. "I have a right to ask. Every child has a right to cry. But not every cry has a right to be answered with a kiss. And not every question has a right to be answered quickly or soothingly."

JOSEPH TELUSHKIN

by KEN GORDON

Rabbi Joseph Telushkin is on the phone. "Larry," says Telushkin, "I gotta get off. Somebody just came into my house." But Larry continues. And Telushkin waits. Politely.

Five minutes go by. Ten minutes. Phone to ear, Telushkin listens as he wanders the book-infested apartment that serves as his office, located on Manhattan's Upper West Side. Telushkin tries again. "Larry, I'm gonna have to get off," but Larry has Telushkin's attention and isn't about to relinquish it. One imagines that Telushkin spends a lot of time here listening to the dilemmas of friends, family, colleagues and acquaintances. When you're a renowned ethicist and Jewish-knowledge specialist, you probably get a healthy number of urgent phone calls. "Larry, I gotta get off," Telushkin says.

Eventually, he hangs up. And he doesn't say a word about Larry. He doesn't even sigh or emit an "oy." It's his first ethical lesson of the day: an embodiment of the idea that we should avoid *lashon hara* (malicious gossip).

Ethical lessons are something Telushkin has devoted a great deal of time and effort to imparting. Whether through his books such as *A Code of Jewish Ethics, Volume 1: You Shall Be Holy*, recipient of the Jewish Book Council's 2006 Jewish Book of the Year Award, his lectures (*Talk* magazine named him one of the fifty best speakers in America), his efforts to create National Speak No Evil Day, his sermons, or even his Hollywood scripts, Telushkin's focus is to encourage people to improve their character. "God's central demand of human beings is to act ethically," he writes in *A Code of Jewish Ethics*.

Doing the right thing isn't so difficult, he explains – and that's his gift. In his hands, ethics aren't abstract and august. The premise of his *Book of Jewish Values: A Day by Day Guide to Ethical Living* (2000), which became the subject of a PBS special, is to make ethical awareness a part of our daily lives.

In terms of accessibility and ubiquity, you can't do much better than an online advice column, and Telushkin's done that, too. In the early 2000s, he spent two years writing "Everyday Ethics" for BeliefNet.com, an interfaith website. In the column, he explored the ethical ramifications of questions posed by readers who wanted to know everything from how to deal with pesky telemarketers to whether it's right for someone in need to receive a kidney from an executed Chinese prisoner. Telushkin's 2003 book, *The Ten Commandments of Character: Essential Advice for Living an Honorable, Ethical, Honest Life*, collects the best of the columns.

"Telushkin was a rare talent – both deep and accessible at the same time," recalls editor Steve Wauldman. Telushkin's column "was not just for Jews, by the way. You always had the sense he was drawing on the wisdom of the ages but he applied it to twenty-first-century dilemmas."

Telushkin, a Brooklyn native, wears a white T-shirt emblazoned with the letters NYC, black pants, black socks (no shoes), and, of course, a kippah. He has a scholar's soft body and inevitable beard. His informal appearance seems at odds with his impressive resume.

He's been a Jerusalem Fellow and sits on the board of the influential Jewish Book Council. To date, he has published fifteen books. His more well-known titles include *Biblical Literacy: The Most Important People, Events and Ideas of the Hebrew Bible* (1997), a Book-of-the-Month Club selection, and *Jewish Literacy: The Most Important Things to Know About the Jewish Religion, Its People and Its History* (1991), which his website reports is "the most widely selling book on Judaism of the past two decades."

Not all of Telushkin's writing is what you would expect of your typical rabbi. There's his series of Rabbi Daniel Winters mysteries and *Heaven's Witness*, the thriller he co-authored about reincarnation. Even more unexpected are his movie and television scripts. He co-wrote the screenplay for the Saul Rubinek film *The Quarrel* (1991) and has penned episodes of *Touched by an Angel, Boston Public* and *The Practice.*

In terms of rabbinic-Hollywood relations, Telushkin is probably in a category of his own. Since the early 1990s he has served as rabbi at the Los Angeles-based Synagogue of the Performing Arts, which he describes as "a very part-time congregation that meets the first Friday night of each month and Rosh Hashanah and Yom Kippur." Telushkin has cut back on his time there to the High Holidays and five services during the year.

What does it mean to be the rabbi for the Synagogue of the Performing Arts? Sometimes it means being privy to confessions that congregants might never tell a rabbi who wasn't also a writer. Take Kirk Douglas, for example, the impetus for a script Telushkin wrote. "Mr. Douglas had said to me, 'Before I die, I want to be in a movie in which I put on tefillin.' It was important for him to do."

The idea became "Bar Mitzvah," an episode from the 2000 season of *Touched by an Angel.* Douglas plays a secular man who owns a string of gyms, clashes with his son about faith, and in the end learns lessons about religion and about himself during his grandson's bar mitzvah preparation.

Asked if he incorporates ethical lessons into his fiction, Telushkin says, "I do. You know, I'm boringly consistent."

While the forms – television, Hollywood movies – are not the traditional platform for Jewish ethics, the marriage of ethics and storytelling is nothing new. "Morality has generally been taught in two ways: through binding legal rules and principles, and through stories. Both exert a profound effect...this is how Jewish tradition has long taught ethics," Telushkin writes in *A Code of Jewish Ethics*.

Telushkin makes liberal use of stories and anecdotes in *A Code of Jewish Ethics*, which he calls his life's work. It was called "a landmark work" by the *Jewish Week*, "the first major code of Jewish ethics to be written in English."

Why the focus on ethics? Telushkin's concern is that over time, Judaism has come to equate ritual observance with religion, with ethics being left out of the equation. "One of the sad things to happen to Jewish life in modernity is that the word 'religious' became associated in people's lives exclusively with ritual observance," says Telushkin. "So that when two Jews are speaking about a third and the question is raised, 'Is so-and-so religious?' He keeps kosher, he keeps Shabbat, he is or he doesn't or he's not, from which one could form the odd impression that in Judaism, ethics are an extracurricular activity."

His goal? "I want to restore ethics to its central place in Judaism," he told *Hadassah Magazine*.

This lack of respect for ethics means a lack of emphasis on kindness, he says. Kindness is sorely needed in our world, and should be one of our highest priorities. And he has an idea about how to nurture kindness, which will in turn influence our world for the better. How? It's simple – praise children for it.

"Parents should reserve the highest praise of their children for when their children perform kind acts," explains Telushkin, who with wife, author Dvorah Menashe Telushkin, has four children. He says that parents praise their children for academic, athletic and/ or cultural achievements, and sometimes even for good looks, but rarely if ever for their kindness. "If children got their highest praise for when they performed kind acts, we'd raise a generation of people who most liked themselves when they were doing kind things.

It would have the capacity down the road to elevate Jewish life and American life."

.   .   .

Telushkin was born in 1948 and raised in a modern Orthodox family. He credits his family with having a strong influence on his life. "I was very deeply affected by my grandfather and my father," he says. "My grandfather was a rabbi in Brooklyn for many years. His first name was Nissan, like the month during which Pesach falls. He was a big scholar, he wrote books. He lived until I was twenty-one, and we learned together. And my father, Shlomo, also had a great effect on me. They were both people who were deeply pious Jews but very much into the tradition of the emphasis on Jewish ethics."

His late mother was also an influence, in a different way. If his grandfather and father (who was also a rabbi, although his career was as an accountant) helped shape the scholar he was to become, his mother played a role in fashioning the dynamic speaker and entertaining writer. She was "a very clear speaker; my mother was very humorous," Telushkin says. She had "an impact on my speaking style. My father was a wonderful person, but not as funny."

Telushkin attended the Yeshiva of Flatbush where he had an academic career that was, to put it charitably, undistinguished. "I was a *terrible* student at school," he says, admitting he graduated in the bottom quarter of his class. But the yeshiva had its good points. The school taught him Hebrew and gave him "a very voluble sense that here's an active Judaism, you can be part of the world, part of the Jewish people, and very Zionist, very bound up with Israel." It also introduced him to fellow student and future collaborator Dennis Prager. "Dennis was an even worse student than me," says Telushkin.

Telushkin didn't grow up planning to be a rabbi; although it was always a possibility, he was more interested in writing, and in college he also became interested in law. "I realized that Judaism was such a passion for me that if I chose another profession, that would be my vocation and Judaism would be my avocation, so there was an advantage to being a rabbi," he told the *Atlanta Jewish Times*.

He attended New York's Yeshiva University for both college and rabbinical school.

While at Yeshiva University in the late 1960s and early 1970s, Telushkin became involved in the movement to get Jews out of Soviet Russia. So did his friend Prager, who now hosts a nationally syndicated radio talk show and is the author of several books, some in collaboration with Telushkin, including their first book, the widely popular *Eight Questions People Ask About Judaism* (1977).

That book developed in a roundabout way, out of other work they were involved in. "I was the co-president of the Student Struggle for Soviet Jewry," Telushkin says. "At around the same time, Dennis was doing the same thing for the Russian Jewry movement. He had gone to Russia, and was one of the early Jews to meet with the *refuse-niks*, and he came out and became a very galvanizing force."

As Telushkin recalls, he and Prager were both giving frequent talks and Prager was struck by the fact that many of the questions people asked, apart from the issues of Soviet Jewry, were very similar. Regardless of whether the questions were from Reform Jews, Orthodox Jews, or members of Hadassah, the things they wanted to know were the same. The two, only twenty-four years old at the time, sat down and made a list of frequently asked questions, which they further developed into the book, *Eight Questions People Ask About Judaism.*

Within six years, *Eight Questions* sold over thirty thousand copies. Telushkin was enrolled in graduate school in history at Columbia and was close to receiving his doctorate, but as the book became a popular success he grew convinced of the power of writing and devoted more time to it. Originally self-published, he and Prager updated the book and added another question, "Is there a difference between anti-Zionism and anti-Semitism?" and Simon and Schuster published it in 1981 as *Nine Questions People Ask About Judaism.*

"The book could not have been written by one of us alone," says Prager. "We were certain that if Joseph had written the book, it would have been nine hundred pages of stories; and if I had written the book, it would have been a fifty-page outline of ideas."

.   .   .

Clearly, Telushkin's natural inclination is to instruct through stories. But he teaches in other ways as well. In addition to all the ways he has found to tell stories that impart ethics, he also conveys ethics through example.

"To me, writing these books on ethics has obviously made me more conscious of my own behavior, and I watch myself more carefully," he says.

"Joseph is incredibly compassionate, first to those around him and also to those he does not know," says Ari L. Goldman, Telushkin's friend, a professor at the Columbia School of Journalism and a former *New York Times* religion writer. "If someone is out of work, he tries to find them a job. If they have a job, he tries to find them a better one. He has helped me with numerous writing projects.

"And now for the people he doesn't know: We live in Manhattan, a place of much noise and many ambulances. If an ambulance goes by with the siren wailing, most people will stop talking and impatiently wait for it to go by. But when Joseph hears a siren, he whispers a prayer: '*Kel nah, refah nah lah.*' That is the prayer that Moses said for his sister, 'God, please heal her.' Moses said it for his sister; Joseph says it for total strangers."

He prays for strangers, and in many ways he prizes his writing for its ability to help him connect to strangers. His work speaks to Jews of all stripes. "There is not a typical reader of my books," he says. "I am as apt to get questions from people in the right wing of the Orthodox world, to people in left-wing Reform, to non-Jews. I think I've managed to isolate Jewish teachings for the human condition."

"No one I know has done more to make Judaism accessible to a wide audience," says Goldman, who sits near Telushkin at Ramath Orah, the modern Orthodox shul they both attend in Manhattan. "His book, *Jewish Literacy*, put our traditions in the hands and hearts of so many people. It is a book that says this is a long and sacred tradition – and it can be meaningful in your life. He writes with joy and clarity."

Telushkin's gift for writing and his passion for ethics came together in 1996, when he dreamed up the idea for a day in which all

Americans refrained from indulging in lashon hara. He pitched the concept to Connecticut senator Joseph Lieberman and Florida senator Connie Mack, who approved the idea and, to Telushkin's surprise, asked him to write up the resolution for what became Senate Resolution #151, National Speak No Evil Day. Alas, the bill failed to pass.

America, it seems, still has a long way to go when it comes to embracing ethics in everyday life. Not many would pass Telushkin's ethical test of going twenty-four hours without uttering an unkind word.

Why is Telushkin so against evil speech? It has to do with the power of words, and the responsibility of wordslingers. As he writes in *Words That Hurt, Words That Heal*: "That words are powerful may seem obvious, but the fact is that most of us, most of the time, use them lightly. We choose our clothes more carefully than we choose our words, though what we say *about* and *to* others can define them indelibly. That is why ethical speech – speaking fairly of others, honestly about ourselves and carefully to everyone – is so important. If we keep the power of words in the foreground of our consciousness, we will handle them as carefully as we would a loaded gun."

If Telushkin was disappointed by the failure of Resolution #151, it has hardly slowed him down. His goal continues to be "to try and express my writing through as many different forms as possible."

And yet, despite all the books, and despite the larger audience reached through television, film and the Internet, Telushkin sees much still to be done. He is at work on the second volume of *A Code of Jewish Ethics*. Subtitled *Love Your Neighbor as Yourself*, it focuses on ethical situations within the workplace and within our communities. After that he'll produce volume three, dealing with ethical issues closer to home, indeed within the home – showing how moral acts deepen our relationships with those we love most – family.

"My work is very much trying to teach the sort of life I should lead and others should lead," he explains. His life is his work, and his work is being a Jewish ethical teacher *par excellence*, a vocation that comes in many forms. Whether it's on the page, at the podium, on the screen or on the phone, chances are good that he's saying something that can help make you a better person or this world a better place. Listen closely.

AVIVAH ZORNBERG

by SARAH BRONSON

Writing a commentary on the Torah is not for the faint of heart. The undertaking necessitates breadth and depth of knowledge in the Bible, Talmud, *midrash* and almost a thousand years of commentary on those texts. And yet, the study and creation of midrash – the interpretation of biblical texts, the search for meaning in enigmatic verses and stories, the quest to "figure out what God really meant" – has been the essence of Torah study for thousands of years.

To tease new meanings and discover hidden nuances in the Torah is a significant accomplishment. In the case of Avivah Gottlieb Zornberg, it is noteworthy on several additional levels: she began her career not as a Torah teacher but as a scholar of English literature; she has developed a unique technique for interpreting the Torah, weaving together ideas from secular philosophy, psychology and literature with traditional Jewish texts; she is the product of an ultra-

Orthodox seminary where the idea of women earning PhD's, and of using ideas from the secular world to shed light on the Torah, is considered unusual at best and taboo at worst; and her work has been published by a general-audience publisher and is read by Christians and secular philosophers as well as Jews.

In person, Zornberg, in her mid-sixties, is a modestly dressed, attractive woman with a calming presence. Her voice is soft, and lilts slightly with a Scottish accent. In conversation, as in her lectures, one listens closely because she speaks quietly; however, there is nothing retiring about her. She is assured and articulate, and the musicality of her speech does not veil the underlying assertiveness.

Zornberg is internationally known as a gifted interpreter and teacher of the weekly Torah portion. For more than two decades, she has taught the weekly portion to thousands of students at women's and coeducational institutions in Jerusalem including Matan, Pardes, Midreshet Lindenbaum, the Jerusalem College for Adults at the Orthodox Union's Israel Center, and at the Kol Rina Synagogue in central Jerusalem. Her lectures regularly draw hundreds of men and women. Bill Moyers chose her to be one of a handful of scholars interviewed in his 1995 PBS series on Genesis.

In describing her teaching style, Zornberg has written that her approach is "to share my own personal struggles for meaning, to discover the ways in which life and text inform each other. My audiences...[are] in the position of 'eavesdropping' on my meditations, on the literary and philosophical resonances emerging from these texts...my way of reading these sources...is a kind of *listening* for the meta-messages in the text."

Her first book, *The Beginning of Desire: Reflections on Genesis* (Jewish Publication Society, 1995; Doubleday, 1996), won the 1995 Jewish Book Award for nonfiction. Her second book, *The Particulars of Rapture: Reflections on Exodus* (Doubleday, 2001), deepened her reputation as one of Orthodoxy's great contemporary biblical commentators.

What makes Zornberg's work unique is the range of disciplines and rigorous application of knowledge she brings to bear on the Judaic texts. Zornberg fuses her mastery of literature and other secular studies, particularly philosophy and psychoanalysis, with her passion for Judaic texts. An instructor of English Literature at the Hebrew University in the early 1970s, Zornberg is just as likely to quote Rousseau as the Rambam, and finds as much inspiration in Thomas Mann as in the Malbim.

"Avivah is a fantastic lecturer," says David Bernstein, dean of the Pardes Institute of Jewish Studies in Jerusalem, and both a former student and an employer of Zornberg's. "She has an extremely broad scope of both Torah and general knowledge. She brings together worlds, which is exciting for listeners. Her training as a PhD in English literature, her command of the Torah, her modern and post-modern analytical tools, create a full and fresh picture of the text. Her approach is rooted in tradition but synthesizes all these fields, and makes the biblical text come alive. I don't think there is anyone else teaching *parsha* [the weekly Torah portion] in the English language who is getting as many people to hear them as she is."

At a lecture at the Pardes Institute, Zornberg discussed the story in Numbers, chapter 27, in which the daughters of Tzelafchad approach Moses and ask why their family should lose its apportioned share of the Land of Israel just because their father had no sons. Moses turns the question to God, who declares that the women are correct, and then proceeds to outline the Jewish laws of inheritance. "Why," Zornberg asked the class, "does the Bible present these laws in the context of a story, rather than simply state the laws outright? What have we to learn from this story of Tzelafchad's five daughters that is so important that the Torah devotes precious space to recounting it?"

Zornberg paused as the students – including several attending the class via two-way satellite video from Boston's Hebrew College – took notes or considered the question. Soon, a few students offered suggestions; Zornberg acknowledged their theories as valid before going on to explain her own in a one-hour lecture.

During the class, Zornberg quoted Ralph Waldo Emerson at length, explaining his ideas about individual autonomy and the process through which a person actualizes his or her humanity. The story of Tzelafchad's daughters was soon transformed into a statement about the importance placed on the individual, the way the Torah sees itself as an organic text, and the ideal, here implied by God, that ideas should first come from the people and if an idea is true, He will countersign it. Far from being a story about inheritance laws, Zornberg said, the anecdote is a statement of God's pleasure in the people, in our ability to interpret and even anticipate His will.

Reading the Torah through the lens of Emerson is not, in itself, a unique approach; many Orthodox rabbis and other teachers will "hook" their audience into a Torah discussion by first quoting a secular source and then showing that the Torah expressed the same idea centuries earlier. But Zornberg does not use secular sources to provide more weight to the Torah; rather, she uses all the texts in her vast memory store as equal players in what she calls the "force field" of interpretation.

"I used to do the fairly conventional thing," she remembers of her beginning days as a Bible lecturer in the early 1980s. "I'd say, 'here is an idea,' and then illustrate it [with a text] from the secular world. And then I began to feel that what I really wanted to do was to weave a tapestry, in which here would be Emerson, and here would be the Sfat Emet [late nineteenth-century Gerer Rebbe], and here would be Rashi [eleventh-century biblical commentator] – and then you can see how one reacts on the other. There is a force field in it that I like, rather than staying within the central experience [of the Torah text] and maybe peeping out every now and then to see what else is going on in the [secular] world."

The traditional *midrashim* – which Zornberg uses in her analysis of the Torah – are commonly taught in Jewish day schools, but Zornberg's approach teases out new layers of meaning that are surprising in their direction and depth.

For example, many are familiar with an ancient legend about Abraham. According to the story, Abraham's father, Terach, owned a shop in which he sold idols. Realizing that a higher power must have created the universe, Abraham smashed the idols, leading his father to turn Abraham over to the king, Nimrod, for punishment. Nimrod and Terach arranged to burn Abraham to death in a furnace, but Abraham miraculously survived the three-day burning unscathed.

Zornberg points out that the simplest explanation for the popularity of this story is that it establishes Abraham's credentials as the progenitor of the Jewish people. But in lectures about the *Akeidah* – the Binding of Isaac – Zornberg says this early event in Abraham's life sheds light on his psychological profile, and helps explain why he was willing to sacrifice his son.

"The Chasidim say that Abraham was confused by God's instructions, and wondered what God had really meant for him to do," she says. "Rashi says that God clarifies to Abraham, when they reach the mountaintop, that He had said to 'raise' Isaac, not to kill him. We must be alive to the implications of this statement. God is saying to Abraham 'you misunderstood me.' But a human being is not asked to consider sacrificing his son, only to have it trivialized by God later."

By applying ideas from psychoanalysis to the furnace story, we can understand how Abraham experienced the mission, she says. "The fact that Abraham's father condemned him to die in a furnace is a repressed level of experience. There was no other way Abraham could have understood God's instructions, given who he was and what he'd gone through. Of course he would hear it [as instructions to kill Isaac]."

The culmination of the Binding, the fact that Abraham "is developed enough to hear the angel calling, stopping him," means that Abraham is now at the point that he can ascribe a different meaning to God's mission, to understand that 'to raise him' means to bring Isaac to the mountain, but that the killing is unnecessary. "He is able to interpret the prophecy now because he is in a different place [psychologically]. This is a story of what Abraham is capable of understanding," she says, adding that by interpreting the story this way, it becomes relatable to anyone who feels that he or she has been "sacrificed by their parents," literally or metaphorically. The Akeidah is, in one sense, the story of the abused child becoming an abuser, and redeeming himself from his trauma just in time to avoid repeating it.

In her approach to the Bible, Zornberg is "trying to make something which hopefully remains authentic, but which touches people, which touches me and other people where they really live, which is often a conflicted place, where there are a number of things going on. [My students] feel that something is speaking to that [conflicted place], rather than looking upwards and trying to simplify, simplify, simplify.

"I don't know if simplifying appeals to me so much," she says. "I like complexifying."

Indeed, most everything in Zornberg's religious outlook and scholarly work is complex, even her description of her ideal student. "I like someone who is curious and creative and seeking, who is clearly an individual and not a type, who is struggling in a unique way," she says. "People who seem to have found too many answers sort of lose me. I like to have young people who are bubbling and still a little bit troubled. I like people who are a little anguished."

Is Zornberg anguished? "Yes," she says, "about death, about bad things happening to righteous people, about the Holocaust. The inner burdens that people have to bear. What it means to be a person. Why is that so hard for so many people? But I'm happy too. I also have great joy and great love."

Teaching is among the highest of Zornberg's great loves, after her husband and three adult children (playing the piano is also on her list of joys). Preparing lectures – facing a biblical text and sculpting something new and unique to say, dwelling in the force fields between every book and every poem she has ever read – is both frightening and exhilarating.

Her favorite verse is Psalms 119:92, in which King David says of the Torah, "If your law had not been my delight, I would have perished in my affliction." Zornberg notes that the Hebrew word "sha'a'shuah," normally translated as "delight," literally means "plaything." The constellation of ideas she has encountered and the questions presented by the Torah's choices of words is her playground.

What is it that draws her to analyze, interpret and reinterpret the same texts year after year? "It's the material, the opportunity to express ideas and feelings," she says. "It's a strange mixture of the didactic and the creative." Forming her lectures into books affords another level of pleasure, since writing allows for more precision and control in articulation, and results in "something you can actually hold onto afterward. In teaching, everything disappears. You hope something has lodged in someone's soul."

. . .

Avivah Gottlieb was born in 1944 and grew up in Glasgow, Scotland. Her father, Rabbi Dr. Wolf Gottlieb, was the head of the Jewish Court there and Zornberg's first and most influential Torah teacher. She attended local secular schools and, after classes, studied Jewish texts with her father.

Studying with her father "was an enviable experience," she recalls, "in the sense of the connection with a world of loving God, loving Torah, loving the Jewish people, loving me. It was an experience of Torah and of a world that is hard to duplicate."

As a child in a small Galician village, Rabbi Gottlieb had shown such promise in Torah studies that his parents, feeling that his potential outstripped their abilities to teach him, sent him to live with his scholarly grandfather in a larger town within Galicia. Eventually Zornberg's father moved to Vienna where he received a doctorate and several rabbinical ordinations. Interested in modern scholarship as well as Jewish studies, Rabbi Gottlieb was "alert and curious and interested in life," Zornberg says. "His mind was open to all kinds of things, and it came across in his way of teaching. There was an openness, not a rigidity, which sat strangely well with his quite serious religiousness. He was a pious person. He had lots of wonderful stories about the world he came from, the Chasidic world."

Even more important than the hours Zornberg spent with her father learning to read Rashi or interpret a passage of Talmud were "the emotional things," she says, "like memories of hearing him chant the words as he studied Talmud. There is something very moving about that melody, something romantic. There is a feeling of a vanished world."

At seventeen, Zornberg left Glasgow for the internationally renowned women's seminary in Gateshead, England. Religiously, she was "on fire, very passionate," she says, in the way that many older teenage girls are fervently spiritual. Her path led her to Cambridge University, where she earned a PhD in English literature. She immigrated to Israel in 1969, began teaching English literature at the Hebrew University, and in 1975 married Eric Zornberg, a physicist from the U.S. with a PhD who decided, upon his immigration to Israel, that he preferred to work with his hands; he has a successful career fixing washing machines and dryers, "to the envy of some of his academic friends," Zornberg notes, smiling.

It was in Israel that she encountered one of her role models, Tamar Ross, a professor of Jewish philosophy at Bar-Ilan University and the mother of seven children, who is just six years older than Zornberg. "When I was at that tentative age, in my early twenties, without any idea what I'd do in the world, she was fascinating," Zornberg says of Ross. "She came from a privileged Orthodox intellectual background. There was a quality that she is who she is and she has got this great mind."

Zornberg was impressed by Ross's "quite daring, quite radical, but well-documented theories about feminism and about many other things. She can't do anything without being both original and extremely thorough. She's very unusual, and very religious, of a type that when I was younger was very important to me."

Zornberg and Ross remain in touch. Ross says of Zornberg, "We were both educated against the stream. My father was a rabbi, her father was a *dayan* [judge in Jewish courts]. Both fathers gave us an intensive Jewish education that was far more ambitious than the norm in those days. And our religious attachments were strong, despite the fact that we were both exposed to a very good secular education. I think what interested her in me was the way I combined the two. To see people who were able to be intellectually honest and nevertheless fervently committed to Jewish tradition was very liberating for her."

Ross was also instrumental in encouraging Zornberg to teach

Torah. In the late 1970s, Zornberg left the Hebrew University, where her lack of published work was threatening her career. "It was publish or perish, and I perished," Zornberg says, and then jokes: "It turned out to be a *tchiyat hameitim* [resurrection of the dead]."

At Ross's urging, Zornberg began teaching at Midreshet Lindenbaum, an Orthodox institution for young women. Over time she was invited to teach Torah at an ever-growing roster of schools, and slowly developed her now-renowned technique of biblical interpretation.

"Dr. Zornberg is a very creative and innovative Torah scholar," says Malke Bina, educational director of the Matan Women's Institute for Torah Studies. "She has created a new, exciting, inspirational and introspective way to learn Torah. If you say that learning can be three-dimensional, I'd say she is ten-dimensional."

The weekly class lectures led to Zornberg's first two books, in which each chapter corresponds to a weekly Torah portion. Like her classes, the books search the verses and themes of the Torah not to find answers, but to find new questions, focusing heavily on the psychological and existential conflicts in biblical characters and texts.

Both books have earned critical acclaim. In a 2001 *Washington Post* review of *The Particulars of Rapture,* reporter and Middle East expert Paul William Roberts wrote:

> [the book] is quite simply a masterpiece. I know of no other book that presents the enormous subtleties and complexities of rabbinic Biblical interpretation with such skill, intelligence, literary flair and sheer elegance of style. Zornberg's dazzlingly eclectic erudition would be oppressive in the hands of a lesser writer, but such is the beauty and succinctness of her writing that her references to Thomas Mann, Wordsworth, Isaiah Berlin, Wallace Stevens, Susan Sontag, and Freud, to name but a few, seem more like the illuminated letters in medieval manuscripts, heightening both beauty and meaning... Her purpose here, however, is not so much to explain the midrashic technique...as to show that technique in action.

Though Zornberg accepts praise of her work with equanimity, she denies that her books are revolutionary. "I just try to convey my excitement about what I'm noticing," she says. "I think what is there, hidden or not-so-hidden in the text is so interesting and so moving, and it addresses people where they really live. And if people haven't noticed it before, well, it always happens, history moves on; someone has to be the first to point out that there is psychoanalytic understandings in the sages, the midrash, and Chasidism. It is very helpful to think a little differently from the way people have thought up until now. In a way, it seems so obvious to me that I do not feel daring about it."

A common observation, especially in Jewish media reviews of her books, is that Zornberg is only the second Orthodox woman after Nechama Leibowitz to publish a Torah commentary. However, being female has never stood in the way of her teaching or lecturing. If there have been criticisms of her writing Torah interpretations as a woman, she has never heard them herself, she says. The modern Orthodox community has embraced her, and reaction from the ultra-Orthodox world ranges from praise to avoidance.

Perhaps this acceptance is because, although Zornberg gives significant weight to secular ideas, she never addresses the questions of whether the Torah is true or not, who wrote it, or why she chooses to observe Orthodox Jewish law. Ross notes that Zornberg's "views in between the lines are more sophisticated than the ordinary believer, so she can accommodate historical analysis and literary criticism, and it doesn't touch her religious approach to the text. She is not bound to a fundamentalist view about how the Torah developed. These topics are not relevant for her. That is what makes her capable of speaking to all audiences."

Looking forward, Zornberg is content to continue teaching, writing, and interpreting. Her next book, about communication and the unconscious in the Torah narrative, is forthcoming from Schocken Books.

"It releases something in me," she says of her studies and her teaching, "almost like poetry. A feeling of creating something beautiful which takes its energy from what I sense in the text. When I'm teaching, when I'm writing, it's not my whole self, but it is the best part of me."

EFRAIM ZUROFF

by DAVID GREEN

How would you picture a "Nazi hunter"? Stern, dour, a chain smoker with angular features and a bad coffee habit? Efraim Zuroff, who has devoted the better part of his career to tracking down war criminals who have at this point escaped justice for six decades, does not fit this description.

He's a cheerful, approachable, gregarious, essentially optimistic ex-basketball player from Brooklyn who ends every phone conversation and meeting by urging his interlocutor to "take it easy." Despite repeatedly confronting some of the darkest behavior in the history of civilization, Zuroff believes that humanity is capable of improving its performance and, through the educational work he does, is trying to bring that change about.

Considering the time that's passed since the end of World War II, one may wonder why Zuroff, who is often referred to as the world's last Nazi hunter, is still at it. Are there even Nazis left to hunt? The answer is: not many. And those who are still alive are generally in their eighties or older, and are often in a physical or mental condition that is more likely to evoke pity than a desire for vengeance. (Zuroff calls this the "misplaced sympathy syndrome.")

But Zuroff's work isn't about vengeance, it's about justice, and in his moral universe, justice can only be based on truth, on historical accuracy. As long as there are individuals who are living on fabricated identities, having concealed from the world the acts they perpetrated during the war – not to mention nations that persist in refusing to acknowledge their recent histories – then the fight for the truth is still being waged, and Zuroff remains a busy man.

But what of the arguments that the remaining Nazis are too old to undergo trials, that they don't pose a threat to society, that they should be left to live out their last years in peace? Zuroff replies to these questions readily; years of thought have honed his responses. He has several answers, among them: "The passage of time in no way diminishes the guilt of the perpetrator," "Killers do not deserve a prize for reaching old age," "Every victim deserves that an effort be made to bring their murderer to justice," "There is such a thing as moral pollution…if society does not prosecute these people. That's a stain on society's morality, and it undermines the underpinnings of society," and that to stop prosecuting people at a certain age would be tantamount to allowing people to get away with genocide.

The home of the Simon Wiesenthal Center's Israel office, which Zuroff has directed since 1986, is a modest office on the ground floor of a small apartment building in Talbiyeh, an upscale Jerusalem neighborhood.

Nazi-hunting today lacks some of the drama that one associates with the kidnapping by Israeli agents of Adolf Eichmann, one of the architects of the Final Solution, from in front of his house in Buenos Aires, Argentina, in 1960. (Eichmann was secretly flown back to Israel, tried and convicted for "crimes against humanity," and executed.)

The type of Nazi-hunting Zuroff does is more likely to take

place in archives than it is in the dark alleys or smoky taverns of South American border towns, and the skills required are those of a researcher well-versed in history, geography and languages. In short, it's painstaking, nitty-gritty research. This makes someone like Zuroff, whose doctoral dissertation in history at the Hebrew University dealt with aspects of the Holocaust, well placed to work in the field.

Zuroff is "a force of conscience internationally" who is "indefatigable in pursuing justice," according to Eli Rosenbaum, head of the Office of Special Investigations (OSI) of the U.S. Justice Department. Zuroff, he adds, "has felt to the depth of his being the stories of the victims and the survivors and devoted his life to acting on their behalf."

. . .

Zuroff had a comfortable upbringing in a middle-class Orthodox Jewish family in Flatbush, Brooklyn. Both of his parents were American-born, and the family was barely touched by the Holocaust. The one exception was Zuroff's maternal great-uncle, one of six brothers, and the only one who remained in his native Lithuania (then Poland) in the decades preceding World War II. A scholar and yeshiva head from Vilna, the uncle was killed, together with his family, by the Nazis in Ponar, in 1941. Confirmation of his death only reached the family in 1948, when Effie's grandfather, Samuel Sar, a communal leader in the U.S. and one of the founders of Yeshiva University in New York, was in Europe, organizing the religious needs of Jewish survivors still living in displaced-persons camps.

Sar's mission in Europe coincided with the birth of his first grandson. When Zuroff's father cabled his father-in-law to tell him he had become a grandfather, Samuel wrote back: "Suggest naming him Efraim," in memory of his murdered brother.

Despite that legacy, Zuroff says that while he was growing up, in the 1950s and '60s, the Holocaust "was not a topic" in his home. In that sense, his family was no different from most other American Jews, including strongly identifying ones. It's not that the subject was forbidden, he says – "it just wasn't of interest." In those years, American Jewry was looking to the future, not to the past, and its mind, he suggests, was set on "achieving material success, into integrating into society, into making it."

He points to two watershed events that caused Jews – not only in America, but worldwide, including in Israel – to begin examining that darkest chapter in their people's history. One was the Eichmann trial, which Israel used as an opportunity to teach the world many details of the Final Solution; the other was the Six-Day War in 1967. That latter event culminated, of course, in a stunning military victory for Israel, but part of the drama derived from the fact that in the tense lead-up to the war, Israel's Arab neighbors were threatening to destroy the Jewish state.

By then, Zuroff was attending college at Yeshiva University, where both his grandfather and his mother were administrators (his father, Rabbi Abraham Zuroff, was the director of a network of modern-Orthodox high schools in New York). Zuroff says that growing up, he hated being the son of a rabbi, even if his father didn't hold a pulpit, and the grandson of someone very prominent in the Orthodox movement. "It's not that I had something against what they did. Actually I thought that what they were both doing was very good. But I didn't want any part of [it]."

Zuroff spent his junior year, 1968–1969, at the Hebrew University of Jerusalem. At the time, Israel was still in something of a state of euphoria, following the victory of a year earlier. It was his first visit to the country, but a year in Jerusalem was enough to convince him that he wanted to return to Israel to live. He felt, he says, that that was "where it's happening. I didn't want to be a spectator; I wanted to be a participant."

Following his graduation from YU, Zuroff returned to Israel as a new immigrant. He received a scholarship from the Hebrew University to study toward a master's degree in history, in its Institute of Contemporary Jewry. When he had to choose an area of concentration, he realized that "the question that interested me intellectually was: How was the Shoah possible?"

Zuroff's graduate work led to a master's degree and later a

PhD, completed in 1997. His revised doctoral thesis was published as a book, *The Response of Orthodox Jewry in the United States: The Activities of the Va'ad Hahatzala Rescue Committee, 1939–1945* (2000). The book is a critical examination of the work of the group, which the rabbis of the ultra-Orthodox community of the U.S. organized in order to save as many Eastern European rabbis and yeshiva students – and later Jews in general – as possible from death at the hands of the Nazis.

That book was Zuroff's second, following a memoir called *Occupation: Nazi-Hunter: The Continuing Search for the Perpetrators of the Holocaust* (1994) in which Zuroff describes how he began his detective work, and some of the more interesting cases he was involved in up to that point. He has also written over two hundred articles and op-ed pieces, chiefly dealing with the Holocaust and related issues.

After finishing his master's degree, and parallel to the years he spent researching his doctoral thesis, Zuroff worked briefly for Israel's Ministry of Religious Affairs in Jerusalem and also at Yad Vashem, the Holocaust memorial and museum. However, it was only in 1978 that he really found himself set on his career path. That's when he was invited by Rabbi Marvin Hier to go to Los Angeles to become academic director of the newly established Simon Wiesenthal Center for Holocaust Studies (as it was then called; later the last three words were dropped).

By that time, Zuroff was married – to Elisheva Bannett, the Israeli-born daughter of Americans who had immigrated to Israel at the time of independence – with children, and he agreed to leave Israel for only two years.

.   .   .

When he returned to Israel, in 1980, Zuroff spent several years doing contract work as a researcher for the newly formed osi, whose task was to identify war criminals who had immigrated to America after the war under false pretenses. Eventually, in 1986, he opened up the Jerusalem office of the swc, whose main pursuit has continued to be investigations.

The Center was named, of course, for Simon Wiesenthal, the charismatic Viennese Jewish Holocaust survivor who lost most of his family to the Nazis and devoted his life after the war to tracking down escaped Nazis. By the late 1970s and early '80s, Wiesenthal, who had been born in 1908, was slowing down somewhat, while at the same time, says Zuroff, "the focus of the hunt was moving to the Anglo-Saxon world, which had admitted hundreds of thousands of refugees after the war, who included thousands of collaborators and perpetrators." And so the Wiesenthal Center, which had been set up principally as an educational and pressure organization, became increasingly involved in the hunt for fugitive war criminals.

When Zuroff was still working for the OSI, he was assigned to the hunt for Josef Mengele, the infamous doctor of Auschwitz. The U.S. government had received information – incorrect, as it turned out – that Mengele had been briefly held by the Americans after the war, and then-President Ronald Reagan ordered the OSI to search for Mengele. During his investigation, Zuroff realized that he could track many escaped Nazi war criminals by using post-World War II refugee records, a discovery that was a major investigative breakthrough.

The postwar report on Mengele's whereabouts had come from a survivor named David Fryman, who as a prisoner had been assigned to Mengele's laboratory at Auschwitz, and the OSI assigned Zuroff the job of tracking down Fryman. A colleague of Zuroff's, who worked at Yad Vashem, suggested he use the records of the International Tracing Service (ITS), which included basic biographical data about everyone who requested recognition by the International Red Cross as a refugee after the war. (As an aside, Zuroff notes that the ITS files comprise "a significant portion" of the contents of the Bad-Arolsen Archive in Germany, which was recently declassified, to significant fanfare. In fact, the ITS portion of the Bad-Arolsen Archive has been accessible to the public for the past five decades at Yad Vashem.)

"My mistake," says Zuroff today, "was that I thought the ITS had files only of Jewish survivors." As he began to look manually through hundreds of records, in search of information about Fry-man, he realized that "there were tons of non-Jews," something that "immediately lit up a red light in my mind. I thought: We know that lots of war criminals registered [with the Red Cross] under their own names, and immigrated to the West posing as refugees. In theory, this archive is a gold mine because among biographical details listed is where people emigrated, what boat they took on what date, etc."

Zuroff says that he undertook a small experiment, taking the names of fifty Latvians and Lithuanians known to have been involved in war crimes, and searching for them in the ITS files.

"Lo and behold, twenty of the fifty were listed, and the beauty of it was that not only were they listed; it said where they went. And, since among the people whom we found were individuals who had entered countries other than the U.S., like Australia and Canada, it was clear that this information had implications that went way be-yond my job as a researcher for the OSI."

Zuroff went to the SWC, telling it, "I have information that could help us identify the postwar escape of hundreds, maybe thou-sands of Nazi war criminals." Even though at the time only the U.S. had an office whose mission was to take legal action against war crim-inals living within its borders, Canada, Australia and Great Britain had investigations of individuals under way or ready to begin.

Zuroff says he told the SWC, "Let's go for the jugular. Let's convince these countries that they have to take legal action against Nazis, and that the best way to do it is to set up a special office that will deal exclusively with these cases." That, recalls Zuroff, "was re-ally the turning point" – when he realized he had become a "Nazi hunter," that he had gone "from being just another researcher to being a person with a vision, whose scope expanded way beyond the initial work for the Americans, and who was basically trying to make a last-ditch effort to upgrade the entire Nazi-hunting effort in several different countries.

"I started churning out lists of suspects for Canada, the U.S., Australia and the U.K. After I compiled a list of seventeen suspects for the United Kingdom, which the Wiesenthal Center submitted on October 22, 1986 to the British consul in Los Angeles, it basically created the problem of Nazi war criminals in Britain. Whereas in Australia and Canada, there were already investigations going on, our lists helped convince the governments that the issue was very important and urgent." For the latter two countries, Zuroff compiled the names of hundreds of suspects.

All three countries – Canada, Australia and the U.K. – "passed special amendments that enabled criminal prosecution of war criminals in their countries," in 1987, 1989 and 1991, respectively. In the U.S., the legal authorities had already concluded that the Nazis among them could not be prosecuted on criminal charges there. "So they adopted what I jokingly call the 'Al Capone compromise,'" says Zuroff. "They couldn't get them on criminal charges for war crimes, crimes against humanity, so they nailed them on immigration and naturalization violations." Violations because someone who had served, say, as a former concentration camp guard generally left that detail off his resume. More often than not, for both technical and practical reasons, it has been easier to prosecute such people on grounds of having lied on their residency or citizenship applications to their new homes than it has been to prove the crimes they committed during the war.

In practical terms, the results of these efforts had more of an educational and political impact than legal results. Very few prosecutions, and even fewer convictions, actually resulted. This can largely be attributed to the number of years that had passed. In retrospect, notes Zuroff, the U.S. decision to pursue these people on immigration violations rather than war crimes was smart: it was easier to build a case, and yielded better results.

"At the beginning," he acknowledges, "we thought it was a copout, but it turned out to be incredibly successful. The Americans have won cases against 107 Nazi war criminals. That's very serious numbers. And out of the sixty-nine convictions since 2000, thirty-four of them have been in the United States."

For five years, between 1986 and 1991, Zuroff and the SWC concentrated on the "Anglo-Saxon" democracies. Then the Soviet

Union fell, and a new world opened up to the Nazi Hunter. "All of the sudden, we had access to the archives, and to the areas where the crimes took place, to the witnesses."

Zuroff explains the significance of this development. "The difference between Eastern Europe and the rest of Europe, in terms of collaboration with the Nazis, is as follows: Everywhere the Nazis came, they found willing, zealous collaborators, even in Denmark. Even in Bulgaria. But the difference was the following: Let's say in Holland, the Dutch police rounded up Dutch Jewry. In Norway, the Norwegian police rounded up the Jews. And so on. But what these local collaborators did in those countries after rounding the Jews up was to send them to a transit camp, and then put them on trains. They did not murder the Jews themselves. That was not the case in Eastern Europe, where local collaborators actively collaborated and participated in mass murder.

"In 1991, for people like me, there was so much to do. And add to this the fact that these countries had been under Communist rule and during that period, they really did not have an opportunity to deal with their own complicity during the Shoah [the Holocaust]. And, since now they wanted to get into NATO, and the European Union, and they're convinced that the road to Washington goes through Israel, they realized that they now had to deal with the Shoah."

By 1991, the window of opportunity for prosecution was clearly not going to be open for long. But in these states, there were other missions to be fulfilled. Dealing with the Shoah in these newly democratic states, explains Zuroff, meant acknowledging what the relationship of their regimes to the Nazi occupiers had been, commemorating the Jewish victims, prosecuting perpetrators in their midst, offering restitution to survivors and undertaking to educate their publics about the Holocaust.

In Eastern Europe today, says Zuroff, "the fight is not only for justice. It's a fight against distortion of the Holocaust, because in these countries, they're trying to do everything possible to minimize the role of their own people in these crimes. They prefer to attribute everything to the Germans and Austrians." At the same time, he works with – and often has to vigorously prod – the governments of former Soviet republics, such as Latvia, Lithuania and Estonia, to come to terms with the Nazi collaborators among them, in many cases prevailing upon those governments to revoke pardons that had earlier been provided to people who had participated in the murder of Jews.

Zuroff says, "This is what I tell the Lithuanians, the Latvians and the Croatians: This is your problem. It's not my problem. You're the ones who want to make the transition to a liberal democracy. You want to build a model society. You can't build a model society on foundations of mass murder.

"My mantra in the past five years has become: What you have to remember is that the Holocaust was not a tsunami, an earthquake or a volcano. It didn't come down from heaven. It was done by human beings to other human beings."

He continues: "The worst thing in the world would be to mystify the Holocaust, as some people do, and say that it's beyond understanding. This is bullshit, in my humble opinion. The Holocaust is incredibly understandable. Because when you break it down into details, you understand exactly how it happened."

Today, the hunt for living Nazis is almost complete. With that in mind, the Wiesenthal Center's Israel Office, together with the Targum Shlishi Foundation (the sponsor of this book) announced, in 2002, Operation Last Chance, which offers cash rewards to people providing information used for the successful prosecution of war criminals. As of spring 2008 the program had launched in nine countries, received the names of 497 suspects and submitted ninety-nine to local prosecution authorities. The information yielded dozens of investigations and what Zuroff terms "six very solid cases which have led to the issuing of three arrest warrants and two extradition requests."

In his career to date, Zuroff has investigated 2,844 suspects whose names were submitted to governments. Of those, he says, "It's hard to say how many were 'seriously' investigated by those governments." There have been approximately two dozen murder investigations opened and less than a dozen convictions.

Rosenbaum of the OSI stresses that the practical results of Nazi hunters' efforts have always been very limited, and sees the main value of their work as "shining the light of truth on the apathetic response of most governments, for decades now, to the problem of unpunished fugitive war criminals."

When Rosenbaum is asked how he justifies the time and expense of the continuing efforts of organizations such as his, and individuals like Zuroff and the late Simon Wiesenthal, to pursue the dwindling numbers of war criminals, he answers without hesitation: "No one who took part in such crimes should be allowed to go unpunished. There are still survivors of these ghastly crimes still crying for lost parents, siblings, even children...beyond that, I think the most important reason is to send a warning to perpetrators of would-be war crimes in the future, to say to them: 'If you dare to act on your horrible impulses, or you dare to follow a criminal order, and you participate in genocide or other crimes against humanity, there is a good chance that what remains of the civilized world will pursue you aggressively, and if necessary for the rest of your life, and that you'll never be able to put this behind you.'

"I want people to see pictures of white-haired old men and women being prosecuted, and to know that the world will never stop."

. . .

Zuroff, who turned sixty in 2008, is not ready to slow down. He says he sees "the fight against Holocaust distortion" as the "next great battle," and envisions himself moving into the field of Holocaust education and information – mainly in Eastern Europe – as the hunt for war criminals winds down. In the past, Holocaust deniers was a term used for those who denied the extent or goals or even existence of the Holocaust. The issue has taken on a new facet in the former Communist republics. Zuroff's struggle is to have those countries acknowledge the roles that their own citizens played, to accept responsibility that they, too, persecuted Jews. Zuroff's goal, he says, "is to set up a foundation to monitor Holocaust distortion in post-Communist Europe and to produce educational material in the local languages."

He laughs as he notes how in certain Eastern European countries he is already considered a "public enemy," at least in some circles. In his office, he keeps a front page from Lithuania's leading newspaper, where his photo was printed at the center of a target. "The message here is very simple: Stop Zuroff. I'm the problem. Kill the messenger."

CONTRIBUTORS

Editorial Advisory Board

Judith Ginsberg, PhD, is executive director of the Nash Family Foundation, which supports underserved Jewish populations anonymously.

Laura Gold is a clinical psychologist, rabbi and the adjunct assistant professor of Pastoral and Professional Skills for JTS Rabbinical School.

Geoffrey Hartman, PhD, is the Sterling Professor of English and Comparative Literature at Yale University (emeritus) and the co-founder and project director of the Fortunoff Video Archive for Holocaust Testimonies.

Karl Katz is the founder of MUSE Film and Television; he was formerly with The Metropolitan Museum of Art in a variety of positions over many years, including as founder of the Office of Film and Television.

Nathan Laufer is a rabbi and founding director of PELIE: Partnership for Effective Learning and Innovative Education, a new national initiative to improve Jewish supplemental education throughout the United States. He is the past president of the Wexner Heritage Foundation.

Deborah Lipstadt, PhD, is director of the Rabbi Donald A. Tam Institute for Jewish Studies and the Dorot Professor of Modern Jewish and Holocaust Studies at Emory University.

Danny Tropper, PhD, is the founder and president of the Gesher Foundation, an organization that promotes mutual understanding and tolerance between the religious and non-religious communities in Israel. He served as special advisor for Jewish Education in the Israeli Ministry of Education and Culture.

Authors

Stephen Hazan Arnoff lives in Manhattan, is executive director of the 14th Street Y, and is pursuing a doctorate at the Jewish Theological Seminary. Previously, he was the managing editor of *Zeek: A Jewish Journal of Thought and Culture*, cofounder of the Artist Workshop Experiment (AWE), founding director of Artists Networks and Programming at the Makor/Steinhardt Center of the 92nd Street Y, and has been on the faculty of several educational institutions. He writes, teaches and consults widely on topics in the fields of Judaism, the arts, music, literature, contemporary creative expression and the study and practice of sacred texts. He has been awarded the Simon Rockover Jewish Press Award for Jewish Arts & Criticism and the New Voices Prize.

Sarah Bronson is a freelance journalist in Jerusalem. A graduate of Barnard College and New York University, she made *aliyah* in 2003. She is a former staff writer for MTV Networks and for *Haaretz* English Edition. Her work has also appeared in the *New York Times, Glamour,* the *Washington Times,* the *Jerusalem Report, Figure* magazine, the *World Jewish Digest,* the *Jewish Chronicle* of London, *Hadassah Magazine* and other publications. Her awards include recognition by the Maryland-Delaware-DC Press Association and the American Jewish Press Association. She blogs about Judaism, politics and life in Israel at chayyeisarah.blogspot.com.

Debra Nussbaum Cohen is the author of *Celebrating Your New Jewish Daughter: Creating Jewish Ways to Welcome Baby Girls into the Covenant* (Jewish Lights) and is on staff at *The Jewish Week,* where she writes about religion, spirituality, Jewish identity and philanthropy. She has written about Jewish life and other religious issues for the *New York Times,* the *Wall Street Journal, New York* magazine, the *Village Voice* and other publications. She lives in Brooklyn with her husband and three children.

Denise Couture worked for a wire service and newspapers before launching a freelance writing career that has taken her around the world. In recent years, she has spent most of her time as a documentary filmmaker and journalism teacher in Washington, D.C., where she is raising her two sons.

Evan Eisenberg is the author of *The Ecology of Eden* (Knópf, Vintage) and *The Recording Angel* (Yale University Press). His writings on nature, culture and technology and his humor pieces have appeared in *The New Yorker, The Atlantic, The New Republic,* the *New York Times, Natural History, Slate* and other publications. He has been a music columnist for *The Nation,* a synagogue cantor and a gardener for the New York City parks department. He lives in Manhattan.

Simona Fuma is Israel editor of the *World Jewish Digest.* She was formerly the publication's editor-in-chief and has also written for the *Wisconsin State Journal, Newcity Chicago* magazine and *The Forward.* She lives in Jerusalem.

Andrea Gollin is a freelance writer and editor based in Miami and the program director of Targum Shlishi. She has been on staff at newspapers and magazines and run museum and university publication departments. Her journalism and book reviews have appeared in many publications including the *Washington Post, New York Newsday,* Salon.com, the *Miami Herald,* and *Entertainment Weekly.* Her fiction has been published in several literary journals.

Ken Gordon is the editor of JBooks.com, the publisher of QuickMuse. com and a freelance writer.

David B. Green is on the editorial staff of *Haaretz* English Edition, where he edits the Books supplement and original opinion pieces. He grew up in Philadelphia, was educated at the University of Chicago and worked at *The New Yorker* magazine, before making aliyah in 1987. Before joining *Haaretz*, he was deputy editor of *The Jerusalem Report* magazine. In 2001–2002, David was a Nieman journalism fellow at Harvard University.

Laura Griffin, a former reporter for the *St. Petersburg (FL) Times* and the *Dallas Morning News*, is a freelance writer, college journalism instructor and girls' basketball coach. Her writing has received awards from the Dallas Press Club, the Society of Professional Journalists, the Texas Governor's Commission on Women, the Associated Press Managing Editors Association, the Florida Society of Newspaper Editors, the Texas Bar and the National Commission on Crime and Delinquency. She lives in New Jersey with her husband and two children.

Barbara Kessel is director of administration at the Board of Jewish Education of Greater New York, the author of *Suddenly Jewish: Jews Raised as Gentiles Discover their Jewish Roots* (Brandeis University Press), and she is a freelance writer whose work appears frequently in Jewish publications.

Francesca Lunzer Kritz lives in Silver Spring, Maryland. A native New Yorker, she attended Touro College and the London School of Economics and has served as a staff reporter for *Forbes Magazine*, *High Technology Business Magazine* and *U.S. News and World Report*. She has been a freelance contributor to publications including the *Washington Post, The Forward* and the *Los Angeles Times* and has been the health writer for *The Jewish Week* since 1996. She is a member of the Kemp Mill Synagogue and of the plenum of the Orthodox Caucus, a division of the Center for the Jewish Future at Yeshiva University.

Ilene R. Prusher is a writer and journalist. Since graduating in 1993 from Columbia University's Graduate School of Journalism, Ilene has written for the *New York Times*, the *Philadelphia Inquirer*, *Newsday* and the *New Republic*, as well as magazines including the *Jerusalem Report*, *Moment* and *Tikkun*. Since 2000 she has been a staff writer for the *Christian Science Monitor* and has served as the newspaper's bureau chief in Tokyo, Istanbul, and currently, Jerusalem. She also writes book reviews for Israel's *Haaretz* newspaper. Ilene was a 2004–05 recipient of the Dorot Fellowship, during which she taught journalism at the Hebrew University of Jerusalem and founded the Creative Writing Workshop at the Pardes Institute of Jewish Studies, where she continues to teach.

Harvey Simon wrote case studies in public policy for Harvard University before moving to Washington, D.C., where he works as a freelance writer and editor. His articles have appeared in the *Los Angeles Times*, the *Boston Globe* and elsewhere.

Oren Baruch Stier, PhD, is an associate professor of Religious Studies and director of the Judaic Studies Program at Florida International University in Miami, where he teaches Judaica courses including "Jewish Mysticism" and "The Holocaust." He is the author of *Committed to Memory: Cultural Mediations of the Holocaust* (University of Massachusetts Press) and co-editor with Shawn Landres of the recently published *Religion, Violence, Memory, and Place* (Indiana University Press). He received a 2004 fellowship from the Center for Advanced Holocaust Studies at the United States Holocaust Memorial Museum for his current project, *Holocaust Symbols: The Icons of Memory*.

Daniel Treiman is the deputy web editor of *The Forward*. He was the founding editor of *The Brooklynite* magazine and formerly served as the editor of *New Voices*, the national Jewish student magazine.

Jane Ulman is a freelance writer, primarily for Jewish publications. Since 1998, she has been transforming the tumult of raising four sons into a column that integrates family observances and humor with the history and *mitzvot* specific to various holidays and lifecycle events. She is also a contributing writer for the *Jewish Journal of Greater Los Angeles*, reporting on religion, education and other issues of concern to the Jewish community. She is a member of the American Jewish Press Association and the winner of a Simon Rockower Award for feature writing. She was also selected to participate as a fellow in the Gralla Program for Journalists in the Jewish Press at Brandeis University.

Jonathan Vatner is a writer and editor living in New York City. He graduated from Harvard University and is a contributing editor at *O at Home* magazine; he was previously a writer for *Meetings & Conventions* magazine. His congregations of choice are Kehilat Hadar and B'nai Jeshurun, both of which approach prayers in innovative ways. He is working on his first novel.

Nancy Wolfson-Moche has written profiles of people ranging from Luciano Pavarotti to Lauren Hutton for books and magazines including *Good Housekeeping, Travel & Leisure, Departures* and *Cigar Aficionado*. She has been an editor on staff at STYLE.com, worth.com, *Glamour, Parents, Seventeen* and *Redbook*. The editor of *Toward A Meaningful Bat Mitzvah* (Targum Shlishi), she has a nourishment counseling practice in New York City where she lives with her husband and daughters.

Carol Zall is a freelance writer and broadcast journalist. Her work has been published in the U.S., the U.K., and Ireland. She has worked in television and radio for the BBC, and is currently a public radio producer in the U.S.